HIDDEN MEANING IN THE NEW TESTAMENT

HIDDEN MEANING
IN THE
NEW TESTAMENT

New Light from the Old Greek

RONALD A. WARD, M.A., B.D., Ph.D.

Foreword by
MARCUS WARD, M.A., D.D.

Introduction by
PAUL S. REES, LITT.D., D.D.

MARSHALL, MORGAN & SCOTT
London

MARSHALL, MORGAN & SCOTT, LTD.
BLUNDELL HOUSE
GOODWOOD ROAD
LONDON S.E.14

SBN 551 05023 3

MADE AND PRINTED IN GREAT BRITAIN BY PURNELL AND SONS, LTD.
PAULTON (SOMERSET) AND LONDON

FOREWORD

IN June 1960 an article appeared in *The Expository Times* under the intriguing title "Pin-Points and Panoramas", written by the then New Testament Professor at Wycliffe College, Toronto. I read it with great delight, for it spoke to my condition and to my need. I had recently returned, after a long interval, to the teaching of New Testament Greek and was encountering something of the climate of resistance which Dr. Ward was later to describe so vividly. In common with many of our colleagues we believe that, once we can persuade, and demonstrate to, our budding preachers and theologians that to be able to read the New Testament in the original still has a point, half the battle has been won. What makes the process of learning such a drudgery, and often more so than it need be or ought to be, is the feeling that the place of Greek in the syllabus, and the inordinate amount of time given to it, especially at the beginning, is simply the hang-over of an older tradition that is no longer relevant. Students will point to the flood of new translations and the copious supply of excellent commentaries and argue that they could use their time and energy better in studying these than in the laborious acquisition of declensions and paradigms. They rarely ask who are to be the translators and commentators of the future. Nor do they normally compare the precision of the Lightfoot era with the tendency to broad generalisation which marks the work of many whose interests are wholly theological and who seem to care little for the exactitudes of grammar and syntax. One sometimes wonders whether in this field, as in so many others, we may not be coming to the end of the time in which we can continue to draw on inherited capital. It must be admitted that the tools provided for the student are not wildly exciting. For many years there has been nothing to match James Hope Moulton's vivid and provocative *Prolegomena*.

It seemed to me that the general approach of Dr. Ward's article gave a proper and welcome lead to those of us who share this concern. Dealing only with "The Preacher's Use of the Aorist" it was but a sample of what might be done. I was able to get into touch with Dr. Ward (and incidentally to enter into friendship with him) in the endeavour to persuade him to develop what he had so well begun. This he has done, and his work, after some vicissitudes, now appears in print. It is all that I hoped it might be. It covers the ground of Greek usage and is written with appealing humour and point. Its wide range of illustration, touching human experience at so many points, seems to me peculiarly relevant to a work dealing with the language of the New Testament which, after all, was written for common people in the language of everyday use. I would not follow Dr. Ward in all his interpretations and suggestions. I know he would not wish anyone to do so. The important thing about this book is that he has shown what a man can do with his Greek once he has mastered the elements. It will surely act as a stimulus to do so quickly. In some of the longer passages selected for exposition he may well introduce some to the declining art of paraphrase.

I sometimes try to encourage my students by saying: 'Your Greek Testament, your Arndt and Gingrich Lexicon, your Moulton and Geden Concordance – and everyman his own Barclay.' Now I must add, at once, 'and your R. A. Ward.' It could be that the use of this book will enable many to understand what the great grammarian-expositor meant when he wrote 'We are saved by the aorist tense and the preposition *en!*'

MARCUS WARD

Richmond College,

University of London

INTRODUCTION

Iᴛ is impossible for me to add the slightest hue of lustre to such a
book as this. I am the one who is honoured by the request, alike
from author and publisher, for something in the way of a preface.
Some years ago, when Dr. Ronald Ward produced his book for
preachers under the rich title of *Royal Sacrament*, I was so struck
and stimulated by the chapter called "The Preacher and His Greek
Testament" that I wrote him a letter of thanks—a small enough
chore which, I regret to say, is performed by me all too seldom.
Anyhow, it is a fair presumption that my note of hearty appreciation
must now be blamed for the request to write an introductory word
about a piece of work that takes the short course offered in a single
chapter in *Royal Sacrament* and expands it into a full-scale (albeit far
from exhaustive) treatment.

Thirty years ago I had the good fortune of sharing a summer
conference platform in Minnesota with Methodist Bishop Frederick
D. Leete. In a day when the Methodist Church had an unhappy
paucity of ministers who exhibited either exegetical interest or
expository skill Bishop Leete would stand up with nothing in his
hand save his Greek New Testament. What followed was a discourse
that was at once scholarly without being "over the head," expository
without being remote, and illuminating without being impractical.

Further to Bishop Leete's credit, let it be said that he wrote a book
which surely falls in the same "line of descent" as this one by Dr.
Ward. Leete wrote about "Picture Words," "Greek Compounds,"
"Potent Particles," "Divinity in Prepositions," "Sermons in Tenses,"
and "Word Favorites." And in it all he acclaimed the men who
taught him to love Greek as "the most perfect vehicle of human
speech."

Now, three decades later, I have before me the fascinating
manuscript by Dr. Ward entitled *Hidden Meaning in the New Testament*,
with the subtitle of "New Light from the Old Greek." And he
writes absorbingly under such heads as "Pinpoints" (the Greek
aorist tense), "Panoramas" (present and imperfect tenses), "Footprints" (perfect tense), "Self-Interest" (the Greek middle voice),
"Relations" (prepositions), "Architecture" (the compounds),

"Sunken Treasure" (figures of speech), and "Near Neighbours" (paradoxical phrases).

It is all delightfully done, with a simplicity which, considering the technical nature of the subject-matter, is quite remarkable. Ministers, teachers, Sunday School instructors, and informed laymen generally —all will find the New Testament coming alive in exhilarating fashion as they follow these vivid studies by Dr. Ward. Here are "wares, ores, and gems" from your Greek New Testament, in possession of which you will find fortune indeed.

PAUL S. REES

Minneapolis, Minnesota

CONTENTS

Timotheo
carissimo filio

AUTHOR'S PREFACE

THIS book has been built up through the years. It sets out more or less formally part of the method employed when I start to make a sermon. The treasures of the New Testament are vast and it is the preacher's privilege to make them available to his people. As Walter Bauer said in a slightly different connection, how great is the ocean, and how tiny the shell with which we dip! It is hoped that the following chapters will prove to be a fragment of the preacher's shell. For a long time I had planned to use "Picture and Movement in the New Testament" as a title, but later counsels prevailed. Pictures vary and movements may be secular, but "hidden meaning" has reminded me of "the treasures of darkness and hidden riches of secret places." It is the task of the preacher to enter the linguistic darkness, find the hidden treasure and scatter it in the full light of day.

I was greatly encouraged when the Rev. A. Marcus Ward, M.A., D.D., urged publication and am grateful to him for writing as he has done. Acknowledgment is also due to the Rev. C. L. Mitton, D.D., Ph.D., the Editor, for permission to use material already published in *The Expository Times*. I am similarly grateful to Dr. Harold O. J. Brown, the Editor of *Themelios*, the journal of the International Fellowship of Evangelical Students. Dr. Paul S. Rees of World Vision International has put me in his debt by his interest and encouragement, and the debt is increased by his contribution to this volume. My wife once more has smoothed my path and cleared away obstacles. In particular she typed the manuscript and compiled the Index, not to mention the long hours spent in helping with the reading of the proofs. I pay my tribute to her for gladly increasing an already heavy load.

I have thoroughly enjoyed—and derived profit from—Dr. Nigel Turner's *Grammatical Insights into the New Testament* but I received it after my own manuscript had been completed. I believe that the preacher should make use of all the scholarship available; but in the last resort it is the man, scholar or not, who must walk with God and make his own discoveries. The preacher deals with words and he may think that he is well versed in them. As Chesterton suggested, he may be confident that he knows the meaning of so

ordinary a word as "hang." But what if William Shakespeare tells
him of

> . . . the winds,
> Who take the ruffian billows by the top,
> Curling their monstrous heads, and *hanging* them
> With deaf'ning clamour in the slippery clouds?

His vocabulary will be enriched and his vision enlarged. If in his
studies of the New Testament he finds that God is speaking to him
in new vision, it will be his joy to translate the vision into words for
the benefit of his people. I hope and pray that all preachers who may
read the pages of this book may find that they are "helpers of your
joy."

R.A.W.

The Stone Church,
Saint John,
New Brunswick,
Canada

Chapter 1

PINPOINTS

IN some parts of the world—and of the Church—the study of Greek is having a hard struggle to survive. Apart from the contemporary emphasis on a scientific education, there are those who see little value in a knowledge of the language and who would dispense with it in the normal training for the ministry. It is argued that if a boy has studied Latin and Greek from a tender age he should naturally continue with the Greek Testament if he is to enter the teaching or pastoral ministry; but if it means beginning Greek when he enters a theological college, then let the attempt be given up: the time spent is out of all proportion to the advantage gained.

We may see here the convergent views of three kinds of people. There is the man who enters the ministry somewhat late in life and has a natural hesitation to embark on a subject which may well prove beyond his reach. His first cousin, so to speak, is the student for whom languages bear the mark of the beast. He has struggled manfully through his theological course and after the miracle of graduation and ordination thankfully begins his pastorate and consigns his Greek to an unlamented end. The third man dogmatically refuses even to consider the study of a "dead" language and concentrates on "practical" subjects in preparation for a practical ministry.

Now the man who enters the ministry late commands our respect and our sympathy. I would not for one moment say that a man cannot be a faithful minister of our Lord Jesus Christ unless he knows Greek. The non-academic man may put the scholar to shame. But given the energy of youth I think that the Church would be denying her ministers an essential weapon for their warfare if she abandoned the study of Greek.

Of all people the evangelicals say that they believe the Word of God written. Then they should read it, study it, read, mark, learn and inwardly digest it. If they cannot or will not study the original, they are at the mercy of any and every commentator or translator, with scant means of checking him. They may even be led astray in their theology.

The preacher has the task of expounding the Word of God. "The old, old story" has to be proclaimed in a thousand variations—the metaphor is from music. Like a composer, the preacher has the tune of the gospel running in his mind, a tune which he sounds forth Sunday by Sunday with different variations.

An ability to read the Testament in Greek is a theological safeguard. It enables the preacher to assess the value of the theories of the commentator and is therefore helpful exegetically. Inasmuch as it may add sparkle to his sermons it is not to be despised homiletically. It is with the last that we are more immediately concerned now.

The Greek language is perhaps the most vivid of all languages. Where we wink or shrug the shoulders the Greek man actually says something, not only to make his sentences sparkle with meaning but to make us *hear* his meaning. He translates his shrug into something audible; his wink is something said, not with a cumbersome accumulation of words but subtly, deftly, by the utterance of a single little monosyllable. In English we emphasise a word by the use of our voice. If our sentence is written down, it takes a sympathetic reader to emphasise exactly the word of our choice, unless the word is underlined or written in italic. A Greek, on the contrary, can draw attention to a word by adding a particle, by actually uttering one little sound.

This vividness of the Greek tongue is not by any means confined to the use of particles. The whole tense-structure makes the language scintillate with meaning, because it is continually bringing pictures before our eyes—always useful for a preacher, because a picture means an illustration, and an illustration means an interested congregation, who are thus mentally prepared for the message of the sermon. In particular the contrast between the aorist and the present and imperfect tenses is highly suggestive. Without referring to the time of an act, past or present, but only to its quality, we may say that the aorist makes a bare mention of an act. It brings its scattered parts into a focus, where they glisten with the brilliance of a single diamond. The present and imperfect tenses, by contrast, are tenses which describe a process, a something-going-on; they imply some sort of activity or movement, to which the Greeks gave the name *kinesis*. The various parts of an act which were concentrated into a single focus in the aorist are here seen in their separateness. Thus the aorist may say "He healed". It says it, and that is that. The present or imperfect says "He is (was) healing", and it brings before our mind's eye a picture of the Great Physician speaking to His patient, gaining his confidence, laying His hands on his head or touching his leprous skin, and so on. The aorist reduces all that to a point, whereas the present and imperfect show us the whole scene. We have the contrast between pinpoints and panoramas, between shooting Niagara and navigating the rapids. The aorist savours of the staccato, of the brisk striking of a note on the piano, whereas the imperfect holds down the keys of the organ. The aorist drops the curtain; the imperfect shows the players acting on the stage. The aorist corresponds to the short squirt from a boy's water-pistol whereas the imperfect is illustrated by the continuous flow of a waterfall. Let us take as an example St. Mark 1: 4–5.

"John the Baptist appeared-on-the-scene in the wilderness . . . (the verb here is in the aorist, and the action is a 'pinpoint' one). And all the district of Judaea was-going-out to him, and all the men of Jerusalem; and they were-being-baptised by him. . . ." The two latter verbs are in the imperfect and they convey to the imaginative eye the picture of two processions; the first shows us the long trail of men and women going out to John, unorganised, unmarshalled, but going out, one on the heels of the other, to see the new prophet. The second picture shows us these same people in their baptismal procession, going down one after another into the water. St. Mark has drawn a simple outline, but it gives to the sensitive preacher the material for the building up of his own vivid description of the events in question. Have the congregation ever seen the unofficial procession of people streaming through the streets towards a national shrine to witness a historic ceremony? Well, it was perhaps something like that.

So much, at the moment, for the imperfect. In this chapter we are thinking more particularly of the aorist. The preacher has to see in his own mind what is meant by the "pinpoint" in question, and by suitable language and if possible by a choice and brief illustration transfer the picture which the scripture has drawn in his own mind to the minds of his listeners. To make the point clearer, think of some of the senses. An aorist of the verb "see" might be rendered "catch a glimpse of". Similarly the aorist "he smelt the sea" might be translated "he got a whiff of the ocean". "He heard" could be "he caught the sound of". "He tasted" would be "He sensed the flavour of". Now with this to guide us, let us look at St. Luke 10: 24. ". . . many prophets and kings desired (aorist) to see (aorist) what you are seeing (present), and they did not (aorist), and to hear (aorist) what you are hearing (present), and they did not (aorist)." The preacher's problem is to find language which will express the "pinpoint". He might start by saying "they felt a sharp desire", but this must be discarded because though "sharp" brings a picture to his own mind it may not necessarily do so to the minds of his audience. It may seem to express only the intensity of feeling. What he is trying to describe in using "sharp" is the experience of a man with a heart attack. He has a *stab* of pain; a *pang* suddenly comes upon him. These are "pinpoint" expressions, and the preacher has to find one suitable and relevant. He might say "many prophets felt the pang of desire to . . ."

The infinitive which follows is also in the aorist. We might start with "to see in a flash", which is certainly "punctiliar", as the grammarians say. But objection might be taken to it on the ground that in a momentary flash of lightning it is the whole panorama which is lit up. In this case, however, the "pinpoint" is not spacial, as it were, but temporal. The duration of time has been brought down to a bare point. (This is quite justifiable, as our Lord says in St. Mark 14: 37, "Could you not watch (aorist) one hour?"—*mian horan*, an accusative of duration of time. The time involved may be quite long. Marcus Dods acutely observes that in Hebrews 11: 27 "the aorist gathers the forty years in Midian into one exhibition of wonderful perseverance in faith".—Expositor's Greek Testament. In Hebrews 3: 17 the "forty years" is specifically mentioned with an aorist. An instance of a "spacial" as opposed to a "temporal" pinpoint is to be found in 1 John 2: 6, "He who says he abides in Him ought himself to go-through-the-process-of-walking (present) just as He walked (aorist)." The spatial element involved in walking has been reduced to a point. The moral walk of the whole life is summed up in the pinpoint of an aorist.) Still, to avoid ambiguity, why should we not say "catch a glimpse of"?

In an exposition the preacher can now paraphrase the text, and the contrast is startling. "Many prophets and kings felt the pang of desire to catch a glimpse of what is continually before your eyes; not a glimpse did they have. They desired (there is no need to repeat the 'pang' unless you want to) to catch the sound of the music which is ever in your ears; not a note did they hear". This is ad-mittedly paraphrase, though we have no doubt met translations which do the same. Even if paraphrase is never legitimate when we are aiming at a translation—which has yet to be proved—it is still a fair practice in the hands of a preacher. It is but a method of ex-position. "The translator," says Monsignor Ronald Knox (*On Englishing the Bible*, p. 12), "must never be frightened of the word 'paraphrase'; it is a bogey of the half-educated . . . it is a paraphrase when you translate 'Comment vous portez-vous?' by 'How are you?' "

Take another example, Hebrews 4: 15. It goes naturally into English as "We have not a High-Priest incapable of a stab of sympathy with our weaknesses. . . ." The metaphor of "stab" suggests a man being "run through" by a rapier; one sharp clean thrust and all is over. It is of the same order as the "pang" in a heart-attack. To complete the picture we must notice the perfect participle, "one who has been tried". A perfect tense can always be turned into an English present state, as we shall see later (p. 42f.), as the perfect expresses the abiding result of a past act. "One who has been tried" as opposed to "one who was tried" means "one who now bears the marks of trial". Again the contrast is startling. Our High-Priest is not one incapable of a stab of sympathy; He is shot through, riddled, with His experiences; He bears the marks of trial which affected Him at every point.

Let us now test this on a larger scale by considering St. Luke 18: 18–30. "A ruler asked Him." The verb is aorist. St. Mark not infrequently puts "he said" into the imperfect, apparently regarding conversation as a process. St. Luke elsewhere (23: 28, 34) distinguishes the tenses: "Jesus said (aorist), 'daughters of Jerusalem. . . .' " But "He kept on saying, 'Father, forgive them . . .' " (*elegen*). How can we bring out the force of St. Luke's aorist in 18: 18? Perhaps by saying "he fired a question at Him", which is faithful to the idea of the pinpoint. The ruler asks, literally, "Having done what (aorist) shall I inherit eternal life?" This recalls the parable of the Good Samaritan (Lk. 10: 25–37), where (v. 25) the lawyer asks the same question. The aorist clearly has some significance, a fact which is shown by the contrasted present in verse 37: "Continue your journey and keep on doing similarly." The ruler in 18: 18 must mean then "What act can I do and have done with, which will give me eternal life?" We must bear this in mind when we paraphrase the whole passage, which we shall now attempt, without going into any further preliminary detail. Notice the force of the aorists.

"And a certain ruler fired a question at Him; 'Good Teacher, what one noble deed am I to do, worthy of a spiritual Congressional medal, which will qualify me for the inheritance of eternal life?' And Jesus said to him, 'Why are you calling me good? No-one is good except One, God. You know the commandments. Thou shalt not commit adultery. . . .' The ruler said, 'All this I kept—from childhood. It is over and done with.'

When Jesus heard this He said to him, 'You still have one thing missing; realise everything; turn it all into cash, rain it on poor men, and you will have treasure in heaven, and come, keep following me.' When the ruler heard this death-knell, grief swept over him, for he was very rich. And Jesus, taking a look at him, said, 'How fussily are the moneyed folk entering into the kingdom of God. For it is easier for a camel to enter through a needle's eye than for a rich man to enter into the kingdom of God.' The listeners said, 'Then who can be snatched into safety?' He said, 'Impossibilities in the home of men are possible in the home of God.' Peter said, 'Look, we dropped our all and fell in behind you.' And He said to them, 'Truly I tell you, there is no-one who dropped home or wife or brothers or parents or children for the sake of the kingdom of God who will fail to get manifold compensation in this season of opportunity and eternal life in the age that is on its way.' "

This mingling of translation and paraphrase, of dignified and colloquial English, reveals something of the possibilities open to the preacher. Clear observation of the aorist clarifies his own mind, not infrequently suggests illustrations, and results in a vividness in preaching. The older English Versions of the New Testament "come to life" in the hands of a sympathetic and skilful expositor.

A few comments on the above translation-paraphrase may not be out of place. The reference to the Congressional Medal is not of course to be found in the original, but the aorist "having done what?" so impressed me with the thought of a single great exploit, which the man could do and get finished for ever, that the thought of a medal was almost automatic. Just as the possession of the Congressional Medal, based as it is on *one* glorious exploit, entitles its holder, however humble his rank, to be saluted by a General; so, the ruler hopes in his inquiry, *one* noble deed will entitle him to the "salute" as possessing eternal life. But it is not one deed of ours but a continuous discipleship which is required as our Lord says (v. 22).

After our Lord's recital of the commandments, the ruler's whole previous moral life seems to have swept into his line of vision, much as a drowning man is supposed to see all his previous life in a moment of time. Commandments? I kept them all, so that is finished and done with. It reminds us of the witty novelist who made one of his characters, a very aggressive Protestant, accuse his minister with the words "I saw the minister last Wednesday practise celibacy in the open street". These reflections are stimulated by the fact that "I kept" is an aorist tense.

"Rain it on poor men" gave me a good deal of trouble. The Greek is an aorist imperative, *diados*, and two ideas have to be brought out; the one is the punctiliar idea and the other is implied by the use of the preposition *dia* in the compound verb. In such compounds *dia* has the force of "in all directions from one original point", and it always raises in my mind the picture of a wheel with the spokes radiating from the centre. I toyed with the idea of "spray it on poor men", but gave it up as inelegant even for a colloquialism. But the word "spray" may give us an illustration of the meaning of *diados*. It makes us see water coming out of the holes of a watering-can when we water our plants in the garden. The water starts from a single source, but in passing through the separate holes in the "rose" at the end of the spout it flows in separate little streams of wider and wider range as it goes down from the can towards the plants. Such at any rate is the picture which *diados* raises in my own mind; other preachers will have others; but it was the Greek word which brought it about.

Again, it was desirable to bring out the "pinpoint" involved in "having heard this", and "death-knell" seemed as good as any word. But it must be confessed that the picture raised by the aorist, faithful to the "pinpoint", was that of a radio quiz. One of the competitors has made his suggestion, which was wrong, and he has been "gonged". Though this could hardly have been brought into the translation, it is mentioned as a further sign of how the Greek aorist suggests illustrations.

"Snatched into safety" was used, not because there is any use of the verb *harpazo*, but because the aorist infinitive suggested the concentration of the saving act to a point; and a snatch is done so quickly, in a "pinpoint" of time, that it seemed justifiable.

One more comment may be given. The word "dropped" is used in social life of people who suddenly, often for good reason, cease to have anything to do with certain members of the community. They may be socially undesirable, and are just "dropped". This is a punctiliar act and at the same time is a fair translation of the Greek word *aphiemi*.

So much, then, for this particular passage. It is hoped that it has shown how the Holy Scripture can come alive to the sensitive preacher. But this is not all: it increases his understanding of the text and may resolve difficulties. The keen difference of opinion between Paul and Barnabas in Acts 15: 37-38 has puzzled many readers. Close study of the text shows that it was not merely a case of a short temper, still less of vindictiveness on the part of St. Paul. Notice the aorist in verse 37. Barnabas was wanting to take-along-with-them the youthful Mark; in other words, to include him in the passenger list, so to speak. Barnabas is thinking of the start of the missionary journey, no more. "Take him or leave him behind? Take him, of course!" That is his attitude. Paul, on the other hand, is looking much further ahead and is thinking of the journey as a whole, of the inconveniences, difficulties and indeed the dangers of having a young man in the company who is likely to want at any moment to "go home to mother". (See Acts 13: 13.) He is thinking, with all the impatience of the missionary, of having to be behind Mark all the time, urging him on, shoving him forward. He did not think it right to compromise the success of the travel and of the missionary work by having "to keep on taking him along with them (present infinitive)", the implication being that young Mark is a slippery customer, and that unless they keep forcing him along with them he will leave them in the lurch. This contrast between the present and the aorist of the same verb throws into high relief the characters of Paul and Barnabas. Paul is consecrated to the apostolate, determined, pressing on (Phil. 3: 14), ruthless in the best sense of the word. Barnabas lacks the foresight of his companion and dwells in the present moment. He is kindly, understanding, wanting to give the lad another chance: the type and example of the older man who is the trusted friend and counsellor of younger ministers. Ultimately, it is perhaps the conflict between the way of wisdom and the way of love. And this insight might never have come to us if it had not been for the use of the same Greek word in both the aorist and the present!

There is an urgency, almost a peremptoriness, about the aorist, which sometimes reveals a high emotional tension. In the last hours before the crucifixion, when the zero-hour of the betrayal is approaching, Satan entered into Judas Iscariot. "Jesus therefore says to him (St. John 13: 27), 'What you are doing, DO—more quickly'." You are already engaged in doing it; then do-it-and-have-done-with-it. Faster! We see here something of a Gethsemane behind closed doors.

Sometimes the aorist, while still a "pinpoint", emphasises the beginning of an action—the so-called "ingressive aorist". We have already had an example of this in St. Luke 18: 28, "we fell in behind you". Other examples are "He burst into tears", instead of the rather colourless "He wept" (Luke 19: 41; 22: 62; John 11: 35);

"wonder fell on them all" (Mark 1: 27; compare 6: 6; 9: 15—astonishment swept over them at the fact that Jesus was present when needed); and "they were gripped by great fear" (Mark 4: 41). One of the loveliest is in Mark 10: 21, which is usually rendered "Jesus looking on him, loved him". The ingressive aorist would be better translated "fell in love with him", if it were not for theological difficulties. How can we compare this with John 3: 16?

The New Testament abounds with aorists like those which have been cited. Think of the urgent "Kyrie eleeson" (Lord have mercy upon us) of Matt. 20: 30; of the vile and vulgar mockery of the peremptory "toss us a prophecy" (Mark 14: 65); of the domestic squawk in "tell her to give me a hand" (Luke 10: 40); of the vivid "a friend of mine descended on me" (Luke 11: 6); of the pain of "compassion pierced him" (Luke 15: 20) and the pathos of "I am no longer worthy to-get-the-name-of a son of yours" (15: 21). (The prodigal lost his qualifications for recovering what he had lost by going into a far country. Had he, beside gathering all together so as to leave no reason for coming home again, changed his name?) Notice how his prepared speech of verses 18–19 is not finished in verse 21; did his father interrupt him? If so, there must be some things which God will not let us say to Him. Observe again the revealing "He put on an act to go further" of Luke 24: 28. These are but examples of the sharpness of outline and of the picturesque vividness of the Greek which should be the preacher's joy.

It will be clear by this time that there is no one expression which will translate a given Greek aorist. It will be determined partly by the fact that it is supposed to render an aorist, and partly by the individual imagination and style of the translator. For example, we might turn Acts 22: 29 thus: "and the colonel got the wind up when he realised that he was a Roman and that he had tied him up." Another man, disliking the extremely colloquial "got the wind up" might prefer to draw on his knowledge of horses, and say "the colonel shied at the realisation that . . ." A country community, men used to the ways of horses, would not fail to appreciate the meaning. Yet a third might be content with "When the colonel realised that he was a Roman . . . his heart sank." The possibilities are almost endless, especially when we realise that literality is not necessarily a virtue in translation. Consider St. John 5: 35, "He was the burning and shining light, and you wished (aorist) to exult (aorist) for a time in his light." It might be said of a man "He got the idea of going to New York," meaning that the idea suddenly appealed to him. He suddenly wished to go, perhaps to his wife's disgust, for she had long wanted to go to Florida, and thought that he was in full sympathy with her. So it is here. As for the "exulting", there is a colloquial pinpoint expression which gives the spirit of it, "to get a kick out of". A kick is a sudden, momentary act, appropriate for bringing out the force of an aorist. Hence we might translate for the purposes of exposition, "You got the idea of getting a kick out of his light for a brief spell."

More dignified methods are open to us. In Acts 18: 27 we can distinguish the tenses thus: "when he was hankering after, longing for (literally 'wishing'—a present), a surge[1] into Achaia the brothers gave him encouragement[2] and told the disciples by letter to *take him to their heart*."[3] Sometimes there is a family conference about what to do on the next public holiday or what present to give to Aunt Mildred for her birthday. At the end of all the discussion the mother may say "We'll *decide*, then, to go to the sea," or "we'll *decide* to give her the candlesticks". So in St. Luke 12: 32 "your Father decided (aorist) to press-into-your-hands (aorist) the gift of the Kingdom" (here are the title-deeds: take hold of them). Compare Romans 15: 26, "Macedonia and Achaia decided to make a fellowship-gift . . ."

It should be emphasised that all these translations are for the purposes of exposition. They represent the beginning of the preacher's work, not the end. Everything depends on how they are used. They are not meant for devotional purposes, like the noble prayers of a stately liturgy. On the other hand, a clearer grasp of the meaning and implications of Holy Scripture should warm the preacher's heart, and through him the hearts of his people. Let us therefore attempt a rendering of another passage before going on to tackle the eleventh chapter of the Epistle to the Hebrews. Let us practise on Acts 19: 1–7.

> It happened while Apollos was in Corinth: Paul traversed the upper region and came to Ephesus and found a bunch of disciples. He said to them, "Did you get the Holy Ghost when you started your faith?" They answered him, "We did not; and what's more, we didn't hear a word about the existence of the Holy Ghost." He said, "Into what baptism then were you plunged?" They answered, "Into the baptism of John." Paul said, "John plunged people into a baptism of repentance, telling them to put

---

[1]Aorist. Professor Kenneth Scott Latourette's great work, *History of the Expansion of Christianity*, will justify the metaphor of the wave of the sea.
[2]He could have said afterwards, "they *pushed* me, gave me a push, into it".
[3]The present infinitive would have meant "to keep on making him at home."

their faith in the One Who was coming after him, that is, in Jesus." When they heard this they were plunged into baptism in the Name of the Lord Jesus. And when Paul had laid hands on them the Holy Ghost swept over them, and they began talking in tongues and prophesying. And the sum total of men was about twelve.

The "bunch of disciples" is not very elegant, but it reduces the scattered disciples, if they were scattered, to a central "point". The word "found" is aorist; if it had been in the present tense it would have suggested a succession of discoveries. If the actual finding is regarded as a "pinpoint" then presumably we may think of the disciples in the same way. There is a phrase in English—used at any rate in England—which might bring out the same thought. "As I was walking down First Avenue I *bumped into* Mr. and Mrs. Jones". It does not mean a collision! It is a pinpoint expression, even if Mrs. Jones was looking into a shop window ten yards behind her husband. So Paul "bumped into" some disciples. It may be argued that the colloquial verb suggests an accident, a chance encounter, and that the apostle was probably actually looking for Christians. In that case we should have to enlarge the Greek by some such rendering as "a glint of discovery came into his eyes as he found some disciples", or else merely say that "he spotted" them. The actual choice does not greatly matter as we are by no means aiming at a literary translation but suggesting a method of interpretation for a preacher.

There is a measure of repetition, to some extent inevitable owing to repetition in the Greek. We might have shown the balance between aorists by rendering "plunge into baptism" and "plunge into faith". Certainly the swift and graceful act of diving into a swimming pool in a moment of time is a fit picture of an aorist. But we are not forced to use this, and no doubt the reader will be able to think of many others.

And now finally, in this chapter on the aorist, let us be more ambitious and try to translate, in the form of an expository paraphrase, the eleventh chapter of the Epistle to the Hebrews.

1. Faith is the ground on which our hopes are built, the proof of facts invisible. For it was by this that the elders gained their place in history. By faith we realise that the worlds have been framed by the Word of God, so that the visible universe has not been brought into being out of observable materials. By

faith Abel offered to God a greater sacrifice than Cain, through which he gained his place in history as Abel the Just: God gave His testimony to him, basing it on his gifts. And through his faith, though he fell dead, he is still speaking.

5. By faith Enoch was moved elsewhere so as not to catch a glimpse of death: continued search for him was fruitless, because God had moved him elsewhere. For he is on record as one who before his removal had given pleasure to God. And without faith it is impossible to light the fire of pleasure within Him; for he who is on the road to God must brace his belief that He exists and proves to be a rewarder to those who are looking for Him. By faith Noah when the news came through about events not yet seen with the naked eye, piously took notice, and constructed an Ark for the preservation of his family. Through his faith he condemned the world and became the heir of the righteousness that is based on faith. By faith Abraham answered the knocking on his door that was calling him to go out to a place which he was to occupy for an inheritance. And he went out without knowing where he was going. By faith he settled, alien as he was, in the land of promise, regarding it as belonging to someone else; he took up permanent residence in impermanent tents (see p. 138), with Isaac and Jacob the joint-heirs

10. of the same promise; for he was intent on the city that has foundations, not guy-ropes, whose Artificer and Maker is God. By faith Sarah herself also got the power to become a mother even after the season of her prime, because she thought the Giver of the Promise credible. And that is also why offspring came from one man, and a corpse at that, as the stars of the heaven in number and as the innumerable sands along the sea-shore. All these died, and their death matched their faith: they got no promises but spotted them far away and hailed them, and admitted that they were foreigners and aliens in the land. For people who talk like this

15. make it plain that they are in search of a fatherland. And if they had always been harking back in memory to the land from which they had set out, they would have had an opportunity to slip home again; but as it is they are longing for a better country, that is, a heavenly one. That is why God is not ashamed of them: not ashamed to go on being called their God; for He prepared for them a city. By faith Abraham during his time of testing offered up the key-man Isaac; yes,

he who had received the promises, to whom it had been said
"through Isaac you will have descendants", embarked upon
the sore task of offering up that only son. Reason showed
him that God was able to raise him up even from the dead,

20. and from the dead also he got him back, figuratively speaking. By faith also Isaac laid his hand in blessing on Jacob and
Esau for their future. By faith Jacob on the brink of the grave
blessed each of the sons of Joseph and did an act of worship-
ful homage to God, leaning over the head of his staff. By
faith Joseph, when nearing his end, made mention of the
Exodus of the sons of Israel and gave instructions about his
bones. By faith Moses, when born, was clapped into hiding
by his parents for a three-month period because they saw
that the child was beautiful, and they did not lose their heads
at the command of the king. By faith Moses, on growing up,
declined to be called the son of Pharaoh's daughter, because

25. he chose to go through hardship with the people of God
rather than to have a temporary enjoyment of sin: he thought
the reproach of the anointed greater wealth than the treasures
of Egypt; for he had his eye on the reward. By faith he abandoned Egypt, not shying at the outburst of the king; for he
held out, as seeing the Unseen One. By faith he celebrated
the Passover and the sprinkling of the blood, in order that
the angel who was destroying the first-born might not lay a
finger on them. By faith they crossed the Red Sea as if through
dry land. The Egyptians had a go at it, and were engulfed.

30. By faith the walls of Jericho collapsed, after being encircled
for seven days. By faith Rahab the harlot did not perish with
those who refused obedience, because she had received the
reconnaissance party with peace. And what more am I to say?
for time will fail me if I relate the details of Gideon, Barak,
Samson and Jephthah; of David and Samuel and the prophets,
who through faith swept kingdoms into subjection, and lifted
justice on high in their administration; promises tumbled *en
masse* into their hands; they put a stopper on the mouths of
lions and smothered the blaze of fire; the two-edged sword
missed them; weak as they were, they tapped the source of
generating power; war unveiled their might, as they rolled

35. back the armies of foreign powers. Women got their dead
as they shot up in resurrection life; others were broken on
the wheel, because they spurned their deliverance so that a
better resurrection might crown their life. Others got the

taste of mockings and scourgings, yes, and of bonds and prison. Stones were showered on them; trials converged on them; they were cut clean in two with the saw; the murderous sword slit their life. They went about in sheepskins and goatskins, feeling the pinch of want, suffering pressure, ill-usage—of whom the world was not worthy—wandering in deserts and mountains and caves, and the crevices of the earth. And all these, after faith had given them a place in history, did not get the promise: God visualised some better gift for us, in order that they should not be stamped with perfection apart from us.

We shall conclude this chapter with a few comments on the above translation. "Abel was witnessed to that he was righteous" (11: 4) is very cumbersome. The fact that he was not a village saint, "born to blush unseen" and after death "mute, inglorious" to rest, but was immortalised in Holy Scripture, justifies his entrance into history. The phrase "as Abel the Just" is much neater than a noun clause. Compare such titles as "Aristides the Just". "Continued search" (v. 5) brings out the graphic imperfect tense. "He was not being found", with its emphasis on continuity, suggests a succession of search-parties, anxious discussions, the passing of days, and does not bring us to that decisive hour when "All search for the survivor was abandoned". As a variant to "light the fire of pleasure" (v. 6) we might say "make His eyes sparkle with pleasure" or "bring a glint of pleasure to His eyes". A charge of anthropomorphism need not worry us: most of our thinking about God is of this order. Does not Scripture speak of the finger of God (Luke 11: 20)? We are in good company! "When the news came through" (v. 7) is an allusion to the tape machine or to a sudden cablegram. It is very bold and may offend some by reason of its anachronism. But we are trying to speak to our own age, and an industrial country will understand this interpretation. As for verse 8, "answered" is in line with Acts 12: 13 (Greek) and "the knocking that was calling" reflects the present participle "being called". So swift was Abraham's answer that the knocking had not stopped but was still going on.

In verse 13 ("spotted them"), I wanted to add in parenthesis "Land ahead, sir," to suggest the sighting of the coast and the signal to people on shore. But it would have been a mixed metaphor as they were already on land. But the suggestion, thus privately given, as it were, does echo the spirit of the text. "The *key-man*

Isaac" (v. 17) is a fair way of rendering the definite article, shows his importance and prepares the path for the following clause with its specific mention of an only son. If a man wants grandchildren, to bear his name, he does not normally begin by killing his only son: such was Abraham's complicated problem which faith solved. Hence the author is at pains to add that he only "embarked on" offering him up—an inceptive or inchoative imperfect tense. He began by saying that he actually offered him up, by faith, because in God's sight his willingness to begin was as acceptable as the completed work. (One day I hope to write a sermon on "The God of the Eleventh Hour", based on Genesis 22: 10, "Abraham took the knife.")

"Lose their heads" (v. 23) could have been, as already suggested, "did not take fright at", "did not shy at". "Tapped the source of generating power" (v. 34) is a metaphor from electricity, and "generating" seemed as good a word as any to show it. For example, a naval dockyard, with its own generating system, may be severely bombed in war and its plant put out of action for months. But by linking on to the "grid" system it is possible to receive electric power from another generating station miles away. "Out of weakness they were made strong." "Slit their life" (v. 37) came into my mind from Milton's

> "Comes the blind Fury with the abhorred shears,
>   And slits the thin-spun life."
>   (Lycidas, 75–76)

This chapter has dealt largely with the aorist tense, though in some measure we could not help anticipating the consideration of other tenses. That was inevitable, as a living language, in contrast to a specially prepared text book, does not give us one chapter of aorists and another of imperfects, all ready-made for us. Even so, the passages we have studied have contained many aorists, and the writer pleads for more ministerial attention to the sheer practical value of the Greek Testament in general and of the aorist in particular. A minister once told me that there was no need to waste time on Greek: "I can find it all in the commentaries." Can he? One can sympathise with busy ministers everywhere but one wonders if they are under-estimating their own powers or even misconceiving the nature of their office. It is doubtful if even the standard commentaries give everything, and if the ministry is a prophetic office, then under the guidance of the Holy Ghost we shall find that God hath yet more light and truth to break forth, not merely from other men's commentaries, but from His Word as we reverently study it. In the thrill of our own discoveries the Word may dawn upon us.

Chapter 2

PANORAMAS

WE have already touched on the uses of the present and imperfect tenses. It was inevitable that we should do so, in order to contrast their meaning with that of the aorist. The time has now come to consider in greater detail the various aspects of meaning associated with them. Whereas the aorist makes but a mention of an act, the imperfect and present give us the picture of an action in progress, of a process going on. The aorist reduces the whole act to a point; the imperfect and present let us see it taking place.

Such a process may be a continuous action, repeated action, or an action attempted or begun. Thus if we say "We were walking along Fifth Avenue when the automobile overtook us", "we were walking" suggests a *continuous action*. It is unbroken and may be represented by an unbroken line, thus ———————————. An example of this in the Greek Testament will be found in Luke 15: 16, "He was longing (imperfect) to plug (aorist) himself full with the husks which the swine were eating (imperfect)". An aorist would have suggested "he felt a stab of desire (i.e. a pang of hunger)"; and "which the swine scoffed (almost in one mouthful)". But as it is we are given two parallel pictures: the swine were eating; look at them, heads down, concentrating hard, shovelling in, working, working, working; and all the time the Prodigal was looking at them in envy, desiring, longing, wishing he could join them. Such is the degradation to which sin brings a man. (The aorist, "plug", is most expressive. Think of the circular, or rather cylindrical, piece of metal which we insert into the bath or wash hand basin to prevent the water from draining away. We plug it in, in one movement. Such is the act visualised by this unhappy man: he was longing all the time to take the swine's food and, in one act as it were, to tip the lot down his throat and so plug up the hole. A coarse and degrading picture, but true to the Greek tenses—and to life.)

A more dignified instance is Philippians 1: 21, "To me to go on living (present tense) is Christ and to fall over the edge of death (aorist of 'to die'), to be halted by death, is gain."

A process may be not continuous but a *repeated action*. This is a subtle distinction, but it is worth noticing. Suppose we say "when he was hitting the boy the policeman arrived". The hitting is not continuous but repeated: first there is a blow with the right fist, then one with the left; then another and another, as blows follow one another successively. Such continuity as there may be is broken. However swiftly the punches are given, there is an interval of time between them. Such an action may be represented by a succession of dots thus: . . . . An example of this may be seen in Mark 6: 56, "as many as touched Him were saved." "Were saved" is in the imperfect tense, and it suggests the succession of cures. All the people who touched Him, one after another, were cured. If we may imagine our Lord keeping a "case-book" after the manner of a modern doctor, the imperfect calls to mind the picture of the doctor at the end of the day turning over the pages. Each page bears the name of a different patient, and on each page is the final result, "cured". As He turns over page after page He describes to Himself the repeated action: "they were cured". Compare the earlier part of the verse. "Wherever He entered into villages or cities or country-districts (possibly 'hamlets') they put (one after another—imperfect) those who were in a state of illness (unbroken continuity—present tense) in the open spaces, and they besought Him (in each successive instance—imperfect) that they might touch (aorist—not present 'fondle') even the fringe (Num. 15: 38–39) of His garment."

In the imperfect particularly, a process may be not so much continuous or repeated as *attempted or begun*. A stock example of this is the verb "persuade". A man might say "I persuaded my friend to buy an aeroplane". He means that he gave him certain advice, supported by all manner of urging, and finally his friend took the advice and actually bought the aircraft. But suppose the result was different and we encounter them when in the midst of the argument and ask what it is all about. "I am persuading him to buy an aeroplane," says the first man. "That is so," says the second, "but now that you have come I have decided against it." Six months later the story is told. "I was persuading him to buy when so-and-so came along and spoilt everything." "I was persuading", a genuine Greek imperfect, means "I was exercising suasion", or, more colloquially, "I was working on him." Such an imperfect is sometimes called the Conative or the Inceptive Imperfect.

There is a good example of it in Acts 26: 9–11. "I decided that I must perpetrate many deeds contrary to the Name of Jesus of

Nazareth; which also I did in Jerusalem. I clapped (aorist) many of the saints in gaols after getting the authority from the High-Priests, and when they were being liquidated (present) I gave my vote (aorist); and often when engaged in punitive expeditions in all the synagogues (present) *I was exercising force on them* (imperfect) to make them blaspheme . . ." Note the succession of aorists: I decided, I did, I clapped in gaol, I voted; then the sudden change to an imperfect: I was trying to force. The church was a harder nut to crack than the persecutor had imagined! You can clap a man in Sing-Sing, provided you can get the authority; you can stow any man away, can kidnap anyone you like, if only you have brains and brawn enough. But you can only *try* to make some men blaspheme. The preacher ought to be able to make something of this. Compare Matthew 3: 14 of John the Baptist "trying to prevent" our Lord from being baptised. In John 10: 33 a conversation appears to take place during a "stoning". The Jews said that "we are trying to stone you" (present)—but in verse 39 they were still seeking to arrest Him!

The pattern of the imperfect and the present tenses is now clear, at any rate in outline. Whereas in dealing with the aorist we had only the "point" to consider, here we have the continuous line, —————————, the succession of dots, ..., and, with the conative and inceptive imperfect, a line or series of dots followed by a space and then an upright "fence", the empty space indicating that the action was but tried: ——————|; . . . . |. Now when we have before us an imperfect or a present we have to decide to which class it belongs. This done, we must visualise the line or series of dots, as the case may be, and see in our own minds what they imply, what picture they conjure up. This has to be transferred, by means of language, to the minds of our hearers, and if we can find a brief and apt illustration we shall be able to bring the force of the imperfect or present to the attention of the congregation without telling them that it is an imperfect or present. The object of art is to conceal art, and the most skilful preacher will always disguise his technique. If the suggested method is successful it should make the New Testament live. Let us test it.

In 1 Corinthians 1: 18 we read "The word of the cross is foolishness to those who are perishing, but to us who are being saved it is the power of God." "Us who are being saved" is a literal rendering of a present participle. Two interpretations are possible. St. Paul may be thinking of salvation as a process which goes on in each individual Christian. (This is not at all meant to deny that a man may be saved now, already, and be certain of it. Cf. 2 Timothy 1: 9, Ephesians 2: 8. If he has laid hold of Christ, then he is saved; and that salvation is developed within him. To put it another way, once he is "over the line" he is saved, but as he grows in grace he advances further and further forwards from that line.) If, then, the apostle is thinking of the salvation of the individual, of "us" made up of individuals, then we might think of a continuous line and translate "to us who are advancing on the road of (not 'to') salvation".

If, on the other hand, he is thinking of "us" as the totality of the church, then he is thinking of "our" number being continually augmented as more and more people are saved. We might then think of a series of dots and render "to us who are going through the turnstile of salvation", and we should picture the crowd at some football match being increased as more and more people came in. Of course there is nothing in St. Paul's mind about turnstiles—or about football either. But if he is thinking about *repeated* action, represented by a series of dots, then a series of individuals doing the same thing one after another (repeated action) in being saved is not unworthily illustrated by the turnstile. Once more, if he has in mind the salvation progressively of the individual, then we have *continuous*, not repeated, action, and "advancing on the road of salvation" is a fair interpretation of his meaning. As for the turnstile, did not our Lord say "strait is the gate and narrow is the way"?

The use of present participles in this very verse (Matt. 7: 13–14) may help to solve some problems. "Enter in through the narrow gate; because broad is the gate and wide is the road which leads to destruction, and those who *are entering* through it are many (but cannot we shout at them 'not that one'? What is the preaching of the gospel for?); because narrow is the gate and a tight fit the road which leads to life, and those who *are finding* it are few (but it may be pointed out to all the rest: again, what is the preaching of the gospel for?)".

If any one is disposed to wonder whether all these distinctions of tense are valid, let him consider Acts 20: 9, where the very difference of tenses adds a lifelike touch. After making the significant statement that there were an adequate number of lamps in the room— and lamps often mean a stuffy atmosphere, when they are not electric—St. Luke tells us that "a certain young man, Eutychus by name, was sitting on the window-sill, *being* (gradually) *overcome* by a deep sleep. And as Paul prolonged his address (one imagines that the room became hotter and stuffier!) Eutychus *was overcome* by the sleep (just mentioned), and fell down from the third floor and was taken up dead." "Being gradually overcome" is a present participle, and shows us a picture of the process going on, of the boy fighting a losing battle; the second "overcome" is an aorist participle; the boy is beaten; he has succumbed to the sleep. In the first case he is "nodding"; in the second he "dropped right off". In paraphrase, we have "being carried to the arms of Morpheus" and "gathered into the arms of Morpheus". In another way, "advancing to the land of Nod", and "arrived at the land of Nod". The congregation will understand, if the ventilation is not good!

Now turn to Luke 9: 23. "If anyone is desirous (present) of coming (present) after Me, let him say—'no'—to (aorist) himself and shoulder (aorist) his cross daily, and let him keep on following Me." "Say—'no'—to" brings out more vividly the force of the aorist imperative than the bare "let him repudiate himself", and at the same time suggests an illustration. According to the "spy" stories, the secret service agent, the member of the "intelligence", if caught spying is disowned by the government employing him. Imagine an agent of the Foreign Office or State Department caught redhanded by a foreign power. In indignation it sends a "note" through the normal diplomatic channels to the government which employs him, in protest. The reply is sent: "We disown him; we repudiate him". That is what the disciple must do to himself every day. Next, he must "take up" his cross. The aorist imperative is so decisive that "shoulder" is the best rendering. What is a cross for? It is for the purpose of one's own execution. It is as if our Lord had said "fling the hangman's rope round your neck"; "pick up the electric chair" (assuming that so weighty an object can be carried), and thereby be *ready* for your own death, and *keep on* following Me. But he can only keep on following as long as he is alive. The point is therefore not "crucify yourself" but "be ready to be crucified". It may never come to that; but you must be ready always. A man can hardly do all this in his sleep, and thus the Christian's daily programme is: 1. a diplomatic note to oneself—"I don't know you"; 2. a legal verdict on oneself; (both of these immediately on waking) 3. a journey for oneself, as long as life shall last. Under the last point a preacher can always encourage himself and his people by reflecting that a. our Lord is always in front; b. always in sight (Heb. 12: 2. Why look if you cannot see?); c. always ready to stop and help,

The variation of tenses in Acts 4: 13-14 is illuminating. "When they were staring (present participle) at the boldness of Peter and John, and it had flashed into their minds (aorist participle) that they

B

were uneducated men and devoid of training ("quacks") their eyes began to open wide in wonder (imperfect; the aorist would suggest "they started up with surprise". Compare the expression "you made me jump") and the recognition stole over them (the idea gradually penetrated their thick skulls—that is the force of the imperfect) that they had been with Jesus. And with the healed man before their eyes (present participle), as he stood with Peter and John, they were lacking (imperfect) any answer to bark out (aorist)." One could wish that the church at large could silence the world's criticism by always and everywhere furnishing the occasion of: a questioning stare, a discerning flash of insight, a growing wonder and a dawning recognition.

Sometimes the grouping of several texts will aid the preacher, especially if identity of tense suggests a theme. Consider, for example, Acts 3: 26, translated by the King James Version, Revised Version, by Moffatt and a number of moderns as "God sent Him to bless you." "Bless" is really a present participle, and the meaning literally is "God sent Him blessing you". We can convey this more idiomatically by saying "God sent Him with blessing in His hands for you". This was after the Resurrection. Before the Resurrection the same is true: "He went about doing good (present participle, Acts 10: 38)". And it is still true, as Luke makes clear in his brief story of the Ascension in his gospel (24: 50–51). Our Lord led His disciples out as far as Bethany, and there He lifted up His hands and blessed them. Now the evangelist is careful not to say "*after* He had blessed them He was separated from them". The use of the present tense implies that *while* the blessing was taking place He was parted from them. If upraised hands are part and parcel of the act of blessing, it is a fair inference that our Lord departed with His hands still raised in benediction, Thus our Saviour Christ gave blessing in the days of His flesh, in the period after the Resurrection, and even when in course of leaving His disciples. St. Luke's story is in accord with John's: "It is expedient for you, it is to your advantage, that I go away (16: 7)." That blessing has never ceased, and "Jesus Christ is the same, yesterday and today and for ever" (Heb. 13: 8).

A somewhat lighter though no less vivid touch is given in Acts 19: 30. A riot had broken out in Ephesus at the instigation of the cynical silversmith Demetrius, who camouflaged a defence of vested interests with a convenient concern for religion. In the confusion and uproar the people rushed into the theatre, and the apostle Paul, always the evangelist, "was wanting to enter into the crowd, but the disciples were not permitting him (imperfect)." This might be a case of continued action: "they were all the time holding him down", but it is more likely to be repeated action. Every time he started up or took a pace forward to go to the theatre, they laid their hands on him to prevent him. At every attempt they blocked his way. It would be amusing if it were not for the seriousness of the situation, but it does give us a picture of the impatient apostle, straining and tugging like a restive horse, every now and then making a fresh effort to break away and not being allowed to. "They kept bringing affectionate force to bear on him to prevent him." Even some of the Asiarchs, the officials who were friends of Paul, had to "keep on saying 'don't go' ". The apostle's wisdom may be criticised, but his courage and spirit are above praise. The church today needs such men in their thousands.

There is an unconscious touch of humour in the silversmith's quotation of the apostle, "They are not gods which are being made with hands" (v. 26). It might be argued that this is repeated action, as one god after another is made, like automobiles coming off the lines in the factory! Following our diagrammatic representation we could write, not a series of dots, but a series of little shrines, one behind the other, neatly arranged as in the car park! But the silversmith is probably giving us a private view over the workshop. Gods are being made: cutting, shaping, polishing, all activity goes to the making of gods that are being produced in the factory. Inhabitants of Coventry or Detroit should see the funny side of this, and a preacher in either of these places ought to be able to speak to the people in their own language.

Sometimes the use of tenses clears up a positive difficulty for the expositor. A notorious problem is Hebrews 6: 4–6, but due attention to the tenses makes it easier to understand. "As regards those on whom the beam of light once fell (aorist), and who smacked the flavour (aorist) of the heavenly gift and crossed the line that made them (aorist) partakers of the Holy Ghost, and got a taste of (aorist) how good the Word of God is and the powers of the coming age, and fall back (aorist)—it is impossible to keep on repeatedly leading them (present) afresh into repentance, seeing that (or while) they keep on crucifying (present) for themselves the Son of God, and keep on putting Him to open shame (present)." Compare Hebrews 10: 26, "if we go on sinning (present) wilfully after we got (aorist) (as decisive as the act of a boy who caught a ball cleanly) the knowledge of the truth, there is no longer left a sacrifice for sins . . ." The experience of missionaries and clergymen generally has been quoted to confirm the truth of all this. The writer is not thinking of an isolated lapse, for which there is forgiveness. He is stating a principle and has in mind the farce of trying to renew repentance in people who have lost their moral sense, and for whom the Cross means nothing. We might compare Mark 4: 16–17.

Sometimes a whole delicate history may be hidden away under an imperfect. Consider Acts 9: 26. St. Paul "arrived on the scene (aorist) in Jerusalem and tried repeatedly (or "made a number of attempts"— imperfect) to weave the threads of his life on to the texture of the disciples' fellowship; and they were all in a state of fear (imperfect) of him, as they were sceptical (present participle) about his being a disciple". We have here a picture of the new convert still in the first flush of his Christian enthusiasm, and of the cold welcome which he received. He must have suffered a number of rebuffs ("Spy!" "Persecutor!"); or else the mere negative attitude which refused to receive him as "one of us". Each time he had to try again, and the brilliant young scholar and aristocrat found much to try his pride. It speaks much for the reality of his conversion that he persisted until Barnabas intervened (v. 27). The details of Saul's endeavours are hidden from us, but a sane and sanctified imagination can pierce behind the screen of the imperfect tense. As to his "weaving the threads of his life", I paraphrased it in this way in order to bring out the force of the present infinitive. The word in the active voice means "to glue", and in the middle and passive "to join oneself closely". If it had been an aorist infinitive the task would have been easy: "he was trying repeatedly to *link on* to the disciples". The picture might be that of a hook, one hook, which in one decisive act joins on to something. But the present infinitive suggests the *process* of joining and weaving seemed as good a metaphor as any. One does not, least of all Saul the former persecutor, dive head-first (a pinpoint idea) into the middle of a mature Christian fellowship. The present infinitive preserves and recognises this thought. This obscure, and we hope brief, period in the apostle's history makes his subsequent behaviour appear all the grander, for it was he who organised the collection of the Gentile churches for "the poor saints" in Jerusalem. This was indeed turning the other cheek. (1 Cor. 16: 1–4; Matt. 5: 39).

We are now ready to attempt the translation of a longer passage, trying to give the full significance to the tenses. Our rendering will not aim primarily at being literary but rather at producing figures of speech which are relevant to the sense. If there is some repetition or if our version grates on the ears, let it be remembered that it is being made as an aid to understanding the spirit of the Greek and not to be read in public worship. Let us take 1 John 3, which contains a large proportion of present tenses.

1.   Take a look at the greatness of the love which the Father has given to us, that we should be dubbed children of God; and we are that. This is the reason why the world does not know us: it did not "discover" Him. Beloved friends, we are now children of God, and the curtain has not yet gone up to show what we shall be. We know that if He comes into our view we shall be like Him, because we shall see Him as He is. And every man who has this hope in Him makes himself pure, just as HE is pure. Every man who makes a practice of
5. sin does the same with lawlessness also; the two are identical. And you know that HE came into our ken in order that HE might bundle our sins away, and there is no sin in Him. Every man who dwells—and stays at home—in Him does not make a habit of sin. Every man who does this has failed to see Him and has not come to know Him. Little children, let nobody deceive you: he who persists in doing righteousness is righteous, just as HE is righteous; he who habitually commits sin traces his origin to the devil, because the devil has been sinning from the beginning. For this purpose the Son of God came into our ken, namely, that He might disintegrate the works of the devil. Everyone who in spiritual lineage has God as his Father does not repeatedly commit sin, because of the law of spiritual heredity; and he is not at liberty to go on sinning, because in spiritual lineage he has God as his Father.
10. This is the test which shows the children of God and the children of the devil in their true colours: every one who is not continually doing righteousness does not originate in God; and no more does he who does not maintain his love of his brother unbroken. Because this is the message which fell upon your ears to bind you from the beginning on, that there should be no intervals in our love for one another. Not as Cain originated from the evil one and ran his brother through with the sword; and for what reason did he run him through? Because his works were wicked, but those of his brother were righteous.
     Stop being surprised, brothers, that the world is hating you. We know that we have changed our residence from death to life, because we are loving the brothers; he who does not love is resident in death. Everyone who cherishes

15. hatred for his brother is a murderer, and you are aware that no murderer has eternal life remaining in him. By this we have come to know love: HE laid down His life for us; and we are under obligation to lay down our lives for the brothers. But whoever possesses the livelihood which this world affords, and stares at his brother in his need and slams the door of his heart against him, how is the love of God resident in him? Little children, let us not love by word or language, but in the realm of deed and truth. By this test we shall find out that it was the truth which brought us into being and shall persuade

20. our heart before Him: if our heart keeps pricking us with condemnation, God is greater than our heart and knows everything. Beloved friends, if our heart does not thus keep on pricking us, we have boldness towards God, and whatever we ask for we receive from Him, because it is our habit to keep His commandments and to do what is pleasing in His sight. And this is His commandment, that we gain a faith in the Name of His Son Jesus Christ and proceed with love to one another just as He gave us commandment. And he who keeps His commandments dwells—and stays at home—in Him, and He in him. And by this we know that He dwells in us: from the Spirit Whom He gave to us.

We must now review our rendering and pass a few comments. "Take a look at" is not too elegant, but it reflects the spirit of the aorist. "Dubbed" is a word which is closely associated with the creation of a knight. The man kneels down in front of the monarch, who strikes his shoulder with the flat of a sword. He kneels, plain Galahad; he rises, Sir Galahad; and the creation of a knight is brought into a focus, a temporal "point", as the sword strikes his shoulder. By that act the king "dubs" him Sir Galahad. It is a good word for conveying the spirit of the aorist "that we should be called" and readers of Tennyson will not miss the aura of romance. "Discover" is written in inverted commas because we have an aorist to deal with once more. An ambitious man sometimes says, perhaps facetiously, "I am waiting to be discovered". The Son of God lived in the backwoods of the Roman Empire and the rulers of this world did not "discover" Him. That is why you are not known either.

"The curtain has not yet gone up" contains a perfect tense, which is necessary in English idiom because of the words "not yet". But the Greek is an aorist, and I have tried to preserve the idea of this tense even in the English perfect by the metaphor of the curtain. When the curtain rises (a "pinpoint" action) it "makes manifest" the stage. To avoid the repetition of the same word in English I have translated the aorist subjunctive in the following sentence, though it is the same Greek verb, by "comes into our view". The picture suggested is that of a man being found in a room when the electric light is switched on, or of a train suddenly being seen when it rounds a bend.

There are a few more aorists, though we now begin to come across some very significant presents, which express continuous or repeated action. This explains the introduction of "practice" (v. 4) in rendering "he who keeps on doing sin." "Came into our ken" is but another variant for the aorist of the former verb, "make manifest". "Bundle our sins away" is a vigorous way of translating an aorist of the Greek verb which is used also in John 1: 29 in the present: "Behold the Lamb of God who is taking away, bearing away, lifting, shifting, the sin of the world". (It is the Greek equivalent of the Latin *tollo*.) As it is aorist the idea of shifting has to be made punctiliar, faithful to the "pinpoint"; and "bundle", used as a verb, visualises all the formerly scattered pieces as united in one bundle; and then in a moment, a pinpoint of time—out!

In verse 6 ("he who continually dwells in Him", present tense) the idea of continuity is indicated by the device "he who dwells—and stays at home". "Habit" is a stylistic variant on "practice". "Does this" merely avoids repetition of the previous idea. "Persists in" (v. 7) is yet another variant on "practice" and "habit" in order to bring out the continuity. So with "habitually" in verse 8. "Disintegrate" represents the aorist subjunctive of the Greek verb "to loose". When an earthquake violently shakes a house the parts which were firmly joined together are loosed and the building collapses: it ceases to be a whole, an "integer".

As a vivid alternative we might say "that He might blow up the works of the devil." "To blow up" will "reduce to fragments", which will certainly "loose" the devil's edifice. Quite involuntarily the picture flashed into my mind of a building "going up" as a result of dynamite. "Repeatedly" in verse 9 is a variant similar to the previous ones. The same is true of "go on sinning". For "at liberty to" as a rendering of "be able", compare Luke 11: 7. "Continually" (v. 10) and "maintain unbroken" are yet further ways of expressing continuity. So with "no intervals" in verse 11. "Ran through" (v. 12) is a case of the punctiliar again. In like manner (v. 16) "we are under obligation" is better than the colourless "ought". "Slams the door" (v. 17) a quick decisive action, is a more appropriate translation of the aorist than the bare "shuts". "Is resident" draws out the continuity in a way that "does dwell" fails to do.

Verse 20 needs a little explanation. "Our heart pricked us" might suggest a pinpoint suitable to an aorist, a single stab. But "keeps pricking" implies a series of stabs. And what is a line of points on paper, which we have used to represent repeated action, if not the result of a number of pricks or stabs or jabs with a typewriter? The meaning of the verb is shown by saying "keeps pricking with condemnation" and it reminds us of the normal English idiom of the pricking of—not the heart but—the conscience. (A possible rendering is ". . . shall persuade our heart before Him whatever condemnation our heart insists on: God is greater than our heart. . . ." In other words, the heart keeps on saying, "you are condemned.")

"Gain a faith" (v. 23) stands for an ingressive aorist. Instead we might say "put our trust in . . ." "Proceed with love to": continuity once more.

Whether all this will commend itself to preachers remains to be seen. But if one's own experience is any guide, it certainly enables the man in the pulpit to bring forth from his treasure things new as well as old. "Keep on becoming doers of the word" says the scripture (Jas. 1: 22). We are like commuters who hear the railroad instructions every day, but need actually to go to the location indicated—the right platform or the right part of the platform—if we are to be "doers of the word". Suppose a commuter wrote a dot on a piece of paper every day he went to the right location. At the end of a month he would have a long line of dots. This is exactly how we represented repeated action, and as I was looking at the Greek word rendered "keep on becoming" I saw those dots and the thought of the commuters occurred to me. It is a very simple illustration, but if a man reads widely, not only theology and church history but biography and novels, he should find that the right illustration jumps into his mind as he ponders the text. The very tense of the Greek will suggest it.

If a man needs encouragement, let him read 1 Corinthians 15: 25: "He must stay-on-the-throne (present infinitive) until He has put all enemies under His feet". Or let him look at the 57th verse of the same chapter: "thanks be to God who keeps-on-giving to us the victory through our Lord Jesus Christ". Is it repeated action, like that of the soldier who keeps on giving out trays of food to the G.I.'s in Fort Monmouth? Or is it continued unbroken, like that of a man paying out a seemingly endless cable?

Or does he seek an example? Look at Luke 23: 28: "Jesus turned to the women and shot-out-the-words (aorist of 'He said'), 'Daughters of Jerusalem, cease your weeping over Me.'" Then look further at verse 34: "Jesus *kept-on-saying* (*imperfect* of "He said"), 'Father, forgive them; for they know not what they do'".

Or would he be moved by the Passion of our Lord? Let him note the fearful words: "Go on with the crucifixion" (Luke 23: 21).

Or does he wish to see how providence can snatch victory out of failure? Turn to Acts 7: 26–29: "And on the next day he appeared to them when they were engaged in a fight, and he put-forth-reconciling-persuasion (conative imperfect), he tried to reconcile them, to bring them together in peace, saying 'My men, you are brothers; for what purpose are you wronging each other?' And he who was wronging his neighbour pushed him away (gave him a push) barking out (aorist participle of verb 'to say') 'Who appointed you a ruler and judge over us? You don't want to bump me off, do you, in the way in which you bumped off the Egyptian yesterday?' And Moses fled . . ." His attempt at reconciliation failed; but what a future he had!

Here are "motels" for life's pilgrimage: "If we keep on walking in the light as He is in the light we have unbroken fellowship with one another and the blood of Jesus His Son *keeps us clean* from all sin." (1 John 1: 7) At every stop on the road there is refreshment and cleansing.

Here is a light to counteract the dark clouds of the gathering storm: "the darkness is passing away (like a sombre funeral procession which does not halt opposite us, but passes on down the road) and the real light (not some artificial, "ersatz" make-do) is already shining" (1 John 2 : 8; compare v. 17).

The processes, processions and panoramas of the present and imperfect tenses should be a god-send to the preacher.

Chapter 3

FOOTPRINTS

Lives of great men all remind us
We can make our lives sublime,
And, departing, leave behind us
Footprints on the sands of time.

WE MAY or may not make our lives sublime but there is a sense in which we all leave footprints behind us. Every time we use the perfect tense we are really calling attention to the footprints which have been left by a former action. For the perfect expresses the abiding result of a past act. Here an illustration may save pages of argument. A mother may say "I dressed William in his best clothes." She says that—and no more. But a thousand things may have happened since then. She may go on to say "It was only ten minutes ago, and now look at him!" He may have fallen down and torn his coat; a class-mate may have thrown mud at him; or he may have taken his father's paint-brush and daubed his clothes to camouflage himself in a realistic game. It might be even worse. The mother might say instead: "That was twenty years ago. He went out at once into the road, was knocked down by a car and killed." But suppose that instead of her original statement she had said "I *have dressed* William in his best clothes". There is a subtle difference here, because she could not have said it if any of the above mentioned unhappy experiences had taken place. If the coat is torn or covered with mud or paint she could not say "I have dressed him", because "have dressed" is a perfect tense, which expresses the *abiding result* of a past action. Such a result can always be expressed, by a slight alteration, in the present tense. Thus William's mother can say "He *is* ready for the party", or "he *is* presentable" or "he *is* respectable" or simply "he *is* in good clothes", which explicitly states what is contained implicitly in the perfect tense. Thus, speaking very metaphorically, we can say that she has left footprints of her former work which have lasted up to the present moment. Hence the title of this chapter which is devoted to the perfect tense. For the sake of completeness we may add that just as the perfect tense expresses the result which lasts up to the present moment, so the pluperfect tense ("I had dressed") expresses the result which lasted up to a certain point in the past.

Now the preacher will do well to pay attention to these variations of meaning, not only because it will enable him to understand the sacred text but also because it should constantly be giving him new ideas for his sermons, or at any rate a new way of approaching old ideas. Consider the noble passage in Romans 8: 38–39, "I am persuaded that neither death nor life... will be able to separate us from the love of God which is in Christ Jesus our Lord". The first Greek word is in the perfect tense and means "I have been persuaded". The preacher's first task is to transform this into its equivalent present: "I have been persuaded" means "I am . . ."—what? "I *am now sure* on the basis of my own experience through the years." There is no reason why he should not change the subject: "With the experiences of life as my teachers it *is* now my firm conviction . . ." What were those experiences? The apostle is ransacking his vocabulary in order to show that the whole universe cannot at any time put-a-space-between (note the force of the aorist) the love of Christ and us, and he has had experience of much of what he outlines. He has not actually died but he has faced death: has seen it threaten himself and seen it take away others. Sir Geoffrey Shakespeare, son of the great Christian leader, Dr. J. H. Shakespeare, has briefly described the passing of his father. "I was with him at the end, and as his spirit sped away he wore a look of inexpressible joy and peace; and his face was transfigured by a smile of sudden recognition as when a man meets a friend."[1] St. Paul would have understood: it was partly the experiencing of such scenes as this that convinced him that nothing can separate us from the love of Christ. Life? For years the apostle's own life had shown him the love of Christ at every point. Angelic beings, that seemed to rule the world and had the prestige now accorded to natural law? They had not succeeded hitherto. The present? He has constantly lived through it. The future? He has always been stepping into it. And Christ, having died once, dies no more. His love ever lives and He Who is enthroned as Lord of earth and heaven will not cease to make His love felt in the apostle's life. St. Paul *has* Christian certainty: that is the force of the perfect tense. In verse 36 he has used another perfect "it has been written". He means that "it now exists in writing". Business men know the value of the written as against the spoken word. To have something in writing means a permanent record which changes not with man's changeableness.

[1] *Let Candles be Brought In, p. 347.*

In Ephesians 2: 5, 8 he says "You have been saved". As I write these words the news is reported that a 20,300-ton liner has run aground on the island of Orleans in the St. Lawrence River just off Quebec. A statement from the ship-owners asserts that "all passengers have been landed". For them it means "You now are on land in safety", which is roughly what St. Paul meant. The New Testament teaches a salvation by grace, and if a man could be saved yesterday and lost today, saved tomorrow and lost the day after, it would not be salvation by grace but salvation by luck: if he chanced to die on a day when he was "saved" all would be well. Thus once again we are brought face to face with Christian certainty. You Ephesian Christians *are* on salvation territory; the danger *is* behind you; you *are* safe. This is a gospel which needs today to be proclaimed from the housetops.

St. John 16: 33 reads thus: "I have told you this in order that in Me you may have peace. In the world you have pressure; but be of good cheer, I have overcome the world." "I have told you" implies "You know My views; you know My attitude; you know My message; you now possess the memory of My Words". All this is a treasure on which they will be able to draw, a perpetual centre of peace in the cyclone of their life. Hence, "you have My message, that in Me you may be in possession of peace (may enjoy peace, cf. Rom. 5: 1, where note present tense). In the world you have (not peace but) pressure; but keep your courage up (present), I have overcome the world". The *message* is a source of peace. In times of stress we look for comfort, to be "mothered": it is significant that our Lord recognised the power of truth. "He caught sight of a great crowd and they pierced His heart because they were as sheep possessing no shepherd, and He began (not to shepherd them but) to teach them many truths." (Mark 6: 34)

There is another source of peace, indeed of courage. "I have overcome the world." This perfect suggests that "the world now lies prostrate in defeat" and there is a sense in which this is true. Try as the world will, it cannot defeat the purposes of God. But there is another sense which is perhaps more helpful. There are certain diseases which medical science today is fighting though victory is not yet in sight. But in some diseases the battle has been won: the cause of malaria has been discovered. "Do not be afraid to go to certain parts of Africa," says the medical profession; "I have overcome the disease. It *is now* helpless before you." So with the disease which is the "world". "Keep your courage up; the world cannot touch you." "Stop being afraid of

those who kill the body but are unable to strike the soul dead"
(Matt. 10: 28).

Something on the same lines is found in 2 Corinthians 1: 8–9; "We
do not wish you to be kept in the dark, brothers, about the pressure
which was switched on against us in Asia; the whole weight of the
excessive blow crashed on our inadequate strength so as to shock us
into despair of continuing our life; but we have got and possess still
(perfect) within ourselves the answer to death, so that we may not
rest our trust in ourselves but in the God whose habit it is to raise
the dead; Who wrested us from so great a death, and will rescue
us; and He is the trustee of our hope (perfect) that He will also still
rescue us . . ." This is a bold paraphrase but true, I venture to think,
to the spirit of the Greek. Any mixed metaphors—and they are not
serious—are hardly more heinous than St. Paul's own combination
of pressure and weight.

Now two perfect tenses suggest two parallel trends of thought.
Death threatens like a truculent frontier patrol, but we have obtained
the answer. Our papers are in order and *we carry them on us*. That
is surely the force of the perfect in verse 9. We do not brazen our way
past him, relying on ourselves, but we rely on our papers which God
has given us. They have got us past the awkward official before now,
and they still do, thanks to the power of Him Who originally issued
them.

As to the future everything depends on that great power (in the
sense in which we speak politically of a country as a "great power").
We *have hoped* in Him. *He* therefore *still carries* our hopeful request
for protection in foreign lands. It has not become out of date, and
He has not ceased to be a great power. Thus *we have the papers* (e.g.
passports, visas etc.). *He is the authority* which makes them effective.
People who have travelled abroad will readily understand the
allusion.

The power of the Greek language to bring pictures to one's
mind is shown in a paragraph about Apollos (Acts 18: 24–28). "He
had been instructed (periphrastic pluperfect) in the way of the Lord"
(v. 25). The implication is that the lessons learnt had stuck. We may
therefore say "He was *familiar with* the way of the Lord". The road
the Lord Himself travelled, or the road the Lord made for us, was
not something outside his own knowledge. He did not feel as a
person feels who plays a piece of music "at sight" or attempts an
"unseen" translation. Like the driver of the swift Greyhound coach,
he knew the road. And yet, despite his familiarity with it, he had
more to learn, more detail to master. Priscilla and Aquila (v. 26)

undertook to teach him, and the Greek aorist ("they set forth the way of God") raises an interesting picture. In the London "Punch", the best of the English humorous papers, a picture appeared during a period of national austerity, poking fun at the socialites who have a carpet laid down at the church steps and down the drive for the bridal procession. The picture showed the happy pair emerging from the church porch, heads high in the air, marching down the long carpet. In front of them a workman, not by any means dressed for the occasion, was unrolling the carpet; behind them another workman was rolling it up! In a time of scarcity, when the carpet may be wanted for another wedding in half an hour's time, such is the device to which fashion will descend. (The reader must not take this too solemnly: *Punch* loves to poke fun and everybody enjoys it.) Now it seems to me that that is exactly what Priscilla and Aquila did. They unrolled the "path" before Apollos, and no doubt pointed out its width, length and patterns. The picture is almost fantastic, but the picture and the Greek word came together in my mind with a click, and a picture will capture the congregation as an argument may not. Such is the power and beauty of Greek.

You can observe the same power in Acts 22: 10, "Arise, resume your journey to Damascus, and there you will be told about all things to-do-which has been assigned you". The last part has purposely been rendered literally to show the structure of the clause. The performance of certain deeds, then, has been assigned (perfect) to Saul. Now the verb "assign" in Greek means "arrange", to "put in its place", so that we might roughly say "the programme of your work has been put in its place and *is now waiting* in its place". This has reminded me of the American system of "checking" luggage. Someone has deposited a detailed set of plans in a locker, where they are waiting for Saul to take them out and act on them. The preacher can say that when Christ lays hold of a man he may look for three things: 1. a journey to be continued (resume your journey— present imperative: Christ sends us on our same way, but different men; the clerk to his office, the farmer to his fields, and so on); 2. a message to be expected (it shall be told you); and 3. a task to be undertaken. Go and find out—it is already waiting for you.

So far we have had a number of other tenses mixed up with the perfects. Let us consider a few perfects in isolation. "I have gazed at the Spirit descending as a dove out of heaven" (John 1: 32) means "I can now visualise the descent of the Spirit"; or "I can now testify to His descent." A bare aorist would leave the door open for a later remark "I gazed—but have forgotten the details; the scene

left no impression on me". "We have found the Messiah" (John
1: 41) means "We know now where He is", perhaps even "We now
have Him". Our Lord's cry from the cross, "It is finished" (John
19: 30), better "It has been finished", implies "The work is now
complete", or even "the gospel is now ready to be preached". "He
has been raised" (1 Cor. 15: 4) re-assures us with its meaning of "He
is now *up!*", that is to say, He is not like Lazarus or the son of the
widow of Nain, who "were raised" (not "have been raised") but
died again. In Acts 18: 27 "those who had believed through grace"
or "those who had gained a faith" implies "those who held in their
hearts a faith by which to live, a working faith", the pluperfect
being re-interpreted as an imperfect. 1 Corinthians 1: 10 is interesting: "I urge you, brothers, through the Name of our Lord Jesus
Christ, all continually to exhibit unanimity in speech and not to
countenance splits in your body corporate, but to be compacted by
the same mind and the same will". The perfect participle "compacted" means "now of one piece"—a noble standard for a local
manifestation of the church. Perhaps we have a picture of a fishing
net: see Mark 1: 19 and compare Eph. 4: 12. "Of one piece" is
obviously of great importance.

In 1 Corinthians 1: 23 the apostle states that "we are preaching
Christ crucified". The perfect participle "crucified" suggests "He has
been crucified". Why does Paul put it in this way? Hundreds of men
had been crucified in the lifetime of our Lord, but they had gone to
their unhappy graves unsung and forgotten. But Christ Jesus is now
One to Whom the perfect tense calls attention: He *is* now One Who
bears the marks of the nails and of the sword—He now understands
human pain; He is now One Who remembers the agony and the
dereliction (Mark 15: 34)—He knows now the loathsome touch of
sin, for He has borne it, and the cost of redemption; He is now the
Redeemer. He knows our pain, and sympathises; He knows our
sin, and intercedes; He knows His triumph over both, and ours
in Him. He has been crucified! He *is* the Christ of the Cross.

Luke 12: 7 says that "the hairs of your head have all been
counted". In other words, "their number *is* exactly known and not
one of them can be removed by an enemy without trace". This
reinterpretation of the perfect in terms of the present saves us from
the naive view of God (the omniscient One!) actually "counting".
In Hebrews 3: 14 "we have become partakers of Christ" means
"we are now taking our share of Him". "Let us take fright, with
fear that . . . any one of you should seem to have been too late"
(Heb. 4: 1) may be transposed to "lest any one of you should seem

to be gazing after a train that has gone", or "seem to be stretching out a hand to what is now out of reach". "We have been evangelised" in verse 2 implies "we know the good news, we know the remedy for sin, we are responsible".

"Has Christ been divided?" in 1 Cor. 1: 13 means the vivid "Is Christ in pieces?" The "having been exercised" of Hebrews 5: 14 and 12: 11 means "fit" in the sense in which an energetic footballer says "I am fit". "You have become dull in your faculties of hearing" (Heb. 5: 11), allied with "You have become in need of milk, not of solid food" (v. 12) almost suggests "You are in your second childhood". "He has taken His seat on the right hand of the throne of God" (Heb. 12: 2) means "He is now sitting". Contrast Acts 7: 56 ("standing") (in witness? Matt. 10: 32) and note that the "heavens having been opened" means "the heavens gaping wide". "Having been begotten again not of corruptible seed but of incorruptible" (1 Pet. 1: 23) means "being now alive in a new world and members of a family that does not die". "He has given us of His Spirit" (1 John 4: 13) means "We are the rightful possessors of a measure of His Spirit". "God has given evidence about His Son" (1 John 5: 9) makes us realise that "the evidence is available" if we care to take the trouble to assemble it to present afresh to the tribunal of our minds. The thought is repeated in the following verse, where in addition we are shown the dreadful picture of God branded with infamy. "He has made God a liar" implies that "God is notorious as One not to be believed"—a fearful footprint for a sinful man to leave behind him. "The requests which we have asked (perfect) from Him", or more idiomatically "have made to Him" (verse 15) brings to our minds the picture of the storekeeper who says to a prospective customer "No, madam, I have not any in stock at the moment, but I *have asked for* them". In other words our requests "are with God" and "they are on the way". And so are the answers to our prayers.

"This has not been done in a corner" (Acts 26: 26) is a vivid expression for those who have eyes to see it. The perfect tense implies that "it is not now lying in a corner". The Greek word for a corner means also an angle, and anything "in" it is presumably between the two arms of the angle and near to the apex. There is only one way in. To find out about anything "in an angle" is like investigating something in a cul-de-sac. It is off the beaten track and may be approached from one side only. In a great city an occurrence might take place here and be undiscovered for a very long time. But "this" is not a bit of backstreet politics; it is not a private liquidation

in streets which the police do not visit; it has repercussions over a
wide area. Approach from any direction you like and you will find
the footprints of the divine.

Acts 13: 48 speaks of "those who had been appointed to eternal
life", "those who had been put in their place with a view to eternal
life". (The word means "to arrange".) The perfect participle suggests "all those who were *in the right group* for eternal life". Only
those of us who were *in the right location* at the Pennsylvania Station,
Philadelphia, boarded that portion of the train which was later to
join the "Texas Special" and bring us safely to Austin, Texas. And so
we paraphrase "All those who through God's grace were in the
right location for eternal life plunged into faith". There is such a
thing as prevenient grace. The preacher must consider whether the
"location" is the Gentiles; the place where Christ is preached; or
the divine enrolment (Luke 10: 20).

There is a subtle difference in the interpretation of the two perfect
tenses of the same verb in 1 John 4: 1–2. "Many false prophets
have gone out into the world." This implies "Many false prophets
are now in the world", and perhaps we may add "telling out their
dreadful doctrines". But "Jesus Christ has come in the flesh" does
not mean "Jesus Christ is here in the flesh", although at first sight
it might appear to do so. It implies rather "The human life of Jesus
has left its mark in the world", and so "His mark is now in the
world". Similarly, "The Father has sent His Son as Saviour of the
world" (1 John 4: 14) does not mean "The Son is now in the world,
saving it", though in another context it might have done. It means
that "the process of saving the world is now in operation".

An illustration may help here. The late Dr. Fort Newton said in a
sermon in Liverpool Cathedral that the English county of Nor-
thamptonshire ought to be annexed as the 49th State in the Union.
Apart from anything else, it had furnished the ancestors of five of the
American Presidents. After the service the Dean of Liverpool said
in mock severity to a member of the Royal Family "What does your
Royal Highness think of the notorious proposal of aggression by
Dr. Fort Newton, suggesting that Northamptonshire be given up?"
The Duke interposed no objection to the evidence, but added that
"since America *has taken* the best of Northampton, it ought not to
bother about the rest!" (Dr. Fort Newton told me this story himself
in 1948.) America has taken; an Englishman might say "we have
given you". Washington had associations with Sulgrave Manor,
Northamptonshire. "We have given you Washington." But this
does not mean quite "You now have this great man", as he has been

withdrawn from this world. It means "The work of Washington still abides". And so our text means that "the saving work of Christ is still going on", and perhaps also "we are in God's debt for Him".

Once more, there is a subtle distinction of meaning in Hebrews 13: 3, "Continue to remember the prisoners, bearing this in mind as you do so: 'we have been bound with them'." "We have been bound" ought to mean "we are in chains", but its meaning is most likely not this but "we know the inside of a prison and are therefore full of understanding". Contrast Mark 15: 7, "in chains", and "stained with blood".

One last example before we pass on to attempt the translation of a longer passage. The Beatitude in Matt. 5: 10 reads "Blessed are they who *have been persecuted.* . . ." It surely implies "Blessed are they who bear the scars of persecution". We can paraphrase: "Blessed are they whose faces bear the lines and whose minds the wounds, of persecution". They, too, can sympathise.

Now let us attempt to translate 1 John 1: 1–2: 29.

> That which was from the beginning, which still rings in our ears, the vision of which is still before our eyes, on which we concentrated our gaze and which our hands felt, regarding the Word of life—and the curtain went up on the life and that first scene left an indelible impression in our minds: we are giving our testimony and bringing to you the news of life eternal which was with the Father and broke upon our gaze—we are bringing to you as well the continuing vision of what we saw and the echoing music of what we heard, in order that you also may march the same road of fellowship with us. And our fellowship also is with the Father and with His Son Jesus Christ. And we are writing this in order that our joy may be full.
>
> 5.   And this is the message from Him which lingers in our ears and which we are passing on to you: that God is light and there is no darkness in Him. If we assert "We enjoy fellowship with Him" and proceed on our way in darkness, then we are lying and truth is not present in our deeds. But if we keep on our way in the light as He is in the light, we enjoy fellowship with one another and the blood of Jesus His Son cleanses us from every sin as it occurs. If we make the statement "We have no sin" we are driving ourselves away from what is right and the truth is not in us. If our habit is to confess our sins He is faithful and just to cut loose the

sins which bind us and to make a wave of cleansing from all
10. unrighteousness break over us. If we say "We have not
sinned—we can find no trace of it" we are making Him a
liar and His word is not in us.

2: 1 Little children of mine, I am writing this to you to keep
you from a crash into sin. And if ever a man does crash into
it, we have an Advocate with the Father all the time, Jesus
Christ the Righteous; and He is the propitiation for our sins,
and not only for ours but also for those of the whole world.
And by this test we know that we have come to a lasting
knowledge of Him: if we maintain the keeping of His commandments. He who says "I have come to a lasting knowledge
of Him" and whose keeping of His commandments does not
last, is a liar, and in him the truth is not present; but whoever
5. keeps His word without a break, truly in him love to God has
blossomed into flower. By this we know that we are in Him:
he who says that he is dwelling in Him is under obligation
himself also to make his way in the manner in which He
covered the course.

Beloved, it is not a fresh commandment that I am writing
to you, but an old one which was in your hands from the
beginning; the old commandment is the word which fell
upon your ears. Again, a fresh commandment I am writing to
you: it is what is true in Him and in you, because the darkness
is passing away and the real light is already shining.

He who maintains that he is in the light and all the while
hates his brother is in darkness until now. He who maintains
10. his love of his brother has his home in the light, and there is
nothing in him which makes other people trip up; but he
whose attitude to his brother is one of hate is in darkness and
is walking in darkness and does not know where he is going.
How is this? It is because the darkness dropped a mist of
blindness before his eyes.

I am writing to you, little children, because you are now
free from the sins which bound you, for the sake of His
Name. I am writing to you, fathers, because you are at the
end of your search for Him Who is from the beginning. I am
writing to you, young men, because you know the thrill of
laying low the evil one. I have written to you, little children,
because you know the Father. I have written to you, fathers,
because you possess the knowledge of Him Who is from the
beginning. I have written to you, young men, because you

are strong and the Word of God has its home in you and you
15. know the thrill of laying low the evil one. Do not let the
world keep its hold on your love; no, nor what is in the world
either. If a man does love the world, the love of the Father is
not in him; because all that is in the world, the desire of the
flesh, and the desire of the eyes and the ostentation of life,
does not proceed from the Father but from the world. And
the world is passing away, and its desire; but he who ever
does God's will continues for ever.

Little children, it is the last hour, and as you heard the
warning shot to indicate that antichrist was on the way,
so now many antichrists are at large. From this we know
that it is the last hour. They went out from us but they
were not "one of us". For if they had been "one of us"
they would have been with us still; but (they went out)
20. so that they might be shown up as being, without exception,
"not one of us". And *you* have a gift with which the Holy
One has anointed you, and you all have knowledge. I have
not written to you because you do not know the truth but
because you do know it and know too that no falsehood is
derived from the truth.

Who is the liar except the man who harps on his denials of
Jesu's Messiahship? This is the antichrist, the man who
unites the Father and the Son in his denials. Every one whose
attitude repudiates the Son has not the Father either; he
whose attitude confesses the Son has the Father also. Let that
remain in you, which fell on *your* ears from the beginning.
If it makes its permanent home in you, you also will have
25. your home in the Son and in the Father. And this is the
promise which He made to us: eternal life.

I have written this to you about those who are busying
themselves with leading you astray. And the gift which *you*
got from Him in your anointing has its home in you and you
have no need for anyone to give you a course of lessons; but
as His anointing-gift covers everything in its lessons and is
true and is not a lie, and as it rammed its teaching home in
you, stay at home in it. And now, little children, stay at
home in Him, so that if the curtain go up on Him our faces
may light up with boldness and not fall with shame before
Him in His presence. If you know that He is righteous you are
aware that every one whose habit is righteousness is a member
of His family by spiritual birth.

We must now attempt to explain and perhaps also to justify some of the renderings in the above. "What we have heard" (1: 1) naturally, as a perfect, suggests the abiding impression which has been made on us, and "still rings in our ears" is a fair way of bringing this out. It keeps to the original reference to the sense of hearing, but at the same time transcends it by being metaphorical. Similarly with "we have seen": we are not forgetting that the experience was concerned with the sensation of sight, and we have kept to this, though metaphorically. "On which we concentrated our gaze" is the result of a long consideration. The Greek verb means to behold, to gaze, to stare at, and seems to imply a sustained effort: there is a difference between "getting a glimpse of" and "having a good look at". The verb, in fact, is connected with the English word "theatre", a place where people "stare" or "gaze" for hours on end. It seems to be the sort of verb which ought to be put in the imperfect tense, because its very meaning points to continuity. But here it is in the aorist and the problem is to combine both the continued gazing and the "pinpoint" of the aorist. Now when we concentrate we make our whole attention converge on one focal *point*, so that "concentrated our gaze" did justice both to the meaning of the word and to the fact that it is an aorist.

"The curtain went up on the life" (v. 2) renders the ingressive aorist. "We have seen" then appears for the second time, and to avoid repetition of "the vision of which is still before our eyes" I have drawn attention to the abiding result which the perfect expresses and at the same time retained the visual reference by saying "that first scene (this is to do with seeing, not, e.g. hearing) left an indelible impression in our minds". "We are giving our testimony and bringing to you the news" represents two present tenses, which show to us the work actually going on, something of that "movement" which the Greek expresses. "Broke upon our gaze" is but a variant for "the curtain went up on the life"; the Greek word is the same and it is another ingressive aorist. Once more (v. 3), we have to find yet another way of rendering the perfects "we have seen" and "we have heard", and though we used the colourless English "we saw" and "we heard", we preserved the "abiding result" of the perfect by saying "the continuing vision of what we saw and the echoing music (metaphorically) of what we heard". "March the same road of fellowship" is an endeavour to make plain the force of the present tense of "have"—"that you may keep on having fellowship with us". "Marching" suggests a process, an action going on, and is suitable. "The same road" may be justified by reason of the word "fellowship". In all fellowship, or, better, community, there is something "common". In this case the road is common to its users and hence it is "the same road".

"We have heard" occurs again in verse 5. These first few verses form an excellent test of our ingenuity in translating the perfect tense. ". . . from Him which lingers in our ears" means just what is meant by "which we have heard from Him". "We are passing on" stands for a present tense—the action is in process. "If we assert" (v. 6) renders an aorist. "If we ejaculate" would represent the "pinpoint" but has been discarded on the grounds that it goes too far. "Assert" will do, provided we remember that we are not saying "insist", which seems to suggest continuity or repetition. "Enjoy" is not meant to refer to our feelings but to the unbroken nature of our fellowship: it is not "a spot of fellowship" or "a dash of fellowship"—to employ the language of a rather light-hearted section of the Christian community—but a deep and settled experience. Compare Romans 5: 1. "Proceed on our way" stands for the present tense of "to walk", and emphasises the continuity. "Keep on our way" (v. 7) does the same. "Enjoy fellowship" is to be taken as in verse 6. "Cleanses us" is a present tense and may be represented by the series of dots, thus: . . . Each dot stands for one particular cleansing, which is repeated time and time again. Hence the rendering, "cleanses us from every sin *as it occurs*". This is not meant to suggest the immediacy of the cleansing, though this may well be true, but is used to draw attention ("as it occurs") to the repeated act of sin which is matched by a repeated act of cleansing. It will be seen how the series of dots suggested the rendering. As an alternative we might say "from every successive sin".

"Make the statement" (v. 8), followed by inverted commas, is an attempt to suggest a "pinpoint". "We are driving ourselves away from what is right" shows us an action in process (present), is faithful to the meaning of the verb "cause to wander" and at the same time to its moral rather than its literal meaning. "If our habit is to confess our sins" (v. 9) is a translation of the present tense and suggests—or is suggested by—the series of dots. "To cut loose the sins which bind us" is a bold way of dealing with the aorist of the verb "to forgive". The verb contains the flavour of "letting go", "throwing", "letting loose", "letting alone", "setting free", "releasing", "slackening", and so on. When it means "permit" you *release* the *restrictions* which hitherto have held a person back; when it means "forgive" you *undo* the *sins* and *offences* which bound him and prevented him from having fellowship with you. We need, then, a metaphor which will retain the idea of "releasing" or "undoing" and at the same time will suggest the aorist pinpoint. "Cut loose" has a peremptory smack about it: the sword flashes through the air and the ropes are cut at one blow. Notice that we could not use, for example, the verb "to hack", which brings to our minds the *repeated* blows of the axe. It is one sharp quick blow which the aorist demands. On the other hand, "snip", though a pinpoint, is unworthy. Similarly, "to cleanse" is an aorist, and "a wave of cleansing . . . burst over us" brings to our minds the picture of one wave, and one only, swiftly enveloping us in a moment of time—the temporal pinpoint.

"We can find no trace of it" (v. 10) states explicitly what is implied by the perfect tense "we have not sinned". This is its "abiding result". Observe the force of "we are making Him a liar". "If we say" is an aorist, though we have not attempted to emphasise it. In utter contrast to this is the horror of the scene which is presented to us by the use of the present: "we are now engaged in the dreadful work of making him a liar": stop! before it is too late.

The second chapter (v. 1) begins with a "crash" into sin. At first I wrote "slip" but dismissed it as being theologically too dangerous: a "slip" is an aorist pinpoint but it might imply that it was not our fault. "Crash" at the very least is neutral, and the picture of an aeroplane hitting the ground with violent force is as good as "slip" for expressing the aorist. "Crash" is repeated in the next sentence, and "all the time" reminds us that "we have" (present) is continuous—not a series of dots but an unbroken line. In verse 3, the perfect tense is retained in the English, though the "abiding result" is preserved by the insertion of the word "lasting". "We maintain the keeping of" avoids saying "we keep on keeping" (present). We have varied this in verse 4 with "whose keeping of His commandments does not last", but the explanation will be clear. So in verse 5, "without a break" preserves the present tense. "The love of God has been perfected" contains the idea of development, and to bring out the "abiding result" we should need to say something like "it is ripe". This would be a fair interpretation, but for the fact that it is not worthy enough. The perfect tense has therefore been kept in English though the last word of the sentence leaves before our minds the picture of the "abiding result": there it now *is*, "it has blossomed into *flower*". "Is dwelling", "is under obligation", and "make his way" all represent present tenses in contrast to the aorist "covered the course" (v. 6).

"Was in your hands" (v. 7) suggests the continuity of the imperfect.

"Fell upon your ears" is clearly an aorist. "Is passing away", "is shining", are equally obviously presents (v. 8). "He who maintains that" stands for a present, and we have gained some variety of expression by retaining the word "hates", which is also present, and inserting "all the while". If he hates all the while, his hatred must be continuous (v. 9). So in verse 10: "maintains his love" and "has his home in" both express the continuity of the present tense. In the next verse we have still to find a way of translating the present tense without a wearisome repetition of "keeps on doing so-and-so"; "he whose attitude to his brother is one of hate" is not unsuccessful. An attitude is settled and relatively lasting, and therefore continuous. Some presents follow which hardly call for comment, and suddenly a vivid aorist is used. This is a minor problem, as our natural English idiom tends to translate it by a perfect: "he does not know . . . because the darkness has blinded his eyes, leaving him blind now". However true this may be in fact, it misses the sharpness of the aorist, which is shown by the device of asking the question, "How is this?" This makes a break with the former present tenses and allows us to say that the darkness "dropped a mist of blindness".

In verse 12, recall what was said about the meaning of the word usually translated "forgive" (1: 9): if your sins have been forgiven, have been undone, have been cut, then (bringing the perfect tense up to the present moment and showing its abiding result) "you are now free from the sins which bound you". Similarly (v. 13) "you are at the end of your search" shows the abiding result of "you have come to know". "You have conquered the evil one" presented some difficulty. We have to choose between saying something in the present tense about the evil one and saying something about the conquerors. The obvious, and here wrong, course is to say "the evil one is prostrate before you" but it is dangerous doctrine, and doubtful. We might say "he is smarting under his blows" or even "under defeat", but it may be questioned if the perfect tense is here used to describe the condition of the evil one. It is surely the conquerors who are in the author's mind. Hence "you know the thrill of laying low the evil one". This avoids saying that he is "down and out", as the boxers say, which is untrue, but does show that he has suffered a defeat. It recalls the temptation of our Lord, after which the defeated evil one "lay off" from Him (as the Americans say) "for a season" or perhaps "until the time of a favourable opportunity". (Luke 4: 13)

"Do not love" in verse 15 is a present imperative and means literally "do not continue to love", and hence probably "stop loving".

This is very harsh and the harshness has been toned down, without doing violence to the present tense, by saying "do not let the world keep its hold on your love".

"You heard the warning shot" (v. 18) is almost startling in its rendering of the aorist. But it keeps to the pinpoint. "On the way" was chosen to represent the present "is coming", or, in reported speech, "was coming" because these phrases are often used in the sense of "going to come". For example, we say, "my son is coming home" and we add in the same sentence "at the end of the year". We mean that "he will come". But our author does not mean that. He means "is on his way", which also preserves the continuity. "Have arisen" goes easily into the present, to express the abiding result, as "are at large". "That they might be shown up" (v. 19) suggests a sudden *dénouement*, and is therefore true to the aorist.

"Who harps on his denials" (v. 22) was brought to my mind by the picture of the series of dots (.......). This kind of harping is a repeated action, and so it reflects the present tense. The same repetition is shown by combining the two objects of the present verb *in his denials*. "Denials" must involve repetition. The same verb appears yet a third time in verse 23, still in the present tense, and for the sake of variety in style we have written "whose attitude repudiates". An attitude, as we have seen, is continuous.

Notice the distinction in verse 24 between "makes its home" (ingressive aorist) and "will *have* your home" (future). If anyone is disposed to argue, with some reason, that the future tense is also punctiliar, like the aorist,[1] he can alter the phrase to read "will *make* your home." We sometimes say after a funeral that the widow "will *make her home* with her eldest son". It clearly marks the beginning of a state, as much as the phrase "he came to the throne".

"Who are busying themselves" (v. 26) is a way of keeping the continuity. So "give you a course of lessons" (v. 27) retains the continuity of the present tense. A variant on this is "covers everything in its lessons". By contrast, "rammed its teaching home" stands for a swift change to the aorist of the same verb. In verse 28, "if the curtain go up", "may light up" and "fall with shame" all represent ingressive aorists. "Whose habit is righteousness" (v.29) brings out the continuity of the present, and the perfect "has been begotten" is brought up to the present moment in "is a member of His family by spiritual birth". That is the "abiding result".

[1]See A. T. Robertson, *Grammar of Greek N.T.* 870–2, but contrast Blass-De-brunner-Funk 318. A short bibliography will be supplied which will include this book. Its description is too long for a footnote.

Chapter 4

SELF-INTEREST

THE middle voice in Greek is a construction which not infrequently baffles us. Its meaning is elusive, perhaps because the Greeks were much more sensitive intellectually, more subtle, than we are. In its widest sense it expresses the interest of the subject of the sentence, and every particular instance of the middle voice gives us some aspect of self-interest. Several different kinds of self-interest have been distinguished. Contrast, for example, the two sentences "He warmed the water" and "He warmed himself." In the latter we could translate the whole sentence by one Greek word in the middle voice, *ethermaineto*. Here the voice shows us the subject acting *on* himself: the subject is also the direct object of the verb. In another sense we find the subject acting *for* himself: the subject is also the indirect object, as in "he provides money for himself". Sometimes it is causative, somewhat like the Hebrew Hiphil, as when we say "he has his son taught". If we had "negative-causation" and the subject did not interpose his prohibition, the causation becomes merely permissive, like "he let his son be taught". Occasionally the middle voice expresses reciprocal action, e.g. "they encourage one another". At times it just draws attention to the subject as possessor or in some other capacity. Students of the Greek language will be well acquainted with these distinctions. Now it is a sound principle for the preacher to ask himself what part the self plays in any given instance of the middle voice. In some texts his task is easy, particularly when the subject is also the object, as in Mark 14: 54, "Peter . . . was sitting with the underlings and warming himself at the fire". In many another context this might be entirely innocent. "Self-interest" is not always wrong, in the present sense of self-interest. Is it wrong for a truck driver to warm his hands while resting on a bitter day in mid-January? But here Peter seems to have been with the wrong people, at the wrong place, doing the wrong thing. Compare 14: 67. A slip of a girl caught him off his guard. But in other texts it is not so easy, and the preacher who puzzles out for himself the position of the self in the sentence may be on the high road to discoveries.

Think of the story of the death of John the Baptist, Mark 6: 21–29. The dancing of the daughter of Herodias had "tickled" (note the aorist) (v. 22) King Herod and his boon companions, and he blurted out at her (aorist) "Hold me up for whatever you are wanting". (The aorist of "ask", uttered with all the peremptoriness of the aorist, suggested the metaphor of the gunman.) He repeated in his oath, "Whatever you hold me up for I will give you, up to half my kingdom". Note here that the verb is twice used in the active voice. The girl went out to consult her mother, and used the same verb. But she did not merely say "What shall I ask for?" She used the middle voice, what shall I ask for *for myself*?" The change of voice from active to middle reflects a subtle change of thought. Herod was prepared to give whatever she wanted it for; she at once thought of what she wanted *for herself*. Strangely enough, though her emphasis was upon herself, she had to seek advice about what she really wanted.

There is a selfishness which never knows what it really wants. Taught by her mother she returned with swift zeal to the king and made-her-request-for-herself to him: "Immediately, the head of John the Baptist on a dish". (Immediately, before the king ceased to be drunk. But her request sobered him, though he insisted on keeping to his oath.) It is a sordid story, and shows up not only Herod and Herodias but also the dancing girl. Her use of the middle voice suggests "the playboy attitude to life". "What am I to ask for myself?" "And she asked for herself." It reveals the playboy, if this term is appropriate for a woman, and it may all be summed up in three slogans: 1. try anything once, to relieve my boredom; 2. spare no cost, so long as I am pleased; 3. neglect any future duty provided I achieve my ends. For suppose instead of asking for the head of this holy man, she had asked for his right hand; it would have been possible, with him still living, for her to have rendered some kindly service. But would she have provided for his needs? would she have cared for his recovery? It is gravely open to question. And the point to observe is this: she represents the logical outcome of that playboy spirit which seeks its entrance into all of us. The middle voice can reveal the depths of character.

But not all examples of the middle voice reveal a character which is to be condemned. "All the things that you are continually praying for, and asking for for yourselves, maintain the belief that you have got them and they will be yours." (Mark 11: 24) "Asking for for yourselves!" The great teaching of this verse is not only the fact that faithful prayer has its answer but also that we can ask God for

things for ourselves. We need to intercede for others; but that is
no reason why at times we should not concentrate on ourselves.
God in His mercy listens to our cry. It may be that such prayers
manifest the true spirit of prayer. For "if two of you come to an
agreement on earth about anything for which they make a request
for themselves, it shall come to them from my Father in heaven. For
where two or three are together in My Name, there am I in the midst
of them." (Matt. 18: 19–20) Mark's demand for reality in prayer is
put in another way: we must forgive whatever we have against anyone, in order that we may be forgiven ourselves. But He does not insist on the assembling of the "two or three." Our Lord speaks in
the singular, not the plural. "Whoever (whatever man) says to this
mountain 'be shifted and be flung into the sea,' and does not waver
in *his* heart but consistently believes that what he is saying is taking
place, it shall be his. *Because of this* I say to you, 'all the things that
you are continually praying for, and asking for for yourselves . . .' "
(Mark 11: 23–24). The faithful prayer of *one* man may have its
answer: therefore, in regard to what you ask for for yourselves,
believe that you have got them . . . How many anxious people would
learn peace of mind if they knew that they could send up a request
for themselves!

The moral value of self-interest, in the sense in which we are using
it, is revealed in a contrast in the use of the same verb in the same
middle voice. "And at festival time he (Pilate) was in the habit of
releasing to them one prisoner whom they used to request for themselves. Now there was the man called Barabbas, lying in chains with
the revolutionaries, who, such was their character, had committed
murder in the disturbance. And the crowd went up and began to
make request for themselves, (for him to do) just as he habitually did
for them." (Mark 15: 6–8, The translation has purposely been kept
as literal as possible.) Matthew 27: 20 tells us that "the highpriests
and the elders persuaded the crowds *to ask for* Barabbas *for themselves*". Luke 23: 23, 25 says that the crowd of people "were pressing
Pilate hard with loud shouts, asking for themselves that He might
be crucified . . . and he released the man who had been flung into
gaol for sedition and murder, for whom they were asking for
themselves . . ." They asked for themselves the release of a criminal,
the murder of the Innocent.

In contrast notice a request which is the same in form but a whole
universe away in spirit. "Joseph of Arimathaea . . . entered in to
Pilate and *asked* for the body of Jesus *for himself*" (Mark 15: 43).
There is no trace of selfishness here. They, immorally, had asked for

a living criminal, Barabbas, and for the crucifixion of the Lord;
Joseph asked for a corpse (v. 45). The use of the word "body"
(v. 43) and "corpse" (v. 45) heightens the effect. Mary Magdalene
can still say "Him", after His death (John 20: 2), not "it". (Cp. John
11: 34) What did he want a corpse for? Why did he want it *for
himself*? He wanted it for himself in order that he might perform the
last kindly offices of love. It was little that he could do: the Lord
was dead. But what he could do, he did.

And, one with him in spirit, the two women called Mary "were
gazing" with love's long look "at where He had been laid" (Mark
15: 46-47). There was nowhere for them to go to, to heal their
heartbreak, and they stayed where they could. The preacher might
sum up his message in the title "The Interim Devotion", suggested
originally to me by the middle voice. When the full light of God's
revelation has not yet shone for us, and our day is sombre with
broken hopes, we can still show forth our devotion to our Lord:
let us do what we can; let us stay where we can; and in God's good
time the fuller blessing will be ours.

The use of the middle voice is not of course restricted to the verb
"ask," but there are a number of very suggestive texts where it is
used. The mother of the sons of Zebedee came to Jesus with her
sons, *asking* that they might take their seats, one on His right hand
and one on His left, in His Kingdom. (Matt. 20: 21) Addressing
them all our Lord replied "You do not know what you *are asking
for yourselves*'" (v. 22) The slight change of voice from the active to
the middle conveys a rebuke which is all the greater for its brevity.
He goes on, "Are you able to toss down the cup (aorist) which I am
going to drink sip by sip (present)?" They may be able—they
themselves are sure of it; but to be on His right hand and on His left
in His Kingdom is not to be arbitrarily given away: it is for those
for whom it has been prepared by His Father, and for whom it is
now waiting in readiness (note the perfect tense). There is a rebuke,
conveyed by the middle voice. But even the rebukes of the Lord are
blessings. In Mark's account of the incident (10: 35-40) they ask to
sit with Him "in His glory". But the cross was His glory (John 17:
1-5). By refusing their request for themselves He saved them from
the horror of the crucifixion: "and with Him they crucify two
brigands, one on His right hand and one on His left" (Mark 15: 27).

We must not dwell too long on one Greek word, but some texts
must not be omitted. "I ask for myself," says the apostle Paul, "I
ask you not to lose heart in my afflictions for you, which are your
glory." (Eph. 3: 13). A noble self-interest—their welfare! He is not

the stern, rigid theologian some people imagine, but the warm-hearted, loving shepherd of souls. In his doxology (Eph. 3: 20) he uses even selfishness to measure the loving power of God: "To him Who is able to do super-abundantly beyond all that we ask for ourselves or think. . . ." Selfishness is deeply rooted within us, and we cannot conceive of the power that would be necessary to satisfy all our desires. It is nothing, cries the apostle in holy ecstasy, to what He can do. If even the wrath of men can praise Him, their very selfishness can be used as a measuring rod of His power and grace: and even this is like trying to measure the equator with a foot-rule. James 4: 2–3 maintains the distinction between active and middle. "You do not have, because you do not ask-for-yourselves (middle); you ask (active) and you do not receive, because you ask-for-yourselves (middle) wrongly. . . ." The mistake does not lie in asking for themselves, but in doing it the wrong way. The background of their prayer is wrong: wars, fights, murder, envy, even taken metaphorically of a quarrelsome church, are not a fit preparation for the suppliant. And the motive of their prayer is wrong, "to blue the lot" (aorist of "spend") in pleasures is hardly worthy. "Ask for yourselves"—but do it in the right way. Armed with a concordance the preacher should find this a rewarding study. 1 John 5: 14–15 will make a good beginning: "And this is the boldness which we have before Him: if we ask for anything for ourselves according to His will He hears us. And if we know that He hears us whatever we request for ourselves, we know that we have the requests which we have asked from Him".

"Put off the old man with his deeds" (Col. 3: 9) looks like a metaphor from clothes ("take off your coat") but there may be more to be said. The middle voice (aorist) may suggest "fling off from yourselves". Think of a footballer, at the bottom of a pile of kicking, struggling players who are holding him down. If he has tremendous strength he may be able to "fling them off from him", and a subtle mind might discern here a resemblance to a schoolboy's rapid undressing before entering the swimming pool. Off comes his coat, shoes are kicked loose here and there, a shirt is torn off and thrown on to a chair, and so on. So we are to "fling off from ourselves the old man with his deeds" like a pack of footballers, which is our temporary "dress". (I am alluding here to a phrase in one of the Greek tragedians, the exact reference to which I cannot trace. He speaks of being "clothed in stones" and bears the grim meaning "being stoned". A footballer is sometimes "clothed with his opponents"!) So we must don, fling upon ourselves (aorist middle again) the new man (v. 10), we must "wrap ourselves in" feelings of pity, kindness and other Christian virtues (v. 12), "holding yourselves back from one another" (v. 13). The latter is better than the ordinary "forbearing one another" of the English versions. The Greek suggests a picture to our minds: if a man has a vicious dog on the end of its lead, and the dog is trying to reach someone to bite him, the owner has to "hold the dog back". So, in our relationships with one another, we are to "hold ourselves back from one another". (Cp. Eph. 4: 2.)

"Redeeming the time" (Col. 4: 5) is a translation which can be improved. A. T. Robertson suggests "buying the opportunity for yourselves out of the open market".[1] But the Greek preposition (ek) may be intensive rather than local, "buying the opportunity for yourselves completely". Now, "buying the wheat for yourselves completely" or "buying it up" as our idiom has it, would mean "cornering the market in wheat". I therefore suggest for the whole verse "Walk wisely in your dealings with outsiders, cornering the market in opportunity". (Cp. Eph. 5: 15–16. Would Wall Street understand?)

2 Peter 2: 22 has an interesting use of the middle voice, "a sow having washed herself turns to rolling in the mire". Is it a genuine middle? It recalls a proverb, which may account for the sow "washing herself". Bigg thinks that the sow "bathed itself in mud",[2] but J. H. Moulton much more attractively recalls the story of Ahikar,[3] from which Dr. Rendel Harris quotes the probable origin of the proverb. "My son, thou hast behaved like the swine which went to the bath with people of quality, and when he came out, saw a stinking drain, and went and rolled himself in it." Moulton regards this as an extremely likely source. If so, he notes that the middle verb is used in its correct sense. The version of Rendel Harris given here differs but slightly from the Syriac and Arabic versions.[4]

How far the preacher can avail himself of a metaphor which borders on the coarse is hard to say: he must certainly be careful. But people in a rural community would understand. The proverb is an apt summary of certain truths which the people in question had not realised. Christian discipleship is not just one thing among many (bath today and mud tomorrow, and something else which tickles our fancy the next day); it is *the* thing. It is not for a brief moment

[1] A. T. Robertson: *Grammar*, 810
[2] Charles Bigg: International Critical Commentary, *Epistles of St. Peter and St. Jude*, p. 287.
[3] J. H. Moulton: *Grammar of N.T. Greek* I, 156, 238.
[4] See R. H. Charles: *Apocrypha and Pseudepigrapha of the O.T.* II, 717f., 772.

but for all our days—and beyond. It is not the fashion of "the quality" (though one could wish that it were), for this is subject to change, but our very life. It is not a matter of mere form but demands our consent, our enthusiasm, our whole will. That poor unhappy animal did not realise what it was doing when it washed itself with the quality!

Compare the aorist middle in 1 Corinthians 6: 11: "you washed yourselves, you dipped yourselves in the cleansing waters". (The picture brought to our mind is not that of a long drawn-out business, like scrubbing, but, as the aorist suggests, of a punctiliar cleansing, like the instantaneous dipping of a hypodermic needle into boiling water to kill the germs and sterilise it.) Compare further the use of the same verb in Acts 22: 16, together with the word "baptise", in a causative middle: "get yourself baptised and get your sins washed away"—appropriate on the missionary field, where converts are "those of riper years". A "negative-causative" or "permissive" middle occurs in 1 Corinthians 6: 7, "why do you not rather let-yourselves-be-wronged, why do you not rather let yourselves be the target of those who deprive you (of what is yours?) (The present tense justifies the "target"; they are continually being shot at.)

A very subtle use of the middle voice which needs a most sensitive feeling for the Greek is seen in Hebrews 9: 12, "through His own blood He entered once for all into the holy place, finding for Himself eternal redemption". (The aorist is one of "coincident action" and need not concern us here.) Now it might be thought, and thought rightly, that our Lord found redemption *for us*; how can He have found it for Himself, Who knew no sin? He found it for Himself as a blessing which He could give to all who call upon Him. (In a time of scarcity a man doing the household shopping might buy the ordinary provisions for his wife, some chocolate for the children, some fruit to give to the people next door, and "some coffee for myself". But he does not take coffee and its absence from the market for months has not bothered him. But he wants it for himself, "to give himself the pleasure of" giving his wife a surprise.) So "for the joy that was set before Him He endured the cross" (Heb. 12: 2). In slight contrast is Acts 20: 28, "the church of God which He gained *for Himself* through the blood of Him Who was His own". Our Lord found eternal redemption for Himself, that He might give it away; God gained the church for Himself, that He might keep it for ever.

A fearful aspect of human character is revealed in Acts 13: 46. "you are pushing away from yourselves the Word of God". The point of the middle voice is that they are not doing it mechanically as a swinging door might push away a small child in its way. Their interest is directed to getting the Word removed as far from them as possible; it is their aim and purpose. God has not done this with His people (Rom. 11: 1), though some have done it with their conscience (1 Tim. 1: 19), and consequently in regard to faith have suffered shipwreck. The deliberate pushing away, emphasised by the middle voice, has reminded me of the story told during World War II. Some Nazis were struggling in the sea after a naval engagement, and some allied sailors tried to haul them aboard and save their lives. In hatred the Nazis spat at them. That was not accidental; that was not a wave of the sea forcing them to push away the help. It expressed the very spirit of the middle voice: *they* pushed away from *themselves* the Word of God.

We have said that the middle voice reveals character. Consider the contrast between Acts 16: 16 and 19: 24. In the former the girl with a spirit of divination—perhaps a ventriloquist—"afforded much business gain to her masters by oracle-mongering". She afforded them gain. In the latter text Demetrius the silversmith "afforded the craftsmen (and himself!) no little gain". The mere use of the middle voice implies "and himself", but so subtle is the Greek as compared with English that we have to add these words. St. Luke thus shows us the motive of the crafty craftsman before he begins to address the members of his "union". People sometimes attack religion as a "vested interest"; here we have a vested interest attacking the Christian faith.

We shall now finish the present chapter by translating a longer passage. By this time it will have been realised that all that may have been discovered in previous chapters (e.g. the way of rendering an aorist) must be used in all subsequent chapters. We cannot limit our attention here to the middle voice. Here is 1 Thessalonians 5: 12–28.

> We are asking you, brothers, to take cognisance of those who are toiling among you, presiding over you in the Lord and giving you warnings; regard them with superabundant affection: their work justifies it. Keep the peace among yourselves. We urge you, brothers, warn the deserters, don't let the timid find that your stream of comfort runs dry, keep your grip on the weak, be long-suffering towards all men.
>
> 15. See that no one returns an evil service with evil, but be always on the trail of blessing for one another and for all men. Don't

let your joy peter out; avoid leaving intervals in your prayer life; in everything maintain the note of thanksgiving; for this is the will of God for you in Christ Jesus. Give up smothering the fire of the Spirit and debunking prophecy;

20. make it a rule to test everything and to retain the good; hold yourselves aloof from every kind of evil. And may the God of peace Himself round you off with holiness, and may your spirit, soul and body be kept in integrity, to be blameless at the advent of our Lord Jesus Christ. He Who is calling you is faithful; He will do it.

25. Brothers, go on praying for us.

Imprint on all the members of the brotherhood a holy kiss of greeting. I am putting you on your honour by the Lord for the letter to be a hand-out, read to all the brothers.

The grace of our Lord Jesus Christ be with you.

Our method hitherto will probably explain the above paraphrase, though a few comments may not be out of place. "Deserters" was used because of its moral flavour. The Greek means people who leave their post, and has almost a military smack about it, and it merges into the meaning "idle". "Don't let the timid find . . ." is a way of drawing attention to the present tense. "Keep your grip on" also brings out the present tense of continuity better than the mere "cling to". Literally the word (it is middle voice) seems to mean "hold oneself face to face with". If "the weak" are the folk who are weak in the faith the apostle must mean that the church must keep close to all who are likely to drop out of its fellowship, be friends with them, "hang on" to them and not let them go. "Returns an evil service" recalls a picture from the game of tennis: if a man "serves" you an evil ball, don't return it. The swift movement of the arm in hitting the ball that is speeding towards you pictures admirably the aorist tense. "Be always on the trail of" is not an unworthy rendering of the present tense. "Don't let your joy peter out" is a negative representation of the continuity in the present "keep on rejoicing always".

The adverb with the verb "pray" comes from a verb which always raises in my mind the picture of a man planting potatoes in a row: he leaves a space between each one, say twelve inches. Now he might be interrupted and omit to plant one potato, which would mean an empty hole, with twenty-four inches between the potatoes on either side. Return now to the text. We cannot be at prayer every minute: the engine driver, the dispenser in the drug store dealing with dangerous drugs, the surgeon performing an operation, may work in the spirit of prayerful trust, but they have to concentrate on their work, and therefore their prayer must be regular, at stated times, but not literally unceasing. The Apostle urges his readers not to leave out one of these stated times of prayer. Hence repeated action of the present tense suggests an inversion: "avoid leaving intervals (this is the meaning of the adverb) in your prayer life ('prayer life' suggests the regularity of the present tense)." Cf. Luke 7: 45.

"Maintain the note of" is the opposite of a staccato aorist—the organ, not the piano. Still we have the present tense, which will explain the subsequent renderings also. "Hold yourselves aloof" is the meaning of the middle verb. "Round off", suggested by the proleptic adjective, also brings out the aorist. "Imprint on" is also aoristic. The aorist of "to be read" was a hard problem until the idea of a hand-out occurred to me, with its picture of a swift passing of a document from one person to another.

We have attempted to say something about the middle voice, in the context of the various tenses and meanings of words. Some scholars may take the view that the treatment has been overdone, and they may be right. But it has been done purposely, to show something of the spirit of the Greek. And if it has in any degree led a preacher back to his Greek Testament, if it has shown him something of the beauty of words or of the pictures and movement which the Greek inevitably suggests, then the task has not been entirely in vain.

Chapter 5

RELATIONS

THE use of prepositions in the Greek language will afford the preacher a happy hunting ground both for new thoughts and for illustrations. Prepositions express a relation between words; originally they were adverbs. Some scholars would say that they were place-adverbs, though this must perhaps be qualified somewhat. But it is true that in many instances place is involved, and where there is a local relation it is possible to see it "with the mind's eye". And where you can "see" something you are on the road to an illustration.

Consider, for example, the somewhat puzzling text in John 1: 16, "of His fulness we all received, and *grace for grace*". "For" is the Greek preposition *anti*, which here seems to mean "in place of". We therefore received grace in place of grace. We must visualise some interchange, some succession whereby one thing takes the place of another. As the picture first came to me it was that of the London Underground Railway, though the New York subway or indeed any busy railroad station would do. Imagine yourself with the passengers who are waiting for the train to come in, though you yourself have a somewhat detached air as you do not intend to travel just yet. It is a busy time, the rush hour. The train comes in, people leave it or board it, and it leaves. Another comes in and the process is repeated; and another; and another. And so it goes on, train follows train, you see train following train, train after train, train in place of train, *train for train*. And that last phrase is exactly what St. John meant. Our Lord gives us His grace, a blessing; and as it is used up and vanishes away, another forthwith appears; and that is used and goes, and yet another follows, grace in place of grace. Or if you like you can be sitting on the seashore and watch the waves come in. One comes, and breaks; another follows; and so on, wave in place of wave. St. John's *anti* makes us see what his meaning is.

A different picture is suggested by Hebrews 12: 2: "for the joy that was set before Him He endured the cross", and it is best interpreted in the light of verse 16 of the same chapter. The meaning of the preposition is derived from "in place of", though with a difference. Esau "(in place of, i.e.) *in return for* one meal sold his rights as eldest son". And our Lord similarly "in return for (i.e. to obtain) the joy . . . endured the cross". This is not an instance of a man enduring the burden and heat of the day in order later to reap his own profit. Here our Lord suffered in order to gain the joy of other men's profit—the redemption of the world. Compare Hebrews 9: 12 and see page 64. There is something of a financial flavour, something of the nature of a transfer deed. Investors on the Stock Exchange and elsewhere will understand the words of the legal document, the transfer deed:

I, A. B., of such-and-such an address, lawyer,
>   *in consideration of* the sum of
>   five thousand pounds,
>   do hereby bargain, sell, assign and transfer
>   to C.D., of such-and-such an address, farmer,
>   his heirs and executors, administrators
>   and assigns,
>   X shares in the Blank Drug and Medicine Company.

"In consideration of" gives the exact meaning of the preposition. An illustration of this order would be talking to some people in their own language.

Apo is another interesting preposition. It means "from" and subsequent idiomatic meanings are derived from that. It is sometimes used "partitively", that is, it helps to suggest the total *from* which something is taken. In the phrase "some of us" the words "of us" are partitive. Now this can be expressed in Greek, and usually is, by a mere genitive, though occasionally the genitive has *apo* in front of it. In Acts 2: 17 Peter quotes Joel 2: 28–32 and says "I will pour out *from My Spirit* upon all flesh". If we say "some of My Spirit" we reflect the meaning of the Greek though the result is unfortunate as it suggests a certain parsimony. But this is not intended.

The promise asserts that God will enrich His people without impoverishing Himself. Paradoxically when He gives His Spirit, the Spirit is present in His entirety, but He does not give all of His Spirit. We could not contain Him. There is thus always an inexhaustible supply, so to speak, left in God. The parsimony is only apparent. The late Mr. Thomas Lamont gave half a million dollars for the restoration of Canterbury Cathedral. It was *from his fortune*, it was *some of his fortune*, but it was far from being mean: it was a princely gift.

We sometimes speak of a man being "filled with the Spirit" and he may be. But it is still only a part of what God can give. For if that man's capacity is enlarged he can be filled again. The tank of an automobile may be full of petrol, but if it is to be driven right across a country it will have to be filled again. Human fullness does not mean divine emptiness but rather the opportunity for human expansion.

A similar partitive use, this time of the preposition *ek*, is to be found in 1 John 4: 13, "He has given to us out of (i.e. some of) His Spirit". The result is the same, but the picture is slightly different. In the former case the gift is merely "from"; here we see, as it were, a hand put right inside the Divine Nature and bringing *out of* it the genuine gift, His Spirit. To complete the story we must refer to another preposition, *kata*, in Philippians 4: 19. "My God will fulfil your every need *according to* His riches . . ." *Kata* implies a standard by which a judgement may be passed. His gift, then, to meet your need will match His riches. The King must give a royal gift. A millionaire might give five dollars *out of* his wealth; Mr. Lamont's half million was "according to" his riches: his fortune set the standard and his gift was worthy of it.

Apo is also used to indicate membership of a party. In Acts 12: 1 Herod the king laid hands on some of "those from the church", to harass them. Perhaps their origin "in the church" stamped them with the marks of membership. Certainly there was a centre, a rally-point, for Christians (Acts 1: 15; 2: 1; 2: 46–47; 5: 12) though it was hardly a fixed locality. They met as one man; and dispersed, though they remained churchmen. A. T. Robertson[1] in a totally different connection asserts that *apo* corresponds closely with the German *von* and the French *de* which came to be marks of nobility. That idea is not inapplicable here, only the church is not a locality (e.g. Philip from Bethsaida; John 1: 44; or, to follow A. T. Robertson, Philip von Bethsaida, Philip de Bethsaida) but a fellowship.

These men, then, in Acts 12: 1 "hailed from the church", from that movable fellowship which leaves its mark on its members, and from the world's point of view they were "party-members", members of a wider group, though they were not at the moment in question assembled. What is involved in "hailing from the church", in being a member of it, belonging to it, coming from it, even though for the time being you may be quite alone as the church is not actually "meeting"?

A man is a member as a response to a call; from choice, not

[1]Op. cit. p. 578.

duress; he supports it with his service, his prayers, his gifts; it has a purpose with which he is in thorough sympathy, to worship the living God and to make known the Name and Gospel of our Lord Jesus Christ. Personal response and choice; loyal service; vital worship; keen evangelism: a preacher could do worse than use this description of the "party" which is his church. And these reflections have come to me as I have brooded over the word *apo*. The politicians ought to follow this exposition without difficulty. And do the individuals strike the world primarily as being Tories, Liberals, Democrats, Republicans—or Christians? So that the question never needs to be asked, "Where do you hail from?"

The preposition *dia* governs two cases. Many students will remember that *dia* with the *acc*usative means "on *acc*ount of" and with the genitive (*-ou*) means "through", "by means of". Let us take the accusative construction first.

The preposition with the accusative expresses some sort of cause. Thus in Mark 2: 4 the mere size and density of the crowd prevented the four men from bringing the paralytic to Jesus. "Not being able to bring him to Him on account of the crowd . . ." Similarly in 2 Corinthians 3: 7 "the sons of Israel were not able to fix their gaze on the face of Moses because of its glory. . . ."

The cause may be contributory and not complete. Paul preached the gospel to the Galatians originally "because of bodily illness" (Gal. 4: 13). It may be that he altered his missionary route for medical reasons; he may have needed a change of air. It depends on the nature of the illness. But there were other causes as well which made him an evangelist!

The cause does not operate in a mechanical way. Our Lord said that His disciples would be hated by all men "because of My name" (Matt. 10: 22). Christ is preached; men do not like it—or the preachers; and consequently they hate them. In the interpretation of the Parable of the Sower we read that the shallow and temporary Christian runs into affliction or persecution "because of the Word" (Matt. 13: 21). But precisely the opposite effect may be produced. Many of the Samaritans believed in Jesus "because of the word" of the woman when she testified. Later far more believed "because of His own word" (John 4: 39–41). The verbal form is identical; the result is different. The phrase *dia* plus accusative expresses what induced men to hate, to persecute or to believe. In fact it illustrates the *schisma*, the split, to be seen in John's gospel (7: 43; 10: 19) "because of Him" or "because of these words" (cf. 9: 16).

The one cause may have different effects. On the other hand the one event may have different causes. The highpriests and elders "delivered up Jesus because of envy" (Matt. 27: 18). They envied His influence and were thus induced to deliver Him up (John 11: 48; 12: 19). But He was delivered up "because of our transgressions" (Rom. 4: 25). We see here the overruling providence of God. He saw our transgressions and this induced Him to deliver Him up. (It was not the only factor: the righteousness and love of God enter in as well, though Paul is not dealing with that subject in the present phrase.)

This raises the whole question: who did deliver up Jesus? We have seen that it was the highpriests and elders. It was also Judas (John 18: 2; Matt. 26: 15–25). The nation was inculpated (John 18: 35). God himself delivered up His son, as Paul explicitly affirms (Rom. 8: 32). And the Son of God delivered up Himself (Gal. 2: 20; Eph. 5: 2, 25).

The cause may have a relatively remote effect. We have seen the phrase, "because of the Word", and noted the diverse result. In particular "the Samaritans believed". Does anything else follow? Our Lord said that ". . . you are clean because of the Word which I have spoken to you" (John 15: 3). It was not automatic. The Word may be spoken and the hearers not made clean. There must be the intermediate step of faith. Thus we have the simple series: Word—faith—cleansing. The faith of the Samaritans was the primary effect; the cleansing of the disciples was the secondary or "remote" effect. The sequence may be discerned in Acts 15: 7–9, "the Word of the gospel", "believe" and "cleanse their hearts by faith."

The cause may have an effect still more remote. When Paul said that "I do everything because of the gospel" he might just as well have said "because of the Word." In form at any rate the phrases are identical. Now we may be sure that the series, Word—faith—cleansing, applies to the apostle. But there is a yet further effect, his "doing everything" (1 Cor. 9: 23). He may have wanted to work with the gospel; or to share it with others. Everything he does is determined by the gospel. The gospel indicates what he should do; and is the "atmosphere" of everything.

In addition to preaching the gospel Paul has other activities. "We are not preaching ourselves but Christ Jesus as Lord (to preach the gospel is to preach Christ), and ourselves your servants (literally 'slaves') because of Jesus" (2 Cor. 4: 5). Jesus is the "cause" of this remoter effect: Christian service. The fact of Christ induced him to serve. We may surmise that he felt the impact of His example

(John 13: 5; Luke 22: 26–27; cf. Gal. 5: 13); was bound by His commandment (John 13: 14–17); and was moved by the needs of pastoral care (1 Pet. 5: 2–3). For the same reason, "because of the Lord," Christians should be subject to human authorities (1 Pet. 2: 13); and "because of Jesus" Paul and his companions "are always letting themselves be delivered up to death" (2 Cor. 4: 11).

Thus the Word (the gospel, Jesus) gives rise to the series: faith—cleansing—service—self-sacrifice. He is the "cause" of them all.

So far *dia* with accusative has looked backwards. "Because of" Jesus we believe, are cleansed, serve, and sacrifice ourselves. But it can sometimes look forwards and the "cause" is a motive. Our Lord was raised from the dead *"because of* our justification"*. (Rom. 4: 25) But the justification had not yet taken place. How could it, if it is by faith? The justification of men is therefore to be regarded as the motive which induced God to raise His son. He raised Him, that is, with a view to our justification. Here the "cause" merges with purpose.

We must now turn to the use of *dia* with the genitive. We begin with the simple command of our Lord: "enter *through* the narrow gate" (Matt. 7: 13). On another occasion He said: "I am the door; if a man enter *through* Me . . ." (John 10: 9). The preacher might well ask himself the meaning of the word "narrow" in this context. When we speak today of a "narrow" person we emphasise the limited range of his thought, knowledge, appreciation and conduct. This cannot be applied directly to our Lord, in Whom are all the treasures of wisdom and knowledge. Cf. Col 2: 3. But it might be a way of saying that "neither is there salvation in any other. . . ." (Acts 4: 12).

For "nobody comes to the Father except through Me" (John 14: 6). In using such a visual image of "those who come to God through Him" (Heb. 7: 25) we must beware of any idea of so going "through" Him that we come out on the other side and go on beyond Christ. The "road" of John 14: 6 is a road to travel on, not to leave; salvation is finally *in* Christ. The "through" expresses mediation.

But how will men know that they can thus come to God? Our Lord prayed for those who believe in Him "through their word" (John 17: 20). Apostolic testimony is the *means through which* men believe in Jesus. It is not a secular means. Men are called "through God's grace" (cf. Gal. 1: 15) and "through our gospel" (2 Thess. 2: 14). And when a man truly believes he is made alive, with a life which lasts until the resurrection, "through the indwelling Spirit" (Rom. 8: 11; cf. 10). The logical consequence of a justifying faith is the enjoyment of peace with God "through our Lord Jesus Christ" (Rom. 5: 1). Through Him is salvation (1 Thess. 5: 9); through Him thanksgiving is addressed to God (Rom. 1: 8); through Him the sacrifice of praise should be offered to God (Heb. 13: 15); through Him God is to be glorified in everything (1 Pet. 4: 11).

A final example will crown the present edifice. "The love of God has been poured out in our hearts *through* the Holy Spirit given to us" (Rom. 5: 5). If it has been poured out (perfect) "it is *now* drenching us, saturating us". But "love" is an abstract term; what does Paul mean? I suggest that through the Holy Spirit the loving God is known in our hearts. We are aware of and we sharply feel the love of God for us because He dwells in our hearts. Through the Holy Spirit our thought dwells on the love of God; our feelings are warmed by the love of God; our will is strengthened by the love of God; and our conscience is taught by the love of God. God is present in our hearts as the One Who is loving us—through the Holy Spirit.

We add a reference to Acts 1: 3. Here the meaning seems to be "He appeared to them *at intervals throughout* forty days". To take a spatial picture to illustrate a temporal meaning, *dia* with the genitive case here may be compared with the statement "the portholes appeared at intervals throughout the length of the ship". If you can "see" those portholes you can "see" the appearances of our Lord after His Resurrection. Now this is illuminating, because it helps us to understand the Ascension. Imagine those forty days; the Lord appears to His disciples, at first to their great surprise. Then He vanishes from their sight (see Luke 24: 31). Then He appears again, elsewhere; and once more He disappears. In time they develop an attitude of expectation: will He show Himself to us this afternoon? And when He does come they find that they do not have to explain to Him all that has happened since He was with them last. He knows it all.

Gradually there grows up within them the realisation that what they say, think or do is known to Him, even though they cannot see Him. Proof of that will come when He appears "next time"; and proof there is. By then the disciples really feel that He is with them, and at this stage there is no longer the necessity for Him to show Himself again and again repeatedly. He therefore gives them one last vision of Himself, and by the acted parable of His Ascension shows them that He will not be seen on earth as before, as He has gone back to His Father. We know now that heaven is not "up in the sky" in the old-fashioned local sense, but they did not know, and our Lord graciously showed them by His act that He was going back to Heaven. What else could He have done? Christians thus have no need to apologise for, still less to explain away, the narratives of the Ascension. We owe something to *dia* and the genitive!

We now come to what Moulton[1] has aptly called the "maid-of-all-work of the New Testament", the Greek preposition *en*. Sometimes its most literal meaning is the best. Thus in 2 Corinthians 4: 3 St. Paul says that "if our gospel is hidden, it is hidden *among* those who are perishing". It would seem that the preacher can start anywhere in this wide world, in the oceans and deserts, in the fields and mountains, in Fifth Avenue and in the slums, and preach Jesus: there is always something of the gospel if only we have the eyes to see it, or the hands to pull it out from its hiding place.

The "man in (*en*) an unclean spirit" (Mark 1: 23) was rendered by Blass[2] "*with* an unclean spirit", apparently with Robertson's[3] approval. But 1 John 5: 19 "the whole world lies in (*en*) the evil one", suggests that it is at least possible that the preposition may mean "in the power of". The man was "in" his own "territory", just as the French in 1940–44 were "in" their own country and yet "in" the power of the Germans. We thus have the picture of "occupied country", a not unfitting description of the sinful unbeliever.

But the fascination of the word appears when we leave behind its literal meaning. "Do you not know that the saints will judge the world? and if the world is judged among (*en*) you, in the midst of you . . . " (1 Cor. 6: 2). This is certainly promising, with its picture of the world with the hang-dog look which characterises the guilty defendant in the midst of the court; but Moulton[4] has shown that in official documents which have survived, our preposition means "in the department of". The church as a bureaucrat! The tables will be turned with a vengeance. Perhaps we might combine the literal and the metaphorical and think of "in your Department of Justice". The strutting bullies will look rather different when they appear there.

"We speak the wisdom of God in a mystery" (1 Cor. 2: 7), says St. Paul. "In a mystery" is puzzling. Robertson takes it to mean "in the form of", though probably something of the literal meaning remains. If by "mystery" we mean, in the New Testament, an "open secret", we have a picture before our eyes. Think of a man who has bought a present for his wife, and suppose that it is wrapped up in

[1]J. H. Moulton: *Grammar of N.T. Greek*, I: 103.
[2]F. Blass, *Grammar of N.T. Greek*, 131. Cf. Blass-Debrunner-Funk, 203 "with an unclean spirit in *him*".
[3]Op cit. 589.
[4]Op. cit. 103.

newspaper. She cannot see the gift, and she is not interested in reading what the newspaper round it actually says. But suppose that very paper has an article or a full page advertisement before her eyes, describing how the gift worked; then she has all the information before her; the "open secret" is just being ignored. Her present is "in a mystery". So Christian truth is available for all to know, in the form of an open secret if you like, wrapped in that which explains it if you prefer it that way.

Note the maid-of-all-work doing double duty in Philippians 4: 19, "My God will fulfil your every need (1) on a scale that matches His wealth; (2) (*in* glory—metaphorical) in a manner which shows His glory, not merely something which He possesses; (3) *in* Christ Jesus, as if the apostle still feared that the glory might be separated from the Giver. We must not separate God's gifts from Him: they are all in Christ. Here is a crescendo: a preacher with a gift for music ought to be able to move stage by stage to the crashing finale.

The root-meaning of the preposition *epi* is "upon"—not merely "over" as the flat top of a table is "over" the floor, but "upon" as the legs of the table, or the carpet are "upon" the floor. From this simple meaning, again one that can be visualised, the other idiomatic uses are derived, with distinctions of meaning determined by the cases. We may feel at times that the Greek language has strayed far away from simplicity into subtlety, but however far it goes it retains the picture of "upon", misty though it may seem. It is difficult to make precise and consistent distinctions between *epi* and the three cases, accusative, genitive, and dative. We must try to "see" how "upon" is to be interpreted in different contexts.

Epi, we say, means "upon". Then it may suggest at times a foundation, a basis. "Man will not live on a basis of bread alone, (Matt. 4: 4) but on a basis of every word coming forth through the mouth of God." We still speak of a basic "diet". The constructors of every welfare state should mark that; the architects of all utopias would do well not to forget that their state must be built on every word of God—not merely the ones they like to pick and choose. "On the basis of the uttered word of Jesus" (Luke 5: 5) let every unsuccessful, defeated man return to his task: he can build (metaphorically) on that, if not on his own works and hopes. Notice how the New Testament speaks of "on the basis of hope" (Acts 2: 26; 26: 6; Rom. 4: 18; 5: 2; 15: 12; Titus 1: 2); and how some foolish people base their trust on themselves (Luke 18: 9). In some circumstances men may "stand on their own feet." Spiritually they cannot stand on their own shoulders.

Paul speaks of placing our trust "upon Him Who justifies the ungodly" (Rom. 4: 5) and "upon Him Who raised Jesus our Lord from the dead" (Rom. 4: 24), with which might be compared the foundation of 1 Corinthians 3: 11. The ploughman ploughs upon the land—but also upon the foundation of hope (1 Cor. 9: 10).

There is a famous text, often misapplied, in 1 Corinthians 2: 9, "What eye did not see and ear did not hear and (what) did not (literally) go up upon the heart of man—how many things has God prepared for those who love Him!" (God revealed them to us through the Spirit.) Now it is not at first easy to see how anything can "go up upon." But "go up" here is appropriate to going aboard ship, to embarkation. Ancient men "went up" and stood "*upon the deck*". Cannot the preacher see that the unbelieving heart is like a ship which will not put in to port and take aboard a fresh cargo? (Cf. Matt. 11: 28) God's truth has not gone aboard.

We may change the picture. The verb "go up" is used of mounting a horse. The horseman "goes up" and seats himself *upon* the horse's back. The human heart is like a restive horse which cannot be mounted. These two pictures may be used to introduce a sermon on the text in a coastal town or rural community, especially if the subject is uppermost in men's minds. There has been a shipping strike; and in a village there may be a riding episode!

We sometimes read exciting stories of men who are trapped in a lift shaft or elevator shaft. Will they be rescued before the elevator comes down *upon* them? With some such picture in mind we might illustrate the text: "The wrath of God is revealed from heaven *upon* all impiety and unrighteousness of men . . ." (Rom. 1: 18). It is similar with Romans 2: 2, ". . . the judgement of God is . . . *upon* those who do such things." (Cf. v. 9)

In John 6: 21 we get vivid good sense if we keep to the simple meaning "upon". Assured that it was Jesus walking upon the sea "they were willing to take Him aboard, and straightway (? in a straight line) the ship (literally) *became upon the land* to which they were going". The aorist verb, associated with the preposition "upon", strongly suggests that "the ship ran aground." This is much more vivid than the bare "at the land" or "towards the land", and in any case the last phrase does not seem to fit the aorist verb. Have you ever seen a boat ride in to the beach on the top of a wave, and heard the grinding noise as its keel makes contact with the shore? "Ran aground" suggests that.

Let the preacher remember that it was dark (verses 16–17); they were making for the shore, but perhaps the sound of the boat running aground, together with the consequent jerk, was the first intimation that they had reached the land. Now either they were nearer the shore than they had realised, or John wishes us to understand that with Jesus aboard they ran a straight course to the shore. (Compare the significant use of the same word in the verb in Acts 16: 11 and 21: 1.) Both thoughts have spiritual truth: with Christ we are nearer home than we realise; with Christ the course is straighter than we dare hope for; and with Christ the sudden jerk and the grind far from being unwelcome, should tell us that one stage of our voyage is over.

Epi with the dative can sometimes imply purpose. Galatians 5: 13 reads that "you were called for freedom." The root idea ("upon") can be brought out by the paraphrase "you were called (by Him) to join him upon the territory of freedom." The active voice is seen in 1 Thessalonians 4: 7. Care has to be exercised to avoid giving a wrong theological impression. "We were created in Christ Jesus on a basis of good works" (Eph. 2: 10) is hardly the correct rendering. How can we bring out the root idea of "upon"? Perhaps it may be done by an inversion. "He created us with the basic purpose of good works." It is not hard to imagine a man replying thus to a question: "I did it for the purpose stated, and *I stand my ground.*"

The root idea of the preposition *kata* seems to be "down". It is not always easy to trace the connection between this and the idiomatic uses of the preposition but the attempt is worth while. Two cases are involved, the genitive and the accusative. We shall begin with the genitive.

Kata with the genitive may mean "down from." The Gadarene swine "rushed down from the cliff into the sea" (Matt. 8: 32). Paul speaks of the churches of Macedonia and of "their down-to-the-depths poverty" (2 Cor. 8: 2). From the thought of "down to" comes the idea of hostility. This is often translated by "against", though it may be doubted if *kata* as such has this meaning. "Against" is our idiomatic usage derived from the context. It would be awkward if we insisted on the vertical picture in a formal translation, though the preacher may find it useful to bear in mind. From "he is against him" it is easy to pass to "he is out to down him." (Matt. 12: 30).

Thus "if you have a complaint against anyone" can be turned into "if you are down on anyone" (Mark 11: 25). "They poisoned their minds against the brethren" (Acts 14: 2) suggests that they put ideas into their heads, they prejudiced them, so that they wanted "to come down on the brethren like a ton of bricks." (Cf. v. 5, "to stone them".)

It would be wearisome to go through all the possible texts which manifest a "down on" somebody or something. But there is an interesting selection. In addition to "us" (Rom. 8: 31 "If God is for us, who could have an effective 'down' on us?") there is the Lord Himself (Matt. 12: 14; Acts 4: 26); the Holy Spirit (Matt. 12: 32); the promises of God (Gal. 3: 21); and flesh and spirit in their mutual hostility (Gal. 5: 17).

2 Corinthians 10: 5 has possibilities for the preacher. Paul is speaking of our mighty spiritual weapons whereby we may demolish strongholds of sophistry and "every high thing (*hupsōma*) that rises against (*kata*) the knowledge of God." Now the "high thing" may be simply pride, which "from its ever loftier ('rising') height looks down in enmity on the knowledge of God." Or we may regard it as a massive fortification to dominate the surrounding country. With the weapons of our warfare we demolish "every lofty fortress which showers (= throws *down*) its missiles on to the knowledge of God." The combination of height and "rising" (*epairomenon*) with "down" is suggestive.

"The document against us" of Colossians 2: 14 is in a sense "the document which sent us down." But Christ has cancelled it and nailed it to His cross. Even so, "I have against thee . . ." (Rev. 2: 4, 14, 20). In what sense is Christ "down on" His church?

We now have to make the difficult transition to *kata* and the accusative. Students have clung to the rendering "according to," but this does not show the connection with the basic "down". We have seen the meanings "down from" and "down to". It may be that "down along" preserves the original idea. But whereas "down from" and "down to" are vertical, "down along" is horizontal. This is strange at first sight. But *kata* with the accusative is used from at least the time of Homer for "down stream." This may show us how the Greek mind worked. Water flows downhill; but to the naked eye a river looks horizontal.

Now that horizontal line will repay study. Think of some such thing as a square table, with a firm flat top. Each side of it is a horizontal, straight line. We could use the side of the table as a means of measuring a length of anything, or of testing whether anything is straight. Figuratively, as in Philippians 4: 19, we can say that the way God meets our need "squares with" His own riches. So in Philippians 1: 19–20 the apostle's knowledge that his experience will turn out to his salvation . . . "squares with" his earnest expectation and hope. Or we might use the expression "in line with". If we want the tenth floor of a building, for example, it is advisable for the floor of the elevator to be "in line with" the floor we need. We can then step off easily, or if we are in an invalid chair we can be wheeled off smoothly. So in Romans 16: 25 St. Paul ascribes his doxology to "Him Who is able to raise you (e.g. in the elevator) to the level of His strength, in line with my gospel and the message which proclaims Jesus Christ (which is on the tenth floor)".

Different preachers will "see" different pictures which are true to the idea of *kata* provided they are suggested by the outline of one horizontal as the standard or norm of something else. Thus "Be it done for you on the line of your faith" (Matt. 9: 29) suggests that the art of healing, like the elevator, is to rise to a certain height, and the mighty work is to be on that (horizontal) level of their faith. Similarly, "do not judge on the level of sight, of outward appearance" (John 7: 24); "you judge on the level of flesh" (8: 15); "I am speaking on the human level" (Rom. 3: 5).

When our Lord sent out the seventy missioners He told them not to stop for "salutations" or "greetings *along* (*kata*) the road" (Luke 10: 5). The same expression is used in Acts 8: 36 of the travel of Philip and the eunuch. Cf. Acts 25: 3; 26: 13. Now "walking" is used of the moral life. We therefore hear of "walking along the road of love" (Rom. 14: 15). *Kata* here expresses a standard. We must not leave this road. But suppose we have difficulty in recognising it? Why, it is that great ten-line highway, flanked by a sidewalk where we should always be. "This is love, that we walk in line with His commandments" (2 John 6). But there are people who follow other roads, dangerous roads leading to disaster: they walk along the road of their own desires (Jude 16, 18). In this day of vast schemes of road-building the preacher ought to be able to draw on some obvious illustrations.

Paul once said that he was running on, with his eye fixed straight ahead (*kata skopon*) on the tape which marks the winning post (Phil. 3: 14). Here is a test of our discipleship. Are we speeding or laggard? Is our gaze concentrated on the one final object?

The original meaning of *para* seems to have been "beside". From this come the later shades of meaning. As a rough division we may say that *para* with the dative means "at beside", with the accusative "towards beside" or "extent beside" and with the genitive "from beside". Let us take the dative first, and see how some of the idioms work out.

Our Lord's mother and some other women "were standing beside the cross of Jesus" (John 19: 25). This is a rare example of the N.T. use of the preposition with the dative of a thing as opposed to a person. But when a Pharisee asked Him to dine with (*para* plus dative) him (Luke 11: 37), he did not mean "beside him" as if they were to stand together at a luncheon counter or snack bar. He meant something like "in his home". So Peter stayed "in the home" of Simon a tanner. (Compare Acts 9: 43; 10: 6 with Acts 10: 32, where the actual word for "house" is used. See also Acts 21: 8.)

But the house or home begins to fade away into something more vague. Paul wanted the Corinthians to "save up" with a view to his collection for the poor saints. Each member should set aside weekly any little extra which had come to him and should keep it "by him". In his home? Possibly; but supposing he were a slave? The picture is of some place closely associated with him, even secret, where the little hoard may be kept (1 Cor. 16: 2). It is clearly external to him. But *para* plus dative may suggest something inner. "God raise the dead? Why is it judged incredible *para humin*?" (Acts 26: 8). If we translate "by you" we lose something. We must combine the inner thought involved in judging with the background of "in your home". The expression suggests a company of men together, thinking their own thoughts and discussing them. The preacher has great scope here for his imagination. Let him visualise a group of men discussing resurrection. They give their arguments for and against and come to their conclusion. Why? The great Joseph Parker once impressively announced his text: "Why should it be thought a thing incredible with you, that God. . . ." Here he stopped. "That *God*." We ought to be able to preach on "The Forgotten Factor" in men's discussions.

Our Lord once said: ". . . we will make our abode *with* him" (John 14: 23). *Para* is not quite the same as *en*. It is roughly the same as "in his heart" (cf. Eph. 3: 17) but the background of "in his home" suggests the influence which such a man exerts. In 1 Cor. 7: 24 we see a slave staying *in* his condition of slavery and also "in the home of God." Can it be that even a slave has the living God as his constant theme and scene?[1]

An interesting development can be seen in the use of *para* with the accusative. First it means "extending along beside", as in Hebrews 11: 12 (Gen. 22: 17 LXX): "like the sand extending along beside the shore of the sea." But in 1 Corinthians 3: 11 there is a subtle change. Paul is thinking of the one foundation, Jesus Christ. Nobody can lay another foundation extending along beside the one lying in position already. So far so good; but the apostle is not

[1] I have tried to work out some of the possibilities of the frequently used N.T. expression "in the home of God" in *Royal Sacrament*, pp. 62–66.

merely thinking of extent. He means "in distinction from." If one foundation lies alongside another, then there are two. No, says Paul. Nobody can lay another *in distinction from* "the church's one foundation, Jesus Christ her Lord."

Consider, again, Romans 1: 25, ". . . they worshipped and served what had been created *para* the One who had created it." How is *para* to be translated here? The background is "beside" which leads on to "in distinction from." But nobody has the right thus to worship and serve. Nobody has the right to place the Creator and the creation side by side and worship the one in distinction from the other. We should therefore translate "rather than", which implies a false choice. (This prepares the way for the "comparative" use in Hebrews.) It also implies "to the neglect of," which is a sin of omission; and "to the dishonour of," which is a sin of commission. Idolatry in any form, physical (an image), mental (a false concept of God), or just plain selfishness and pride, is a false choice, a neglect of spiritual duty and a slur on the living God. There is not much room here for the plain man's "doing no harm" and "being as good as his neighbour".

The expression "in distinction from" branches out in yet another way. Paul was accused of persuading men to worship God "*para ton nomon*" (Acts 18: 13). They did not mean that he was, so to speak, a Free Churchman with a form of worship in distinction from their own, with an emphasis on grace rather than law. He was acting "contrary to the law," just as the troublemakers of Romans 16: 17 were stirring up strife "contrary to the teaching" which had been given and received. But how far does one have to go to be "contrary"?

Paul told the leading Roman Jews that he had done nothing contrary (*enantion*) to the people or their ancestral customs (Acts 28: 17). It is conceivable that he might have done something or some things so contrary. James can visualise a man keeping the whole law with the exception of one point, in which he fails (Jas. 2: 10). The handwriting or document which our Lord cancelled and nailed to the cross, which was against us, was completely against us. (Note *kata* plus genitive and *hupenantion* in Col. 2: 14.) But how shall we interpret Galatians 1: 8–9? Paul pronounces a solemn anathema against angel, apostle or any man who preaches as gospel that which is contrary to the gospel preached by him and received by the Galatians. Does he mean contrary at every point? Or is it rather "contrary in any essential point"?

This is not merely an academic exercise. It has been the fashion to speak of the different theologies of the New Testament—Johannine,

Pauline and the rest. And we have been told of the "different approaches" to the Christian faith and so on. Paul's anathema is too solemn to be disregarded. It is not going too far to assert that the whole ecumenical movement depends on the right interpretation of his use of *para*. And the problem arises long before re-union schemes are brought to fruition. For example many of us who are content to recline happily on the ample bosom of the Anglican communion are glad to take the Holy Communion with Anglo-Catholics, Free Churchmen and members of the Brethren. But if some who have attained to notoriety were given a position of ecclesiastical authority over us, where should we stand if we were summoned to some kind of ecclesiastical gathering in which we were expected to attend a service of Holy Communion celebrated by a heretic? Can you communicate with and utter an anathema upon one and the same person?

We pass now to the use of *peri*. Its root meaning is "around", "about", and the exercise of a little imagination will bring to our minds the picture of a circle. The preacher will not use the idea slavishly but it is a good point of departure. He may not find *peri* with the accusative particularly helpful. John the Baptist had a leathern girdle round his loins (Matt. 3: 4) and was "encircled in a belt". The gardener of Luke 13: 7 spoke of digging round a tree and surrounding it with manure. The "circle" is used metaphorically when Peter went up to pray *about* midday (Acts 10: 9).

These examples illustrate; but *peri* with the genitive is more rewarding for the preacher. In Luke 4: 37 "rumour (news) went out about him into every place in the neighbourhood" and "the story about Him spread the more" (Luke 5: 15). "About Him" suggests that all the talk *enclosed* one topic.

This is perhaps a neutral or colourless use of *peri*. But it can express interest or concern. When our Lord caught sight of the crowds "He was moved with compassion for (*peri*) them" (Matt. 9: 36). Can we not say that "His compassion enfolded them"? It is perhaps too deliberate to think of "He brought them within the circle of His compassion," as if our Lord weighed up the matter and finally decided to be compassionate. But if His compassion was spontaneous it might be reflected in "they fell within the circle of His pity."

We read in Matthew 26: 28 that "this is My blood which is shed for (*peri*) many." It is in their interest, for their benefit. The preacher will see that the Saviour shed His blood "to bring them within the circle of God's fellowship." Without His blood they will stay outside. ". . . you who once were far off were brought near by the blood of Christ" (Eph. 2: 13).

It is well known that the phrase "concerning (*peri*) sin" is frequently used in the Greek Old Testament for the sin-offering. (See Rom. 8: 3; Heb. 10: 6–8.) It is perhaps impossible to find out with absolute certainty the motive of the original translators, but the "circle" of *peri* offers a challenge to the preacher. Does the preposition suggest the taking away of sin? Then either we are entangled in its encircling coils or we are trapped and besieged by it.

But suppose, with the great A. T. Robertson, we think of being liberated from sin, "from around" it. Then the picture is of men gathered round a central fascination, spellbound. All the illustrations of the order of "bees round a honeypot" are relevant here. Not for nothing did the writer to the Hebrews speak of "the enjoyment of sin" (Heb. 11: 25).

The "concern" which we have seen associated with *peri* comes out clearly in the passages in the New Testament which refer to prayer, either as petition or as thanksgiving. "Keep on praying for those who mistreat you" (Luke 6: 28) can be turned into the pedestrian "keep them within the circle of your prayers." But we might elaborate and say "do not let them escape beyond the horizon of your prayerful interest." Our Lord prayed for Peter, and told him so (Luke 22: 32). He "made him the centre of His prayer." The writer to the Hebrews wanted his readers to have the habit of "surrounding us with your prayers" (Heb. 13: 18).

This idea of the circle which we have tried to express in a variety of ways, should be the beginning of an illustration. Others should spring to mind. For example, we have heard not infrequently of men escaping from prison. When the news comes over the radio or television we are informed that within a very short time "the police threw a cordon round the area". While this is fresh in the minds of the congregation, cannot the preacher urge his hearers to "throw a cordon of prayer round" the person in need? In rural areas farmers have a wire running round a field through which is a small electric charge. The cows touch it—and that is enough! The slight shock keeps them in the field. Cannot the country clergyman illustrate prayer from this?

As we are not seeking to be exhaustive we shall consider but one more preposition, *pros* with the accusative. It is not necessary to go into the question of whether its root meaning is "near "or "towards". For our present purpose we shall incline to "towards" and hope to show how it works out. In the majority of uses *pros* seems to express some kind of *direction*.

It is used in a literal sense in Luke 7: 44, "He turned towards the

woman." So also "He withdrew towards the sea" (Mark 3: 7).
Cf. Mark 6: 45. The evildoer does not direct his steps "towards the
light" (John 3: 20). A vivid picture is given in Matt. 3: 10 and Luke
3: 9. "Already the axe is put (*keimai* is used as passive of *tithēmi*)
towards the root of the trees," is being levelled at it, aimed at it.
The eschatological wrath is seen in the picture of the divine Judge,
axe in hand, about to strike. The edge of the axe is at the correct
angle, directed towards (not a branch but) the very root. This must
be the end of the tree. Will anything stay His hand? And does it
help if we translate John 12: 32 by "And I, if I be lifted up from the
earth, will draw all men *towards* Me?" Will they arrive?

In the literal sense *pros* does at times express both direction and
arrival. "Which of you will have a friend, and he will go to him at
midnight . . ." (Luke 11: 5). Paul can tell the Corinthians that "I
came to you" (1 Cor. 2: 1, 3).

But it may express the direction indicated by the body without
any actual movement. The two disciples "found a colt tethered . . ."
(Mark 11: 4). Surely not "to the door"! "Towards the door" must
mean "facing the door," that is with its head to the door. An advance
on this suggests the direction of both body and of attention. When
our Lord used a boat as a pulpit and "sat in the sea" all the crowd
were on the land "facing the sea". But their interest was not in the
seascape but in the Preacher (Mark 4: 1). A similar combination of
"direction and attention" may be seen by a comparison of Luke
22: 56 and Mark 14: 54. Peter sat "facing the fire." This is the
"direction." Attention? He was warming himself. Speaking "towards the ear" (Luke 12: 3) implies the direction or inclination of
the head and the attention given to whispering a secret. An analogous idea is apparent in "face to(wards) face" (1 Cor. 13: 12). Cf.
2 John 12; 3 John 14; and perhaps Luke 10: 39. Mary sat facing our
Lord's feet and attending to His word.

A "direction of attention" is seen in Matthew 19: 8; Mark 10: 5.
Moses permitted divorce "in view of your hardness of heart." This
expresses reflection, not purpose. Cf. Luke 18: 1. "He spoke a parable
to them *directing attention to the fact that* they must pray always and
not faint."

In other instances we have a "direction of words." "He said to
them" (Luke 11: 5) means that He directed His words towards
them. Cf. Mark 10: 26.

Words and attention are combined in Mark 9: 14, "scribes arguing
with them." An interesting "secondary direction of words" is a
development in Luke 20: 9, 19. Our Lord spoke the parable *pros*

the people (v. 9) and *pros* them, i.e. the scribes and the highpriests (v. 19). What is the difference? The former is simple enough: He was speaking to the people and what He said was the Parable of the Wicked Husbandmen. In the second case the meaning is that the parable, though spoken *to* the people, was *aimed at* the scribes and highpriests. We can get the flavour of the expression by saying that "they had spotted the fact that He had spoken this parable *at* them." Cf. Mark 12: 12 and Matthew's explicit *peri* (Matt. 21: 45).

The "direction" may also indicate purpose, when *pros* may be translated by some such phrase as "with a view to." "The harbour was unsuitable for the purpose of wintering" (Acts 27: 12). The cross of Christ was "with a view to the demonstration of God's righteousness" (Rom. 3: 26). The wanderings in the wilderness after the Exodus were recorded in the Old Testament "with a view to our instruction" (1 Cor. 10: 11) as they were "pattern" events. In the church everything should be done "with a view to consolidation" (1 Cor. 14: 26; cf. v. 12). Under this head comes the construction of *pros* with the accusative of the neuter definite article and the infinitive.

In some passages in the New Testament the "direction" is highly metaphorical and complex. Paul tells the Galatians that he went up to Jerusalem to visit Cephas and "stayed *with* him a fortnight" (Gal. 1: 18). Later in the letter (4: 18–20) he was wishing "to be *with* you at the present time and to change my tone." The "with" (*pros*) is more than a mere physical presence. If the apostle had been present his torrential arguments (he hopes) would have ebbed as the church responded to his persuasive exposition of free grace. *Pros* in this context must mean roughly "in contact with" you or "in fellowship face to face with" you. However we translate it the meaning seems to include some sort of "dealings", though not of course commercial dealings.

Similarly Paul thinks joyously of being absent from the body and "at home *with*, in experiential fellowship with, the Lord" (2 Cor. 5: 8). An apt comparison is his desire for more than a mere "stopover" with the Corinthians (1 Cor. 16: 5–7). Note again his behaviour in his association *with* them (2 Cor. 1: 12). Colossians 4: 5 can be a trap for the unwary. It lends itself to the rendering "walk with wisdom towards those who are outside" but it really means "behave wisely *in your dealings with outsiders*."

"Are not (all) His sisters (here) with us?" (Matt. 13: 56; Mark 6: 3) implies that "we know them; we have had dealings with them; they are an ordinary crowd!" Once more, in Mark 9: 19 the *pros* is more than a mere juxtaposition: "How long shall I be with you? how long shall I put up with you?" (Cf. Luke 9: 41.) Our Lord's endurance of the persons in question suggests that His time *with* them included the interplay of personalities. Cf. 1 Thessalonians 3: 4; 4: 12; 2 Thessalonians 2: 5; 3: 10; 2 Timothy 2: 24; Titus 3: 2.

With this as background we turn to what is perhaps the most elusive use of *pros* in the New Testament, ". . . the Word was with God" (John 1: 1). It is impossible in translation to exhaust the meaning of *pros* here in one English word, but we may be able to attempt an exposition. It would seem that the Word is to be regarded as "facing God", with a purposive attention which is expressive of interest and of experiential fellowship. Light is thrown on the subject from elsewhere in the fourth gospel.

Only Jesus "has seen the Father" (John 6: 46). The perfect tense is significant. His intent gaze has left its mark. He gives utterance to what He has seen in the home of the Father (*para* plus dative. John 8: 38). He can do nothing of Himself; He cannot act at all unless He sees the Father doing something, which He "copies". The Father shows Him everything that He Himself is doing (John 5: 19f.). Again, "As I hear (from the Father), I judge" (5: 30). "As the Father taught Me, I speak" (8: 28).

It is plain that the words "attention" and "interest" are relevant. Indeed the fellowship is close and intimate, closer even than "having dealings with". He knows the Father (17: 25); He loves the Father (14: 31); does the will of the Father (6: 38); and positively seek the will of the Father (5: 30). To do the Father's will completely is meat and drink to Him (4: 34) and He always does what is pleasing to the Father (8: 29).

In view of all this, John 1: 1 suggests that the Word faces the Father with close attention and interest; gazes with rapt attention and listens in the same way. The Word "has dealings" with the Father and is in the most intimate fellowship with Him.

It is on these lines that we must begin to understand the meaning of the fact that "the Word was *with* God."

Now let us see what can be done with St. Paul's Epistle to the Galatians. We shall give a translation first, and then some comments.

Chap. I: 1. Paul, a man of apostolic office—men were not the fount of it, no individual man was the channel of it. I was made an apostle through Jesus Christ and God the Father Who raised Him out of the company of the dead—and all the brothers with me, to the churches of Galatia: grace to you,

and peace, from God our Father and the Lord Jesus Christ,
Who bowed to death for our sins so that He might wrest us
out of the evil secular present, thereby reaching the level of
God our Father's will, to Whom be glory for ever and ever;
amen.

6.   I am amazed that you are so soon on the move from Him
Who by the grace of Christ said to you "Come!" and are
going over to an alternative gospel, which is not just "another
version" of the true one; amazed—unless there are some who
are disturbing you and wishing to distort the gospel of
Christ. But even if we or an angel out of heaven drive a
gospel into you contrary to the one we drove into you, let
him be anathema. As we have said previously, so now I repeat,
if anyone is hammering a gospel into you contrary to what
you received, let him be anathema.

10.   For am I now persuading men or God? or am I seeking
to go on giving pleasure to men? If I were still pleasing men
I should not be a slave of Christ. For I make known to you,
brothers, that the gospel which was preached by me is not
based on a human foundation. For even I did not take it
over from a man nor was I taught it, but it came through a
revelation of Jesus Christ. For you heard, like a clap of
thunder, my kind of life at one time in the Jewish religion, how
that I was overdoing it in persecuting the church of God and
trying to devastate it, and in the Jewish religion was pioneer-
ing my way forward beyond many contemporaries in my race,

15.   overflowing all the time with fanaticism for my ancestral
traditions. But when He, Who ringed me round from birth
and called me through His grace, made up His mind in my case
to drop the curtain that veiled His Son, for the purpose of
my preaching Him among the under-privileged non-Jews,
at once I did not have a word with flesh and blood nor did
I go up to Jerusalem to my seniors in the apostolate, but I
went off to Arabia, and again I returned to Damascus. Then
after three years I went up to Jerusalem to have a look at
Cephas and I stretched my fellowship with him to fifteen
days; but I did not catch a glimpse of another apostle, except

20.   James the Lord's brother. Before God I am not telling
lies in what I am writing to you. Afterwards I went into the
territories of Syria and Cilicia. But my face was unknown to
the churches of Judaea in Christ. Only the news was coming
through to them: "Our quondam persecutor is now preaching

as a gospel the faith which once he was trying to devastate".
And in my case they were glorifying God.

Chap. II. 1. Then after an interval of fourteen years, I went up
again to Jerusalem with Barnabas (I had added Titus to our
party as well); my visit was based on a revelation; and I put
up to them the gospel which I spend my life preaching among
the non-Jews, but privately to the reputable members, for
fear that I might somehow be running to no purpose—or
had run. But not even Titus who was with me was forced
to be circumcised, though he was a Greek. It was all because
of false brothers who had slipped in, who butted in to cast
a spy's glance down on to our freedom which we have in
Christ Jesus, that they might fling a lasso of slavery around
5. our neck. We didn't budge an inch before them or yield
them a moment's subjection, in order that the truth of the
gospel might survive the storm and reach you intact. But
by those whose reputation had some weight—it makes no
difference to me what sort of people they once were; God
does not accept a man's face-value—for the men of reputation,
I say, did not have a word with me at all, but, on the contrary,
when they spotted the fact that the gospel of the uncircumcision was in my hands as a trust, just as the circumcision
gospel was in Peter's (for He Who had been active in Peter
with a view to the apostleship of the circumcision had been
active also in me in regard to the non-Jews), and realising, I
say, the grace that had been given to me, James and Cephas
and John who had the reputation of being pillars, clasped our
hands in fellowship, so that Barnabas and I might go to the
non-Jews and they to the circumcision; only they wanted us
to keep the poor in mind; the very thing I had an urge to do!
11.   But when Cephas came to Antioch I took my stand and
resisted him to his face, because his conduct had condemned
him. For before certain people came from James he had been
in the habit of eating in the company of non-Jews; but when
they came he began to trim his sails and to fence himself off,
through constant fear of the circumcision party. And the rest
of the Jews also played up to the rôle he had assumed, so
that even Barnabas was drawn into the march of their pretence.
But when I saw that they were not going straight with their
eyes on the truth of the gospel, I tackled Cephas in front of
all of them: if you, being a Jew all the time, live like a Gentile
and not like a Jew, why are you forcing the Gentiles to live

15. like Jews? We are by nature Jews, not samples taken from Gentile sinners, but we know that a man's acquittal does not originate in works of law; he is not acquitted except through faith in Christ Jesus. Hence even we directed our faith into Christ Jesus, so that the seal of our acquittal might be derived from faith in Christ and not from works of law, because no mortal man will find his acquittal in works of law. But if when seeking the verdict "Not Guilty" in Christ we were found to be sinners ourselves also, is Christ a servant of sin? Heavens, no! For if I build again the edifice of law which I tore down, I constitute myself a transgressor. For I through law died to law that I might come to life in God's sight. I am dead; when they crucified Christ they crucified me; it is no longer I who am alive, but Christ is alive in me; and the life which I now have in the flesh I am living in faith in the Son of God Who set His love upon me and gave Himself up for me. I am not cancelling the grace of God; for if righteousness came through law, then Christ died—and got nothing out of it.

Chap. III. 1. O senseless Galatians, who cast a spell over you, before whose eyes Jesus Christ was placarded as "One Who bears the marks of crucifixion"? This news-flash alone I want to get from you: you took the Spirit—was that involved in works of law or in hearing and believing? Are you thus senseless? After beginning in the Spirit are you now being completed with flesh? Was so much done to you in vain?— IF it was in vain. Therefore I ask: the activity of Him Who supplies you with His Spirit and operates powers among you —did it start in works of law or in hearing and believing? Just as Abraham believed God, and it was counted to him as righteousness.

"A man of apostolic office" (1:1) is better than the bare "apostle" because it was the apostleship which did not come "from men". Notice that "fount" is suggested by the preposition "from" (*apo*) and "channel" by "through" (*dia* with the genitive). But "through" has been retained later in the verse because Jesus Christ and God are not channels in the same sense: it was through them, by means of them, that St. Paul became an apostle. "Out of the company of the dead" (*ek*) shows that before the resurrection our Lord was inside the group suggested by the plural; and "company" is necessary because we can hardly say merely "out of the dead". "Bowed to

death" (v. 4) is a punctiliar phrase, to bring out the pinpoint in the
aorist of "gave Himself". It is the same with "wrest us", which raises
the picture of a man swiftly plucking a diamond necklace out of the
fire into which it has fallen. The text, of course, has nothing in it
about necklaces, diamond or otherwise, but the pinpoint expression
conveys that to me. Other preachers will find that other pictures
occur to them, though the one aorist is the starting-point.

"Evil secular present" is an inversion. It is so easy to say "present
evil world", and so liable to misunderstanding. The Greek word
aiōn really means an age. Christians are not taken out of the world
(*kosmos*) though a few may try to escape by going into a monastery.
Our Lord does not wrest us out of the world. "No longer am I in
the world, and they are in the world . . ." "I do not ask that Thou
shouldst remove them out of the world, but that Thou shouldst
keep them out of evil." (John 17: 11, 15) But He does wrest us out
of the age: He does deliver His people from the spirit of the age,
and "secular" just preserves the essential flavour of "age". It is
well that our Lord does so deliver us, for, as Dr. W. R. Inge has said,
"If you marry the spirit of your own generation, you will be a widow
in the next". Compare 2 Timothy 4: 9–10. "Reaching the level" is
suggested by the horizontal line of *kata*.

"On the move" (v 6.) is a modern phrase used to describe restless
people who never seem to have a permanent home. They come to a
town, buy or rent a house, but within a short time grow tired and
seek a home elsewhere: they are "on the move" once more. The
present tense of the Greek verb shows us the action going on:
"they are engaged in putting themselves" is the meaning of the
simple verb, and the addition of the preposition (*meta*) to it brings in
the idea of change, as is so frequent with this preposition in compound
verbs. Compare the Greek verbs behind the words *meta*morphosis,
*meta*noia (repentance). "On the move" seems to include both the
idea of change and also that of the action actually going on.

"Said to you 'come!' " contains the sharp monosyllable "Come"
which admirably gives us the spirit of the aorist "called". "Are
going over to" picks up the ideas of change and action-in-process
in "on the move". "Drive a gospel into you," "drove into you"
(v. 8), is an attempt to render the pinpoint once more. A man is
depicted driving a nail into a board with one swift blow of the ham-
mer. By contrast, "is hammering" (v. 9) shows us the act going on,
as blow follows blow.

"Based on a human foundation" (v. 11) is the picture raised by
the horizontal line in the preposition *kata*. "Like a clap of thunder"

(v. 13) is a pinpoint expression; note that it is not a roll of thunder, which would imply a present or an imperfect tense. A "clap" is sudden, startling, almost instantaneous. "Overdoing it in persecuting" can be justified. The verb must be an imperfect in English, and "I was persecuting" with the adverbial phrase "in line with excess", "excessively", is awkward, apart from the fact that it might be thought that you could persecute provided you did not take it too far. "Overdoing it in persecuting" avoids this. "Was trying to devastate it" stands for a conative imperfect; compare Acts 26: 9–11 and see page 30*f.*

"Overflowing all the time with fanaticism" (v. 14) needs a little explanation. The Greek participle means "being in a state arising out of the previous same state". Hence the phrase "all the time". The Greek adverb comes from a word which sometimes means "odd", not in the sense of strange or queer, but "odd" as opposed to "even". It always raises in my mind the picture of the even numbers "pairing off", like choirboys leaving church with the "odd" one left over, an extra. So the adverb here suggests "with an extra", "with a surplus", and so "overflowingly". "Being . . . overflowingly a fanatic" may easily be transposed into "overflowing all the time with fanaticism", and the preacher has a choice of illustrations before him. Overflowing? Like a river? Ask the people of Winnipeg or Northern Italy who know from experience. Like a pot boiling over? or a volcano? The preacher will know and choose for himself.

"Ringed me round" represents the aorist participle of a verb connected with our word "horizon" and with a Greek noun meaning "border" or "boundary". Reading the Greek here brings to the mind a picture of a photograph of a group, say a group of class-mates. Sometimes parents put a ring round one of the faces in the photograph, to indicate to distant relations which is Charles or Robert or as the case may be. So when God looked upon all the world there was a ring about Saul of Tarsus: He had marked him off to bear His Name among the nations.

"To drop the curtain that veiled" (v. 16) represents the aorist infinitive of the verb "to unveil", and the punctiliar nature of the action is retained in "drop". The swift fall of a curtain is a fair example of a pinpoint. "Have a word with" connotes something of deferential intimacy, and the slight emphasis on *one* word, not many words, again reflects the pinpoint. "Have a look at" (v. 18) in much the same way retains the flavour of the aorist. The reference to "fellowship" arises in the preposition (*pros*). "The news was coming through" (v. 23) stands for the periphrastic imperfect tense, "they were hearing", aptly represented by a series of dots (see page 30). "Our quondam persecutor" is a fair rendering of what seems to be a present participle; but the present participle does duty in Greek for an imperfect one too. "Trying to devastate" is conative imperfect as in verse 13.

"Added Titus to our party" (2: 1) recalls Acts 15: 37–38, where the same verb is used. Note that the verb here is aorist, and see the discussion on pages 19*f*. "Based on a revelation" (v. 2) comes from the horizontal line in the preposition (*kata*). "Put up" happens to be a literal translation, but it was not chosen for this reason. There is a use of this verb in English by clerks and other subordinates, when they are going to suggest some policy to the people in power. This is not to say that St. Paul was a subordinate, but it may reveal his tact and courtesy, his nice choice of words.

"Butted in" (v. 4) brings to my mind the picture of a man standing on the sidewalk and slipping into a procession that is already half-way past. He has no right to do it, and our English expression "to butt in" suggests this. Its reminiscence of a goat which put its head down and "butted someone" is true to the aorist. "Cast a spy's glance" is once more a pinpoint phrase; and so is "fling a lassoo of slavery". The true Greek text here may be a future indicative, but this tense is also punctiliar. In verse 5 the aorist tense is brought out in "didn't budge an inch", and this is combined with the ideas of time and subjection in "yield a moment's subjection". The apostle can hardly be insisting on a literal hour. The vigorous language is in accord with his rising emotion, which is seen all the more clearly in the broken sentences which follow. How many preachers in the heat of their argument have lost the thread of their sentence and have had to begin again, or finish the sentence as if they had begun it in another way! "Survive the storm and reach you intact" combines two thoughts. The verb means "remain throughout", but it is aorist, and "survive" sums this up. The preposition (*pros*) presents the picture of the truth of the gospel going "towards you," and hence the double translation.

The broken and involved constructions in verses 6–10 have been kept, in order to show the apostle's white heat of passion as he tries to develop his theme. In verse 6 the apostle seems to have been about to say "from those whose reputation had some weight I received nothing", but he breaks off, and after the parenthesis starts again with "the men of reputation did not confer anything on me". For the verb, compare 1: 16. In 2: 7 "spotted" is a pinpoint. "Was in my hands as a trust" represents the perfect tense in historic sequence.

The perfect can always be transposed into a present, and this, in English, becomes a past when in historic sequence. "Realising" (v. 9), though an English present participle, stands for a Greek aorist. To "realise" is what happens when something suddenly occurs to you, and "realising" is thus after all a pinpoint. "Clasped our hands" again is a pinpoint. "Keep in mind" (v. 10) renders a present tense: the picture is not that of a G-man saying to an arrested man "Try to remember the exact time", i.e. try to call back into consciousness. It is rather that of a football captain who tells his men before the game "remember all the time to work together as a team". "Had an urge" is yet another pinpoint expression. By this time, if not before, the reader will distinguish such for himself.

Note the imperfects in verse 12, "began to trim his sails and fence himself off"—a swift succession of metaphors. "Constant fear" shows the continuity of the present participle. "Played up" (v.13), or "fell in with his game" colloquially expresses the force of the aorist of the verb that is associated with acting a part. "I tackled" (v. 14) is punctiliar: watch a footballer! And an argumentative man will often say "I tackled him about it," when he merely means "I said". "Samples taken from" (v. 15) is suggested by the preposition "out of" (*ek*); similarly, (v. 16) "originate in" is justified by the same preposition. "The seal" suggests a punctiliar act. "Acquittal *in*" because derived *out of* (*ek*, once more). "You will not get money out of that game" means "you will not find money in it". "The verdict 'not guilty'" (v. 17) is a pinpoint. "Come to life" (v. 19) stands for an ingressive aorist. "I am dead . . .": the perfect can always be made into a present. "Set His love upon me" (v. 20) is more punctiliar than the bare "loved". So, too, with "cast a spell" (3: 1), and "news-flash" (v. 2). "One Who bears the marks" (3: 1): present for perfect. "Involved in" (v. 2) because "derived out of" (*ek*). So with "start in" (v. 5).

This chapter has largely dealt with prepositions when they govern nouns and pronouns; they will appear again in verbs.

Chapter 6

ARCHITECTURE

ONE of the fascinating and rewarding studies for a preacher is the examination of compound verbs, that is, verbs which are made up of a simple verb with the addition of one or more prepositions. We have the same sort of thing in English; we speak of "stand" and "understand", or "give" and "forgive". Often we can see how a certain Greek word gains its meaning by the addition of a preposition; this may suggest a picture, and when that has been done we are on the track of an illustration. Take the Greek word *diadidōmi*, which means "I distribute". The simple verb means merely "I give". Now in many instances the addition of the preposition *dia* to a verb adds the meaning "in all directions from one original point". (See page 19.) In this connection it is worth saying again that I can always "see with the mind's eye" the spokes of a wheel, which start from one original point, the centre, and go out in all directions. Is not this precisely what happens when we distribute anything? "We" are the centre; each receiver is at the end of a spoke.

Now, with this in mind, consider Romans 5: 12, "through one man sin entered the world, and death through sin, and so death *passed* to all men . . ." The Greek verb (*diēlthen*) contains the preposition which we have been discussing, and it bears the meaning "went in all directions to all men". Some translators give "spread to all men", but the rendering which occurs to me is "fanned out". During the fighting in World War II the newspapers used to say that "tanks had punched a hole in the enemy lines, and breaking through had fanned out". That is exactly what death did, in the apostle's thought, and the illustration of the tanks was suggested by the Greek compound verb.

Take another example, Mark 11: 23, "whoever . . . does not waver in his heart . . ." The compound verb is *diakrinō*, which, according to the lexicon, means "separate", "distinguish", "discern (one thing) from (another)"; in the middle and passive voices it means "doubt", "hesitate", "waver". Now the simple verb means "I judge". The addition of the preposition suggests some such meaning as "I am judging in all directions". In other words, the subject looks at one possibility, and then he looks at another; and so the process goes on, as his thoughts and judgements, starting from one centre, his mind, like the spokes of a wheel, keep on directing themselves towards something different. This certainly separates one thing from another, and in the middle voice the verb looks at separate objects and regards them as "good for *me*". This is obviously "wavering" between one and the other.

We clearly can find an illustration in some form of oscillation. Some people are like the pendulum of a clock; they can never make up their minds but are always wavering. But the swinging of a pendulum is a slow, solemn business, and some people dart from one possibility to another much more quickly. Then think of the sport of archery. The bowman shoots an arrow and it enters, say, a gatepost. There it sticks, *quivering*. Rapidly it oscillates, from one side to another, several times in a second. If you were to look down on to it from above it would appear like a section of a wheel, the successive positions of the arrow taking the place of the spokes. Oscillation! It is that which prevents faith from gaining the answer to its prayers.

Again with the wheel and the spokes in mind, look at Mark 8: 25. It concerns the blind man of Bethsaida. At the first imposition of our Lord's hands he saw men walking, "as trees". His vision was blurred: there is no clear outline of the men; it was as if he were looking at trees and the leaves are not distinguished one from the other but "overlap". But when our Lord laid His hands upon him the second time "he saw clearly". The Greek verb is *dieblepsen*. Men are no longer seen as trees. Each part, as it were, is no longer overlapping another part; he sees each thing where it actually is. That is to say, his lines of vision go out from his eyes like the separate spokes of a wheel, and the ends of the spokes are not confused: each separate thing is seen in its separateness, though united in the one inclusive view. May not the preacher see that when Christ lays His healing hand on a man, he sees things as they are, sees everything in its right place, does not confuse rites and morals, faith and works, external observances and inner piety, nature and grace, world and church, the authority of the church and the liberty of the individual member? This insight originated in the use of the preposition *dia* in a compound verb.

The sense of discrimination, of keeping apart the ends of the spokes, is seen in the verb *diaginōskō*. Notice how the verb is followed by a plural in Acts 23: 15 and 24: 22, and the use of the cognate noun in 25: 21: St. Paul wanted the emperor to "sort things out and keep them separate," which is what a legal "diagnosis" is. Observe further the three distinctions in 1 Corinthians 12: 4–6: distinctions of gifts (we have different kinds of talents); distinctions of services (we use our talents in different ways); and distinctions of results (we achieve different things). The word is found in English as "diaeresis", which is used for the two dots above a vowel to show that it must be distinguished from its neighbour in pronunciation, not joined with it: as in coöperation.

This ramification, this dividing up into its separate branches—or spokes, to keep to the figure of the wheel—is again seen in Acts 13: 49, "the word of the Lord was spread abroad through the whole territory". "Spread abroad" is *diephereto*, and means "was being carried in all directions". We see here the good news in actual process of being carried, not merely by a horseman who speeds through Main Street shouting out his tidings, but by innumerable individuals who take the tale into the side-streets, into the separate homes, even into the separate rooms of the houses. The preacher will surely see that the gospel is not only for the main street; deals not only with broad principles; inspires not only sermons on "The Church and the Atom Bomb", "The Church and Democracy", and so on; but goes into separate houses, has a message for the family as well as for the state, for flesh and blood as well as for institutions; and also goes into private lives, to separate individuals who fling themselves down on to their beds in frustration, sorrow or chagrin, who turn their faces to the wall and will not eat bread, for very sickness of soul.

A rather different picture is suggested by John 6: 18. A violent wind was blowing and the sea was being "raised". The verb is *diēgeireto*. To grasp the picture, think of a chess- or draught-board. You see the separate squares in their separateness. Now the sea may be likened to a chess-board, and the preposition *dia* suggests that first one square was raised up, then another, and then another, and so on, all separately. In other words, there was not a swell, as we sometimes say of the sea, but it was "choppy". The swell suggests one whole surging mass; "choppy" on the other hand implies that separate waves keep rising in different places. It is a graphic picture, and it is a nice question which is worse; the one great heave or swell, or the separate waves all over the surface of the sea. The preacher will see that his message is sometimes for people who have to face one mighty swell, and sometimes, as here, for folk who see separate waves wherever they look: waves of trouble, of temptation, and of anxiety. But despite the choppiness, our Lord walks on the sea. Which is a parable for all discerning hearts.

But the preposition *dia* when used in compound verbs does not always have this meaning. Sometimes it retains the meaning of "through". The lexicon and the context will be the preacher's guide. One of the happiest examples is in the use of the verb "to go through" in Acts. Thus in Acts 13: 6 we read "having gone through the whole island . . ." (*dielthontes*). There is reason for thinking that the verb is used in a semi-technical sense: business men "go through" their books; a teacher of music will "go through" a piece for the benefit of a pupil; a train will "go through" without the necessity of a stop-over; and Paul and Barnabas "go through" an island, not in the bare sense of travelling through it but in the deeper sense of evangelising it. They go through it with a tooth-comb; go through it conducting "mopping-up" operations. There is a lesson here for all travellers; what do we think about, for most of the journey? The two apostles went through, systematically making known the Name of Christ.

We have spent some time on one preposition, in order to show the possibilities. But we are by no means limited to one. Consider for instance, *kata* in a compound verb.

St. Paul speaks of men who "hold down the truth" (Rom. 1: 18). Sin not only coils itself around us (cf. page 84), but it would suppress truth itself, and it is the nature of truth to seek lodgment in human minds. The crowds once were trying to "hold down" our Lord, to prevent Him from leaving them (Luke 4: 42). But He had to preach the kingdom of God to the other cities also. There is the sin of opposition to the truth, and there is the sin of monopoly of the truth, when men will not support foreign missions.

"The Son of man must suffer many things and be rejected by the elders and highpriests and scribes . . ." (Luke 9: 22). "Rejected" (from *apodokimazō*) is an interesting word. The simple verb means "to test", "to examine", and the addition of the preposition with the meaning of "away from" turns it into "disqualify", "reject after an examination". It suggests a picture of examiners giving an oral test to a candidate. After the usual questions they "fail" him. The aorist infinitive, requiring a pinpoint expression, almost makes us see these irate examiners standing up and shouting as one man "failed! away, candidate!" Have you ever preached on "The Man Who Failed an Examination?" It would be a good subject for a University sermon. Why did He fail? Brilliant grasp of His subject, clear and forceful exposition of His themes, superior knowledge, all failed to convince these prejudiced men. One day they will be examined . . .

Sometimes the prepositions are piled one upon another, as in the Greek word *anekdiēgētos*. The simple verb, *hēgeomai*, means "to lead" or "to think, regard, deem". When *dia* is added to it the meaning becomes "to narrate", and if we put *ek* in front of that it adds a touch of completeness, "to set out in complete detail." In the adjective the *an* is privative like the English (through the Latin) privatives in- and dis-. Thus in 2 Corinthians 9: 15 the apostle is thankful to God for a gift "which cannot be described completely". Let the preacher try to do it: it is too big for him to handle. With the passing of time more and more of it comes into view ("to grasp with all the saints . . . " Eph. 3: 18). With the continual growth of the church, new experiences of the love of Christ are learnt, and so more and more of His gift is seen; additions are continually being made to it.

God's gift then, cannot be described in detail. Some aspects of Christian experience must not be. St. Paul, caught up to paradise, (2 Cor. 12: 4) heard words which were *arrēta*, "not to be spoken". (*a* privative again, and the root *re*-). And St. Peter (1 Pet. 1: 8) speaks of a joy which is *aneklalētos*, "incapable of expression in speech." You cannot (*a* privative, with the helpful *n* in front of a vowel) speak it out (*ek*). Here is a theme for the expositor. He knows a gift, a personal message, a joy, an experience, call our knowledge of Christ what you will, which in one sense can only be partly told because there is so much of it; which in another sense must not be told at all because our Lord speaks words to the individual, words of love and grace for him alone ("tell His disciples and Peter" Mark. 16: 7), and which in yet another sense cannot be told because the greatest literature and the noblest style are poor instruments— it would be like wooing with a megaphone or asking a colour-blind man to describe a sunset.

Consider the architecture of the apostle's word for "exceeding abundantly" in Ephesians 3: 20, *huperekperissou*. Part of the word we have met before (see pages 83*f*). The compound starts from the preposition *peri*, around. Now if one thing is around another it is surely greater. Think of the arms of a huge man which he puts around his tiny son. Or if you think of a besieged city, you can put more guns round it, because you have ample space, than it can train on you. From the preposition *peri* thus comes the adjective *perissos*, "more than the regular number or size". It denotes something "extra". Cf. Matthew 5: 37, 47. The Jew has an "extra" (Rom. 3: 1). *Perissos* also means "odd" as opposed to "even"—one extra after the other numbers have paired off. Cf. p. 92.

But the apostle also adds the preposition *ek*. It suggests that what is round is not close-fitting like the cylinder round the piston of an automobile, but stands *out* from it, like a wall round a house *and its lawns*. Finally the apostle also adds the preposition *huper*. (This appears in English as "hyper"; there are Calvinists and hyper-Calvinists.) It means "beyond" or "above". Thus if we think, not now of a wall, but of a circle of tall trees, they are "round" the house and its lawns, they thus stand "out" from it, and they are "above" it blessing it with their shade.

How can all this be applied? I think of a friend who spent eighteen months in the desert of North Africa during World War II; when they advanced they did not quite reach a city; when they fell back they again did not go far enough to reach civilisation. Imagine the heat and dust, and his longing for a square yard of shade: some people find life like that, and God is able to give them not a mere square yard of shade in the desert, but a circle of lofty, shady trees around them. It is more than they ask—a square yard; it is more than they conceive—a shelter over their heads; to be in Christ is to be in a palace, surrounded by fair lawns and noble trees. So the apostle (1 Thess. 3: 10) throws up a protective covering of prayer, and later (5: 13) in the same letter bids his readers regard their pastors and leaders "in love". If they are there, they have a wall around them and a roof over them: intruders will not come on the ground, for a wall prevents them, and they will not come from the air, for a roof will keep them out. The "objectionable people" will not be able to get in.

The addition to a simple verb sometimes gives us an elusive play upon words, the jingle of which is not easy to reproduce in English. Thus we might attempt to paraphrase Romans 12: 3 thus: "I tell everyone in your company, through the grace that was given to me, not to think above himself. (We speak of a man "getting above himself", when he has "high notions".) This contrasts ill with the level at which he ought to think; let him think at a level that brings him down to moral sanity in his thinking. This is somewhat cumbersome but it retains the repeated "think". The compound *huper-phronein* suggest a picture of a man who, in his own estimation, is head and shoulders *above* his fellows. The combination of the preposition *para* with the vague cognate or internal accusative governed by *phronein* (the antecedent and the relative are here telescoped into the one relative pronoun, by a normal Greek idiom) suggests a picture of two men: the one, much taller, as he himself thinks; the other, on the proper level of self-estimation. The first man is as he is; the second is as he ought to be. Has the preacher, has the congregation, ever read *Alice in Wonderland*? The tall man needs to eat, as Alice did, and become shorter! The very preposition suggests the illustration.

Take another instance: "Where therefore is boasting? it is excluded" (Rom. 3: 27). The verb is an aorist: "the door was slammed". It also has attached the preposition *ek*: the door was slammed and boasting was shut *out*. The dullest preacher will see here a pursued figure reaching the sanctuary of his home and hastily banging the door in the face of what was hot on his track.

The same simple verb, with a different preposition (*sun*), is used in Romans 11: 32, "God shut up all in disobedience . . ." Again we see a door slammed, this time on people inside; the preposition implies that they are shut up *together*. How vivid is the picture suggested! All of them, bundled in, herded together, with the door slammed after them. Who can fail to think of the Black Hole of Calcutta? Or of the political policy of "encirclement"? But this has a beneficent purpose: "that He might show mercy to all."

The addition of a preposition to the same simple verb sometimes yields a neat and arresting rendering. In 2 Thessalonians 3: 11 the apostle says: "we are hearing that some are walking in disorderly fashion among you, in no way *ergazomenous* but *periergazomenous*". We can render this "not busying themselves but busybody-ing".

Sometimes the addition may be a noun as well as a preposition. Take the word *apokaradokia*, often translated "earnest expectation". It is used in Romans 8: 19 of the creation waiting for the revelation of the sons of God. The *-dokia* part suggests the waiting; *kara* means a head, and *apo* means "away from". Can you imagine a man in prison climbing the wall of the grounds and looking out anxiously, with his head stretched as far as possible away from the wall, to see round the corner if his rescuer is coming? That is the picture. St. Paul uses it again in Philippians 1: 20, where it opens a window into his mind: he stretches out far over his prison wall, as it were, to catch an early sight of the processions of events which will pass by shortly, assured that whatever they are, whoever they are, he himself will suffer no shame and Christ will be magnified. A noble eagerness with which to face the future!

Let us now apply the knowledge we have so far gained in attempting the translation of the Epistle to the Ephesians. It may be that a new approach will yield us treasures of thought, pictures, still and moving, and from them illustrations of the truth of God.

I. 1.   Paul, an apostle of Christ Jesus through the will of God,
to the holy members who are located in Ephesus in body and
in Christ Jesus by faith: grace and peace to you from God
our Father and the Lord Jesus Christ.

May the God and Father of our Lord Jesus Christ be blest:
He blessed us and thereby crowned us with every spiritual
blessing in the heavenly realm in Christ, to match the way in
which He picked us out for Himself in Him before the found-
ing of the world. His purpose was that we should be holy
and blameless when He looks upon us; He set us in the
5. circle of His love, where we were reserved for adoption as
His sons through Jesus Christ, to meet the good-pleasure of
His will and to inspire praise for the glory of His grace which
He bent low to give us in Him Who is the Object of His
long love. In Him we have redemption through His blood,
the liberation from our false position, on the scale of the
wealth of His grace, which He made to burst into our bay
like a tidal wave. He was entirely wise and understanding
when he made us to realise the open secret of what He willed.
It followed the pattern of His goodwill, which He displayed
10. in Him for the purpose of His managing the fullness of the
times: to sweep up all things into Christ as head so that they
stem from Him, both on the plane of heaven and on the plane
of earth: in Him, in Whom we were also chosen for His
particular care when we were roped off in advance in the field
of the purpose of Him Who makes the operation of all things
to fit in with the counsel of His will, so that we who lead the
procession of those whose hopes live in Christ might be
instruments of the praise of His glory.   In Him you also, when
the word of truth, the gospel of your salvation, fell upon your
ears and found a lodgment in believing hearts, in Him you
were stamped with the Holy Spirit of promise, Who is the
first instalment of our inheritance, an experience which leads
on to the ransoming of the possession, to the praise of His
glory.
15.   Because of this I also seeing that I caught the strain of
your concerted faith in the Lord Jesus and of the love to all
the holy members, am not bringing my thanksgiving to an
end. I raise a protective covering of prayer over you bearing your name, prayer that the God of our Lord Jesus Christ
the Father of glory may find an entrance in you for His gift
of wisdom which will tear away the bandage from your eyes

so that you fully know Him; that your imagination may have the light playing on it, so that you may know what the hope is which His call inspires, what is the wealth of the glory of His inheritance in the holy members, and what is the surpassing magnitude of His power toward us who are keeping our faith alive, in virtue of the active operation of the might of His strength, which He has set in motion in Christ by a

20. twofold act: He caused Him to burst into the world from the company of the dead and to take His seat on His right hand in the heavenly realm, in rank outsoaring every rule and authority and power and lordship and every name that is named, not only in this age but in the future age as well. He lined up everything in subordination under His feet, and gave Him to the church as head over everything, seeing that the church is His body, full of Him Who sees to the completion

II. 1. of all reality in its every part. And when you were dead, killed by your trespasses and sins in which you at one time strode as directed by the secularism of this world, following the bidding of the ruler of the authority of the air, the spirit that is now active among the family of the disobedient (among whom also all of us at one time showed our hand in lives immersed in the desires of our flesh and the fulfilment of what flesh and intellects willed, and were by nature deserving of wrath like the rest also); God, being rich in mercy, because of His deep love which He focused on us, you included,

5. when we, too, were dead, killed by trespasses, started the pulse of our common life with Christ—it is to grace that you owe your present state of salvation—made us to surge up with Him and in that fellowship to take our seat in the heavenly realm, in Christ Jesus, so that in the coming ages He might floodlight in His kindness streaming towards us in Christ Jesus the surpassing wealth of His grace. For you now enjoy a salvation which grace created and faith canalised. The whole experience did not start in you but is the gift of God. It did not start in works, so that nobody should utter a

10. boastful word. For we are a piece of His handiwork (see p. 121), not self-produced, since we were created in Christ Jesus for the purpose of good works, which God got ready in advance for our life's walk.

Therefore, keep in mind that once you, Gentiles in the flesh, people who are called uncircumcision by what is called handmade circumcision in the flesh, were at that season apart

from Christ, a blank space on the citizen roll of Israel, to
whom the covenants of promise were foreign privileges;
you were in the world, without a hope and without God.
But now you, who were once far away, in Christ Jesus swept
home, brought in by the blood of Christ. For He is our
peace, Who united both parties, and made the wall between
them collapse—the barricade of hostility. In His flesh He
15. cancelled the law of commands consisting in decrees, so that
in His creative work for peace He might link the two into
one new man in Him, and reconcile both groups in one
corporate body to God through the cross, using it to deal a
death blow to the hostility. And He came and preached
peace to you who were far away and peace to those who were
near; because through Him we—both groups—have the
entrée on one spirit to the Father. Therefore you are no
longer aliens and foreigners, but you are fellow-citizens of
20. the holy members and are God's own, a building raised on the
foundation of the apostles and prophets, with Christ Jesus
Himself as the corner-stone, in Whom every building, by
joining the common framework, gains a larger part in a holy
temple in the Lord, in which you also are being built in
together to make a dwelling-place of God in the Spirit.

Many of the renderings we have given will carry their own explanation. Even so it may not be without value to show how we
have arrived at a number of them. In chapter 1, verse 1, for instance,
it was the contrast between the two uses of the preposition *en* which
started a train of thought. In the end "located" was chosen and the
problem was how to bring out the contrast. Obviously "body" is
implied in the first part. In the second the "believing" are in Christ
"by faith": it is a fair inference from the adjective to the noun. Cf.
1 Thessalonians 2: 14.

"Blessed us and thereby crowned us with" (v. 3) repeats the idea
of "blest" and also is a pinpoint expression: it is not quite enough to
say "crowned us with blessing" because this omits one use of the
thrice uttered idea (blest . . . blessed . . . blessing). In "crowned"
we can "see" the human dignitary place the crown on to the head of
the king: a not unseemly human illustration of the divine.

"To match the way in which" avoids the hackneyed "according
to" which is frequently used to render *kata* and its associates. "Picked
us out for Himself" (v. 4) combines the meaning of the aorist and
the middle, and suggests a picture: we can "see" a hand grasp and

take. The infinitive of purpose easily allows us to begin a new sentence with "His purpose was".

At the beginning of verse 5 the aorist participle (*pro-orisas*), connected with our "horizon", always suggests to me a fencing round, a marking off: imagine yourself on an ocean liner, with the ring of the horizon all round you. Now "God marked us off in love, or lovingly". What is more natural than to combine the ideas by saying "He set us in the circle of His love"? If it is objected that He loved us before He put us into the circle, the answer is clear: the circle is not that wherein alone His love is found, but is the circle which His love created. But what about *pro-*? What of the fact that He did it "beforehand"? This is brought out by an inversion. "He marked us out in advance for adoption" means "He marked us out . . . reserved for". Note the two uses of *eis*, which we have toned down to ". . . as His sons". *Eis* indicates movement, direction; once in that circle we were to move *to* adoption, *to* Him. Notice then, the four pictures: picking out (watch your wife actually take a jewel out of a tray in a shop in Oxford Street; only we were not jewels, but paste); encircling; adopting; keeping, as a son.

"To meet the good pleasure of His will" is a variation, once more, on the theme *kata*. Think of two tables placed side by side, the one "flush with" the other. "He bent low to give" (v. 6) expresses the pinpoint in "He graced us". It is true in idea also, for grace is love bending low. "His *long* love" is an unsuccessful attempt to plumb the depths of the perfect tense here: "in Him Who has been (and still is) loved".

"Liberation from our false position" (v. 7) once more contains a picture. *Aphesis* implies a loosening, and an undoing, and the word for "trespasses" means a "fall beside" the right path. Suppose a man has fallen from the narrow road into a quagmire or bog, or from a causeway built over quicksands. A rope, a helping hand from a firm position, will loosen him from the spongy mass that sucks him down: such is the forgiveness of trespasses. "On the scale of" represents the ubiquitous *kata*; the elevator (see p. 79*f*) with its horizontal floor has come up to the right level.

"Made to burst into our bay. . ." (v. 8) may be compared with the treatment of words cognate with this on pages 92 and 99. "Burst into" represents the pinpoint of the aorist; "our bay" (a locution for "us") prepares the reader for the overwhelming "tidal wave", a not unworthy figure of the verb. A new sentence is now begun, "entirely" of course standing for the "all wisdom". "Made us to realise" (v. 9) is punctiliar, and corresponds to the "click" in our minds when we say "as soon as I realised (e.g.) that it was after midnight . . ." "It followed the pattern of" is yet another way of turning *kata*. But how can following suggest a horizontal line? A typist takes a carbon copy of the letter she is typing, and when the task is done she lays letter and copy horizontally on the desk: the writing on the paper underneath "follows the pattern" of the top sheet. So it is with every copy. In embroidery a woman follows the pattern lightly drawn on the material.

"To sweep up all things into Christ as head so that they stem from Him" (v. 10) may seem a lot for the meaning of a single word. "Sweep" is a pinpoint. The rest will be clearer by the aid of an illustration. We may think of the nervous system, with the nerves of the body gathered up into the controlling brain; or of the millions of telephone wires that receive their importance solely because they are joined to the central exchange—otherwise they are little more than long bits of metal; or we may think of the British Commonwealth. It is not always realised that, e.g. Canada, Australia and New Zealand are independent nations. They are self-governing and could go out of the British fellowship tomorrow if they wanted to do so. How then are they connected? The Queen of England is also Queen of Canada, of Australia, of New Zealand, and she is the sole constitutional link between them. In a sense she gathers them all up into herself, and they "stem" from her. Without her they are separate entities.

Somewhat similar was the ancient Roman Empire. The various nations which composed it were linked in the person of the Princeps or Emperor, and Professor J. B. Bury pointed out that as the Principate was in theory elective, strictly speaking the Roman Empire ceased to exist, when an emperor died, until the appointment of his successor. Note the use of the preposition *ana-* in the verb: His purpose was to make all things "head *up*" into Christ.

"Chosen for His particular care" (v. 11) is better nowadays than "chosen as His portion". "Roped off in advance" may be compared with verse 5. Sometimes on a sports ground a special part of the turf is protected, and people are prevented from walking on it until the team itself comes to play. This applies particularly in cricket, where the pitch is roped off. Notice how the metaphor is kept up in "the field of the purpose": if it is "in" that purpose it is surely "according to" it—a new way of getting round the elusive *kata*. Similarly with "fit in with": I nearly wrote "to cog in" with, with the picture of two horizontal cog wheels. "All things", did we but see it, take their plane and their pace from that omnipotent wheel of God's counsel.

"We who lead the procession of those whose hopes live in Christ" (v. 12) stands for a perfect participle. "Lead . . . " is suggested by the preposition *pro* in the verb. The perfect implies "have set our hopes in Christ and they are still there in Him", which justifies writing "live". "Fell" and "found a lodgment" (v. 13) bring out the pinpoint, and because the grammar is a little awry we may link them. "Were stamped" is more faithful to the pinpoint than "were sealed" might have been: to stamp with a seal is a momentary, decisive act. Cf. Matthew 27: 66.

In verse 15 note the somewhat vague musical allusion in the English "caught the strain of your concerted faith". "Caught the strain" is of course a pinpoint. But how are we to render *kath' humas*? For better or worse I can "see" a platform with an orchestra sitting on it, not in tiers, but all on the same level: here is the horizontal line. "Your concerted faith" just retains that musical flavour of a concert party. The preacher may care to develop this. As there are different kinds of instruments in an orchestra, so there are different kinds of "believer" in the church; but all join to make one united work of praise to God. (Note the distributive use of *kata*.)

Verse 16 again brings its picture. The apostle speaks of "making a mention" and of "on my prayers". We have attempted to combine these in "I raise a protective covering of prayer over you, bearing your name". It suggests a roof over their heads, with a name or a device written outside on the roof. Some factories have their name written in large letters on the roof, to be seen from the air. The preacher has perhaps read of wounded soldiers, far from a city, being tended in tents which bear the mark of the Red Cross. The tent affords shelter from wind and rain; the Red Cross is to give protection from aerial attack. Such is the covering of the apostle's prayer.

"Find an entrance in you for His gift" (v. 17) reveals the pinpoint more than "give" by itself does. Verse 18 has been rendered very freely. "Eyes of the heart" is a strange expression, probably meaning what we mean by "imagination". "May have the light playing on it" stands for a perfect tense with its abiding result. "My eyes have been illumined" means "I can now see" or "I am in the light".

"Keeping our faith alive" (v. 19) emphasises the continuity of the present participle. "Burst into" and "take His seat" (v. 20) are both pinpoints. "Outsoaring" (v. 21) is for the compound "super-above". "Lined up" (v. 22) is a pinpoint; "made them to fall in", as a military man might say, is rather long, whereas the crisp "lined up" seems more punctiliar.

The first seven verses of the second chapter reveal the apostle thinking at such high speed and with such emotion that he seems to get involved and to lose the thread. He starts off with a participial phrase in the accusative, suspended in mid-air as it were until a main verb can come along and take it down; but he follows with subordinate clauses, and forgetting to put in the main clause starts off again in verse 4. There is a link, however, in verse 5, which we have tried to show: a participial phrase not unlike the one with which he started in the first verse. We have retained the long complex sentence in order to show the pressure under which the apostle's mind was working.

"Strode" (2.2) is punctiliar, summing up the past life. We might have expected an imperfect. "As directed by" (v. 2) stands for *kata*. "Secularism" (*saeculum* in Latin is an age) is a fair inference from the Greek *aiōn*, which means an "age", almost "the spirit of the age". The meaning is decidedly *not* "the age of this world" in the sense of so many centuries old. "Secularism" means living within the age or epoch as if it were self-contained, with nothing outside or beyond it. "Following the bidding of" stands for the familiar *kata*. "The family of the disobedient" is a variant of the Hebraistic phrase "sons of disobedience". The Hebrew mind thought of the completely disobedient as having a family likeness to disobedience itself. "The cogenitally disobedient" might be an alternative. "Showed our hand" (v. 3) is a pinpoint: the verb means "to conduct oneself, behave oneself (not necessarily well), live in a certain moral and religious way, good or bad"; its spirit is that of the old-fashioned noun "deportment". We have saved this reference to living by adding "in lives". This enables us to move on to "immersed in", which is true to the preposition *en* and also to the idea of continuity in the present participle which follows.

"Which he focused on us" (v. 4) is a pinpoint for the aorist and its cognate accusative. Notice in verse 5 how we have added "you included", to try to pull the participial phrase in verse 1 into the structure of the sentence. "Started the pulse" is a pinpoint: we sometimes read in the newspapers of a doctor who has made a man's heart start beating again after he was "dead". "Common life" draws attention to the preposition *sun-* in the verb and prepares us to overcome a difficulty a little later. "It is to grace that you owe your present state of salvation" is an inversion in order to show the present force of the perfect tense. "Made us to surge" (v. 6) is a pinpoint. "In that fellowship to take our seat" performs a twofold task: it expresses the pinpoint of the aorist, and it avoids a rather awkward incongruity. If we say "He made us to sit *with* Christ" we have to add "*in* Christ Jesus", and "with" and "in" do not quite march together. The reference to fellowship avoids this difficulty though it does retain the force of *sun-*; and we prepared the way for it with "common life" in verse 5. If, on the other hand, the *sun-* means "together with one another", then we have a fellowship implied anyway. Either we have avoided the incongruity or we have retained a slight touch of vagueness in the original.

Notice the picture in verse 7 suggested by the pinpoint of the verb and the construction. In the dim evening light there stands a massive building. Suddenly someone presses the master-switch and the whole pile is bathed in light. In the text the building is "the surpassing wealth of His grace". The light which floodlights this building is "His kindness streaming towards us in Christ Jesus". In a word, His rich grace is floodlit by His visible kindness. There is metaphor within a metaphor—hostile critics would even say a mixed metaphor —but everything said about matters not perceived by the senses is metaphorical and if we dig deeply enough we shall find many mixed metaphors. The preacher will gladly pay the penalty in return for picturesque illustrations.

"Streaming towards us"—the cause of the trouble about metaphors —is suggested by the preposition *epi*. When anything comes towards you, makes contact with you, it may be one of three kinds of things: it may be a bullet, corresponding roughly to a mathematical point; it may be a wire or cable stretched across the road to sever your head when your car hits it at speed (as the writers of thrillers tell us), corresponding roughly to a horizontal line; or it may be a wall of water, as when the sea rushes into an inlet in the coast, corresponding to an area. The last is the picture suggested here by *epi* and the accusative—a wall moving towards you, an area, not a bullet or a wire. Hence comes our phrase "streaming towards us". If we can imagine Niagara Falls streaming into the Arizona Desert we have something of the idea. Mixed metaphor? Better that, with a rapt congregation, than an icy correctness and restive inattention.

On the other hand we may be reminded that not infrequently games are played at night and a whole stadium is floodlit. Then we may see the light streaming down *upon* the pitch. Or we may prefer to illustrate:

The quality of mercy is not strain'd,
It droppeth as the gentle rain from heaven
Upon the place beneath . . .

Merchant of Venice: Act IV, Scene I.

Or even:

How sweet the moonlight sleeps *upon* this bank

Ibid: Act V, Scene I.

"Enjoy a salvation" (v. 8), with "now", legitimately turns the perfect tense into a present. The ideas in the prepositions have been emphasised by being altered into verbs. Instead of saying "by grace" we have said that grace did it. When we might have said literally "through faith" as a channel we have shown this by saying "faith canalised it". Without faith as a canal, salvation has no direction, does not reach us: it is the contrast between a marsh and a river. "The whole experience" is much better than "and that not of your-selves", because "that", or more strictly "this", suggests faith, whereas it is neuter, and does not mean faith, as "faith" is feminine. "Did not start *in* you" is but an inversion of *ek* (*ex*). So it is in "it did not start in works". "Utter a boastful word" is a pinpoint.

In verse 9 "a piece of His handiwork "deserves mention. It is not "His handiwork", "His product", but "a product of His." The indefinite article ("a") implies that there may be other handiwork which He has produced: we are not the sole effect of His work. The "His" is emphatic, which is shown by the position of *autou*, and we have therefore inserted "not self-produced". "Got ready" (v.10) is a pinpoint, like the following "for our life's walk".

"Keep in mind" (v. 11) represents the present, as distinct from the aoristic "call to mind". "A blank space on the citizen-roll of Israel" (v. 12) is an attempt to do justice to the perfect tense with-out overdoing it. "Having been alienated" means "now being aliens from the country which once was theirs". But they were members of it only ideally, so that we must say nothing that would suggest that they have had their citizenship cancelled or have been deported. "A blank space" just hints at the loss of an ideal position without implying that they had never been members even ideally. The alteration of order avoids the familiar "without God-in-the-world".

"Swept home" (v. 13) is a pinpoint. "Made . . . collapse" (v. 14) is similar. The verb means "loosed": you can almost see the indi-vidual bricks going their several ways as that which holds them together and makes them *one* wall is disintegrated. "The middle wall of partition" has been made clearer. "Of partition" is a geni-tive of apposition—"the middle wall which barricades". That middle wall is the hostility between Jew and Gentile, and we have quite legitimately united the idea of barricade with that of hostility—wall and hostility are in apposition. (A picture of part of the literal "middle wall", a marble barrier of the inner courts of Herod's Temple at Jerusalem, may be seen in Deissmann's *Light from the Ancient East*, p. 75. It bears an inscription in Greek, warning foreigners to "keep out" on pain of death.) Smashed! exults the apostle. What an illustration for the preacher! And how relevant to the Berlin wall!

In verse 15 "consisting in decrees" has the great authority of J. H. Moulton behind it. "In His creative work for peace" is true to the continuity of the present tense and also makes sure of bringing in the idea of "create". This leaves us free to concentrate on the pinpoint, the laconic monosyllable "link". "Deal a death-blow" is again punctiliar.

Verse 21 is not without its difficulties. The picture seems to be that of *every* building (not "the whole building") being "fitted together" with the main building: each one is added as it is ready. But how can a building "grow" or "increase"? The main one may, as parts are added to it, but each separate part does not grow: hence our rendering, faithful to the present tenses: "every building by joining the common framework, gains a larger part. . ."

Chapter 7

SUNKEN TREASURE

WE have already noticed (page 109) that language about subjects not perceived by the senses must be the language of metaphor. We "see" through a man's pretensions—or even the man himself—we "follow" the argument which he "advances". We "cast" our eyes round the room or "throw" a glance over the scene. In none of these, and countless other instances, can the meaning be literal; even when we "reflect" we cannot literally "bend the mind back", which is the real meaning of the word. In all such cases the rock of the literal meaning has been submerged by the advancing tide of metaphor.

Now if the preacher can realise the presence of the rock he will find that, for him, it is not a rock after all; certainly not a rock which will wreck his ship, but rather a treasure in the ocean which can be salvaged by him. For, once again, metaphor contains the elements of an illustration. His first task is to recognise the presence of a meta phor. Very many people go through life without realising that they are using this figure of speech. They speak of "squares", they see a man "curb" his passion (as if it were a restless horse), they hear that a man has "laid the foundation" of scholarship, and they know that familiarity "breeds" contempt. If this treasure can be brought to the surface the preacher will be amazed and thrilled at the riches in his hands.

This reference to metaphor can be extended. Whether or not a metaphor is involved a word has a whole history behind it. It has associations with other contexts and it may suggest allusions. All this may prove part of the immense amount of "sunken treasure" which the preacher may raise to the surface. We shall try to illustrate this, without limiting ourselves to metaphors.

Consider briefly the passage in 1 Cor. 15: 53: "this corruption must *put on* incorruption" or "this perishable thing must put on imperishableness". Notice the aorist verb used twice: it is used of putting on clothes. Cannot the preacher arrest the attention at least of the ladies in his congregation by a preliminary word about fashions? There was once some talk of "the new look" in women's dress. Here it is, never to be superseded: we have to "slip it on" – note the pinpoint.

There is an interesting word in Acts 2: 14: "Peter took his stance with the eleven and *lifted up* his voice and gave utterance to them. . . ." It is used also in John 13: 18, "he who eats my bread *lifted up* his heel against me", where the picture is that of the kick of a horse. Peter spoke on the day of Pentecost, with a voice like the kick of a horse. This can be the manner of the Christian preacher: He is supported by the listening church ("with the eleven"); he is sure of his message (like the kick of a horse); he has the gift of the Holy Spirit ("gave utterance": notice the same word in verse 4 of the gift of the Spirit). This must not be identified with mere "noise".

I was reading Aristotle's *Parts of Animals* and came across the word *laktizein*, "to kick" (IV.10.690a.21). As never before the words to the apostle on the Damascus road burnt themselves into my mind: "it is hard for you to kick against goads". The familiar words this time brought a picture with them—an angry beast, lashing out continually (note the present tense of the infinitive. Acts 26: 14) and in vain: for its master held it firmly, and if he were riding it, how could kicking do him any hurt? I could see clearly the struggling beast as it kicked fruitlessly. How irrational and vain is it to struggle when Christ has laid hold of us! to kick into the empty air. Folk living in horse-rearing communities, or who have seen a horse broken in will understand the force of all this. The preacher might consider what constitutes the "hardness" to those who resist Christ. Is it uneasiness, unhappiness, or something deeper still?

There is a contest which may be observed on the Sports Day at many an English school called "Throwing the Cricket Ball". The object is to throw the ball the farthest, and he who does so wins. Eph. 3: 19 never fails to remind me of this: the apostle prays that his readers may discover the love of Christ which "over-throws" knowledge. Knowledge is advancing at a rate unparalleled. A doctor has stated categorically that there is nothing, positively nothing, which science cannot investigate. It is a proud claim, for apart from a multi-dimensional realm of which we three-dimensional creatures know nothing and can investigate nothing, the living God is not a subject for scientific investigation. But, however far knowledge may go, the love of Christ has gone farther; it is ever in front. Let knowledge reach the farthest limits of the universe, and it has not reached the limits of the love of Christ.

There is another way of taking this text. Some scholars find here a reference to the work of the auctioneer. Knowledge makes its "bid" but the love of Christ outbids it. Knowledge, that fascinating pursuit, increases its bid more and yet more for the allegiance of men, but the love of Christ can always offer a bigger price. His love will always do more, pay more, give more, than anything else in the world.

There is a Greek word, (*polu*)*poikilos*, which is often translated "manifold", which has rich associations for the preacher. Its meaning is "many-coloured" (with variations such as "spotted", "mottled", "pied", "dappled"); in music, "with a changeful strain"; and "intricate", "complex". It has connections with embroidery and tapestry. The apostle uses this word to describe the wisdom of God (Eph. 3: 10). It is a noble epithet. Think of the first meaning, "many-coloured". The implication is that we can see all the colours at the same time. Thus at any given moment there is variety in the wisdom of God: He knows and understands the different characters in one family, the different classes and nations in the one world; the different hopes and fears, joys and sorrows, of different people.

Further, the "many-coloured" is rather of a special order, hinted at by e.g. the word "dappled". The wing of a bird may seem one colour when you look at it from one angle, and another colour from another angle. We know perhaps what is meant by "shot" silk: a necktie looks somewhat red when you look from the left, and somewhat green when you look from the right. Such is the wisdom of God: at the same moment it looks different to different people. That may account for the vitality of some controversialists. God's Sovereignty and man's freewill, for instance, the preaching of the Word and the administration of the sacraments, natural and revealed theology, are subjects of controversy, and the tendency is for men to say "either . . . or". Neither side will give way, each believing that he sees the wisdom of God. He probably does, but he does not realise that he sees but one colour of it, and his antagonist sees the other: both their views are reconciled in a higher unity.

By contrast think of a piece of music "with a changeful strain". First we have the crashing notes to represent the storm, and then the tinkling ripples of music as the thunder has died down and we hear the plashing of the limpid brook. What is to be noticed is that, whereas in the former example all the colours were visible at the same time, even though to different people, here we must of necessity have succession: first one type of music and then another. It accords well with the wise providence of God in history and in individual lives. There is the storm of war and the quiet of peace;

there are times of rapid expansion and times of rest; booms and slumps—all in the history of the nations or of the individual. And there is that in the wisdom of God which can order and guide through these successive phases.

If we are impressed by the vast scale of life and the intricacy of the issues involved there is comfort and inspiration for faith: God's wisdom is intricate too. He can match and control the most complex of human situations.

But how does He do so? In all His variegated wisdom there is His variegated grace (1 Peter 4: 10). His love which bends low to our human need reveals itself in different "colours" to meet our varying needs: temptations of varying colours assail us (James 1: 2), catching our eye and luring us on; temptations of siren-music, with sweet sounds and alternating strains, which give delight in turn and only seem to hurt us not; temptations intricate and complex, in whose labyrinthine mazes we are lost unless loving, intricate wisdom can guide and rescue us. In all this, flashing colours attract us, successive sweetness assails our ears, the toils entrap us—unless loving wisdom, iridescent, softly sounding its successive airs, charm our eyes with nobler colours and our ears with lovelier melody, and, master of intricacy, unweave the bonds that are tightening around us. Not for nothing did the writer to the Hebrews (2: 4) speak of the "variegated powers" of God: in glittering colours, tuneful changes and vast complexity they match the wisdom and the grace of God. There is no dull sameness in Him.

So we might go through the New Testament, finding our metaphors and allusions on every page. The apostle prays (Eph. 3: 17) that his readers may be "rooted and grounded in love". He wishes them to have a firm foundation in love, not running away from it, not toppling down; and at the same time not to be a dead building but a living plant, drawing sustenance—from love—through the roots. He tells us that "knowledge puffs up, inflates, but love builds" (1 Cor. 8: 1): are you a toy balloon that may be pricked by a pin, or a massive building which can weather many storms? "Quench not the Spirit" (1 Thess. 5: 19, see page 66): some people throw cold water on to the fire of other men's enthusiasms: will they throw cold water on to the fire of the Spirit? We might preach on the "Undesirable Fire Brigade".

"Necessity presses me hard," says St. Paul, "woe is me if I preach not the gospel" (1 Cor. 9: 16). Compare Acts 27: 20, of the storm at sea "pressing hard". The urge to preach the gospel is a wind howling about a man's ears, a surging of the deep, which will shipwreck his very life unless he finds the calm of having proclaimed the Word of God.

When President Roosevelt died Mr. Truman succeeded. I shall never forget hearing the broadcast, relayed to England, of his first meeting with Congress. He stood up and began: "Mr. . . ." but before he could continue, a voice was heard, not meant for American ears, nor for English ones. It was the voice of the Speaker, Mr. Sam Rayburn, whispering to him: "Just a minute, Harry; let me introduce you to them first." I was deeply moved by the quiet friendliness of it all, the kindly understanding of the mood of a man who has suddenly been thrust into great office, the affectionate use of the Christian name. This incident has come back, with all its deep feeling, as I read just now Romans 6: 13: "Cease introducing your members to sin (as if it were some august body which has to have people presented to it; as if it were a king giving audience or holding a levée. 'Let not sin continue on the throne . . .' verse 12) as instruments for carrying out an unrighteous policy. Present yourself to God . . ." (This must be used with care: it will not do for Acts 1: 3.)

The apostle wishes his young friend and disciple to "keep on fanning the flame of the gift of God which (was in him) . . ." (2 Tim. 1: 6), that the red-hot coals may give not only heat but light through its flame. Poke the fire! He wishes men to be "boiling in spirit" (Romans 12: 11; compare Acts 18: 25). He himself has the desire to "slip his cable", to "weigh anchor", to "loose the ship of his life from its moorings" (Phil. 1: 23) and be over the sea with Christ.

Consider the word *sundesmos* (Eph. 4: 3). The unity of the Spirit can be broken if Christians engage in mutual hostilities. They are kept together by peace, which flows from love (Col. 3: 14). Loving Christians are peaceful Christians, and thus they stay together. But what starts "trouble"? It is often just talk. Now it is not entirely fanciful to recall that *sundesmos* also means a "conjunction."

We do not really think well of secret discipleship, like that of Nicodemus (in its early days). And similarly Christians ought not to be permanently silent (Acts 8: 1, 4; 11: 19). In the complete witness of the church each man can be regarded as a sentence or a clause, testifying to Christ. And they are joined together by "conjunctions" —or should be. Are you also an "and" or a "but"? Do you add your testimony to the one witness or interpose an objection to it? Christians should "say the same thing" (1 Cor. 1: 10) without being parrots; and have the same, one, mind (Phil. 2: 2) without being machines. Be a peaceful conjunction!

St. Paul tells the Galatians that he bears the brand marks (*stig-mata*) of Jesus in his body (Gal. 6: 17). We may see here the signs of the ownership of a slave; a religious tattooing which points to the God Who is worshipped; the scars of Christian service (? Acts 14: 19); and perhaps also the marks of divine discipline or training. This can provide a starting point if a preacher wishes to challenge his congregation.

Herodotus (VII. 35) has an interesting story which is relevant here. The Hellespont had been bridged from Asia to Europe but a storm smashed and scattered the work. Xerxes in futile anger ordered the sea to be scourged with three hundred lashes. Herodotus has also heard that the king sent tattooers to brand the Hellespont as a mark of disgrace. This is a piquant tale which the preacher can use. There are people who profess to bear the indelible marks of baptism. Has their baptism become unbaptism, just as circumcision has become uncircumcision? (Rom. 2: 25) Were the "marks" of Christian discipleship ever on them? If they are believers is there no sign of it? Are they like the Hellespont? Could the "temporary" of Mark 4: 17 have a more apt illustration? Which are they: persons bearing the signs of their allegiance or a mere watery surface which retains no mark? (The connection here consists of the "sunken treasure" of the words *stigmata*, *stigeus* and *stizo*.)

The writer to the Hebrews (10: 35) tells his readers not to "cast away their boldness." The verb from *apoballo* is used by Aristotle in the *Nicomachean Ethics* (III. i. 1110a. 9). Nobody would do it voluntarily, he says, but in a storm at sea all men of sense will *jettison* their cargo to save life. "Do not jettison your boldness (*parrēsia*)." But that is just what some people have done. In Christ we have boldness of approach to God (Eph. 3: 12; cf. Heb. 10: 19); boldness in prayer (1 John 5: 14); boldness at the day of judgement (1 John 4: 17). The secret is to take God at His word and to abide in Christ (1 John 2: 28). Some have not heard the gospel in these terms. Some have heard it and have ceased to abide in Christ. Others, strangely enough, not only do not possess boldness but seem actually to resent it and reject it. Conversations can be revealing. "Do not jettison your boldness." It is not a piece of cargo which can be spared but the very life-blood of the Christian. What is its "reward"?

In his great chapter on the Resurrection St. Paul speaks of the Lord's appearance to him as to "one born out of due time" (1 Cor. 15: 8). He uses a single noun for this expression, with the definite article (*to ektrōma*). It means "miscarriage" and is not perhaps the

best of words for polite society or the drawing-room. But why "*the*
miscarriage"? It has been reasonably suggested that it is a coarse
nickname given by enemies, perhaps Judaisers. It is a mark of
humility that the apostle uses the term here, when he need not have
done. And just as "methodist" became an honourable term after a
controversial beginning, so Paul lived to show that "miscarriage"
could have its glorious side.

For "miscarriage" implies that he had been born dead. If in his
preaching Paul spoke about being "dead to the law" (Gal. 2: 19 AV;
cf. Rom. 7: 4) the Judaisers could have seized on this and retorted:
"Precisely; as you say, you were born on the Damascus road—
dead." The apostle, however, would have the last word. "Thank
God," he could say, "you are right. I have been crucified with
Christ . . ."

"Miscarriage" has a further implication. It means that he was
"born too soon." It was an untimely birth. From the beginning he
was not fully developed. Again he has his answer. "I know that,"
he could say; "I was born blind (Acts 9: 9). And it is entirely by the
grace of God that I am what I am now (1 Cor. 15: 10). I have a long
way to go, but I am speeding on in my search to know Christ fully—
and I must be conformed to His *death*! (Cf. Phil. 3: 8–14)

"But I have been given an advantage," Paul might continue.
"I was born long in advance. I have seen the Lord in His glory.
Most Christians will have to wait until the End for this (Acts
22: 6, 11). I can take my place with the apostles who witnessed the
Transfiguration and likewise saw His glory" (1 Peter 5: 1).

The background of trade should be understandable by most
congregations, even in this age when "communication" is supposed
to be such a problem. Paul asserts that he and his companions do
not "corrupt the Word of God" (2 Cor. 2: 17 AV). His verb is
kapēleuō, which describes the work of the retailer rather than the
wholesaler; the small man at the corner store rather than the merchant.
From this may be inferred the fact that the preacher and evangelist
is not engaged in a petty activity but a vast operation. He is not
selling bootlaces on a tray. He is concerned with the greatness of
the gospel.

He is not hawking, peddling, driving a bargain, or "doing a
deal", but ultimately commanding. Some men disobey the gospel
(1 Pet. 4: 17) and they have no right to disobey it. God commands
that men should repent. The preacher must not forget the authority
of the gospel.

And he is not auctioneering to the highest bidder but offering a gift. He has no business with buying or selling. His "business" is the grace of the gospel.

When some of the "sunken treasure" has been salvaged it will be found to be remarkably modern. All the "athletic" words may be included here. Sometimes the reference is direct: running and boxing, for example, in 1 Corinthians 9: 24–27. But what of *sunathleō* in Philippians 1: 27 and in Philippians 4: 3—women who had worked with Paul in the gospel; and the *athlēsis* which had been endured in Hebrews 10: 32? *Agōn* and its compounds may be suggestive; and *gumnazō*—"train yourself for godliness" (1 Tim. 4: 7). It raises the whole question of the place of effort in a religion of grace. We might add "You were running well" (Gal. 5: 7); growing weary (2 Cor. 4: 16—*egkakeō*); and "crumpling up" (Gal. 6: 9, *ekluomai*).

There is a Greek adverb, *ontōs*, which is generally translated "really, actually". Now when the old Greek philosophers were thinking about reality, particularly reality as opposed to appearance, they spoke of *to on*, or, in the plural, of *ta onta*. The adverb consequently suggests where it occurs that we are concerned with reality, not with that which merely seems to be. The crowd really considered that John the Baptist had been a prophet (Mark 11: 32). It raises interesting points about the depth of public opinion: what is the preacher doing and saying to convince men of the truth of his ministry and office? Do they respect a clergyman but in their heart doubt what he says? Is their attitude one of mere appearance?

If we hold that we ought to interpret the Greek as "they held that John had been in reality a prophet" it still raises questions. What is a prophet in appearance? And, what in contrast, is a prophet in reality? What is a man who is *becoming* a prophet? What are the *essentials* of the prophetic office? Not the clerical collar or clerical dress generally: a prophet is one who has been chosen by God to utter His will in and for the world. Is the preacher that? And does he pay attention to Him Who is *Prophet*, Priest and King?

The centurion at the Cross saw our Lord commit Himself into His Father's hands, and declared Him to be *in reality* a righteous man (Luke 23: 47). Readers of Plato's Republic will remember the early discussion between being and seeming good. If we regard our Lord as truly righteous, we are under an obligation not to be content with a reputation. He has left us an "example" (1 Peter 2: 21) and the purpose is for us to "follow His tracks". The "example" means outline, an artist's sketch, which we have to colour or fill in ourselves, not a complete and detailed picture which we have to copy slavishly in all its minutiae. There is freedom in the Christian discipleship.

To keep to the metaphor of the tracks or footprints: His feet might be much larger than ours; His stride might be longer than ours. Our feet could not then fill His footprints and even if they could, if our stride is short, we might not be able to make the length of our steps agree with His. But we can follow His road, go where He went, and take our direction from Him. For His life was in reality on the road of moral goodness.

St. Luke also says (24: 34) that the Lord was risen in reality. His Resurrection was no mere appearance, the survival of ideas which are immortal, a misinterpretation of shadows, the result of imagination's wishful thinking. *He lives:* not only in men's hearts, but objectively in His own right, as it were, whether our hearts possess Him or not. He is not just an atmosphere, a moral consciousness: not just a spirit surviving into the great beyond; Jesus of Nazareth is alive, actually, truly, in reality. There is a touching line sometimes written in memorial notices and on tombstones, "to live in hearts we love is not to die." Alas, it is. Ask any widow whose husband lives in her heart if he died or not. That is the tragedy; and it is because he did die that she feels her anguish. But Jesus Christ is alive, and the Living Christ can bring peace and comfort to her heart.

What does He do when He comes into our hearts? He gives us a freedom which is freedom in reality (John 8: 36). There are freedoms which are offered which are but freedom in appearance. The world likes to do as it likes, and calls it liberty, little thinking that it puts itself at the mercy of its own instincts and ties itself up in knots. Real freedom is freedom to do the right, to serve and to love God. They who are tied to Christ are free indeed; with Him as Master the slave enjoys the royal freedom of the sons of God. And a congregation of God's people thus living and thus knowing their true freedom will cause the unbeliever to realise that "God is in reality among you" (1 Cor. 14: 25). For it will be clear that they have laid hold of a life which is greater than, different from, the life of those whose ambition it is to "see life"; for they will have laid hold on life which is life in reality (1 Tim. 6: 19).

Consider again, John 14: 1, "Let not your heart be troubled"— let the trouble stop. The verb in question is used not infrequently of political agitation, disorder and anarchy. Some republics are a by-word for their "troubles", with presidents rising and falling rapidly. The "trouble" of a divided state and an unstable government with its swift succession of presidents would be avoided if there were one ruler and everybody loyal to him. So it is with the human heart. The "troubles" of indecision, of the divided allegiance, of having one "ruler" after another, would come to an end if the whole heart gave itself in utter loyalty to Christ. "Believe also in Me."

It is stated in Ephesians 2: 10 that "we are God's *handiwork*." The Greek word *poiēma* means something which has been made, and at times it has the particular meaning of "poem". The preacher can illustrate his sermon by the use of this category, especially if he has to preach the annual sermon to the Literary Society. "We are God's poem." We may then infer that He took pleasure in making us, spiritually; and that one of our many duties is to be a joy and a solace to others. Think of all that poetry means to the discerning: the music of words, the pictures that speak, the balm that soothes every mood of the human heart. Further, a *poiēma* may have reference not only to a whole poem but to a single line. It is said that a great poet may spend hours, even days, "polishing up" the lines he has written, so that there may be nothing to jar, nothing to spoil the picture or the music of his words. In like manner we may think of the Lord God polishing up His people to "literary" perfection.

But a single line, by itself, has not great value as a rule (though admittedly we quote it) apart from the other lines of the context. Thus our religion has a social reference. We are to be associated with other "lines" in the great poem. In literature we speak of purple patches, where some lines have far outshone the average of the book. So in that vast poem which is the Church some lines are nobler than others. We call them Saints. But it is God's purpose so to polish all the lines that in the end there is one perfect poem, with no word or syllable misplaced.

I once took a very dim view of the apostle Paul who, so my grandmother informed me in a moment of rebuke, had learnt to be content (Phil. 4: 11). But I doubt if he meant "content" in the sense in which we generally understand it. His word is *autarkēs*, which appears in the modern noun "*autarky*". It means self-sufficient or self-contained. It is a good Stoic word and is an instance of a philosopher's word which has been baptised into the Christian faith. The cold grim creed of the Stoic may have little attraction for the radiant disciples of Christ, for the Stoic made the human heart a desolation and called it peace. But the technical term "autarky" was a worthy candidate for baptism. The Stoic "wise man" is independent of his circumstances; he can discard all the adornment and amenity of life because whatever happens is on his theory determined by sovereign reason. Material good may be far removed from him, but it does not matter: reason decreed it, and reason is good, and the wise man needs nothing apart from himself and his attitude. He is himself (*autos*) able to suffice (*arkeō*) himself. Now when St. Paul speaks as he does he is not saying what a wonderful man Paul is. If we may put it so, he is speaking geographically and saying where his resources are located.

We sometimes speak of a block of apartments or a vast hotel as being self-contained. We imply that it has its own shopping arcade and other amenities. You do not have to go outside to get what you need. That is precisely what the apostle means, for he has within him the living Christ. He can always travel light. He is not cumbered with the luggage which the world must carry if it is to be amused. He need not bother to ensure his supply of drugs to relieve his boredom and dope him into unconsciousness: he has it all within. "Thy word have I hid in mine heart." In a deeper sense than Zeno the Stoic ever dreamed, he is self-contained.

Observers of political and economic life will be able to illustrate the apostle's meaning in other ways. We are told, for example, that Greece can never be self-supporting as owing to the mountains and the general roughness of the soil she can never produce enough food for her population. Again before World War II Germany embarked on a scheme which would render blockade fruitless in any future war in which she might be engaged. What would be the use of denying imports to a country if she already has ample stores of everything she might need? Her aim was "autarky". For Paul it meant that he never need fear a blockade. All is within, Christ in you the hope of glory.

Here then, are some of the treasures in the New Testament which await our discovery. Evangelicals hold strenuously that God speaks to them through His Word written, and He sometimes says what is not to be found in the commentaries. Study the commentaries by all means, especially the best ones; try to arrive at the right exegesis. But remember Dr. Helmut Thielicke's striking characterisation of Spurgeon as a "charismatic listener", with an "inimitable immediacy . . . to his text." Get everything you can out of the Greek text *before* you consult the commentaries. Use all your academic equipment but listen with the hearing of faith. For "it would only indicate that we had been driven mad by the art of hermeneutics if we were no longer capable of accepting and valuing, as a corrective of our perfect exegesis, the childlike candour of a preacher who could 'listen like a disciple'."[1] That is wise counsel.

[1]Helmut Thielicke: *Encounter With Spurgeon*, London 1964, p. 3.

Now let us attempt a translation of Ephesians 3–4.

3:1   For this cause I, Paul, the prisoner of Christ Jesus for
the sake of you Gentiles—you'll see the point of that, if you
heard tell of the management of God's grace, grace pressed
into my hands for you: on the top deck of revelation the
light of the secret pierced the cloud and reached me, as I
wrote earlier in a brief word, reference to which enables you
to realise as you read my ability to put two and two together
5. in the open secret of Christ. In other generations it did not
reach the minds of the sons of men in the manner in which it
burst into the open before His holy apostles and prophets in
the Spirit. The secret means this: the Gentiles are heirs along
with the rest; are members of the Body, along with the rest;
and along with the rest have a share of the promise, in Christ
Jesus through the gospel. I stepped into the position of
"minister of the gospel", along the line of the free gift of
God's grace, grace given to me in continuation of the operation
of His power. To me who am more insignificant than the
most insignificant of all holy members was this grace given, to
sound the note of the gospel to the Gentiles of the unexplored
wealth of Christ, and to throw a spotlight on to the question
of what is the management of the secret which has been hidden away from the successive ages in God Who touched off
the creation of all things, in order that the iridescent wisdom
10. of God might now by means of the church catch the eye of
rules and authorities in the heavenly realm, to square with
the purpose of the ages which He brought to a head in Christ
Jesus our Lord, in Whom we have boldness and a place for
our ship to put in with confidence, through faith in Him.
Hence I ask you to give me this: stop losing heart on those
occasions when the life is being squeezed out of me for your
sakes, seeing that it is your glory.

    For this cause—to resume what I started to say—I am
15. kneeling down to the Father, from Whom every family in
heaven and on earth derives its name, in prayer that He may
put into your hand a gift on the scale of the wealth of
His glory: that His Spirit may complete the circuit that brings
power for you to be reinforced in the inward man; that Christ
may settle in your hearts through faith; that you, with roots
spreading and foundations deep, in love, may get the strength
to grasp with all the holy members what is the breadth and

length and height and depth, and to come to know the love of Christ which overshoots knowledge, that you may be filled to saturation point with all God's fulness.

Now to Him Who is able to produce a superabundance beyond all that we ask for ourselves or conceive on the production line of the power that is active—not quiescent—in us, to Him be glory in the church and in Christ Jesus up to all the generations of the age that crowns the ages. Amen.

4:1   I therefore the prisoner in the Lord am beseeching you to make your step worthy of the call "Come!" with which you were summoned. Always have a spirit that is willing to lie low; restrain your strength; go on and on without an explosion; lovingly keep your hands off one another; ever show swift zeal to keep uncut the Spirit's oneness: peace is the cord which binds the parts together in one. There is one Body and one Spirit, just as also the call "Come!" raised in

5. you one hope. There is one Lord, one faith, one baptism; one God and Father of all, the One Who is over all, penetrates all, and dwells in all. Now to each one of us was given grace that reached the measure of the free gift of Christ. That is why it says

> He went up on high and brought captives
> into captivity; He gave gifts to men.

Now what does the relative term "He went up" mean except that (He had to start by being "down" and so) He also went down into the lower parts of the earth? He Who went down

10. is Himself also the One Who went up far above all the heavens in order that He might permeate everything. And He did give: some men as apostles, some as prophets, some as evangelists, some as pastors and teachers, with a view to the fitting of the holy members for the task of service, for the building of the Body of Christ, to go on until such time as we all touch down at our triple destination: at the oneness of the faith in and of the knowledge of the Son of God; at the Perfect Man; at the measure of the maturity of the fulness of Christ. The purpose is that we may cease to be infants, raised aloft on successive waves and swung right round by every gust of teaching in the sea of the trickery of men who stop at nothing in their schemes

15. to mislead but by maintaining the truth in love may make everything grow into Him Who is the Head, Christ. Then—

working now not into Him but from Him—the whole Body, as it is assembled and united through the provision of every necessary fastening, goes on growing as each separate part duly performs its function, and so tends all the time to a building of itself in love.

I therefore am telling you and charge you in the Lord no longer to go on walking as the gentiles also do in the emptiness of their mind: darkness enfolds their reason; the life of God is a foreign country to them—all because of the persistent ignorance in them, because of the hardening of their heart. True to type and past feeling, they delivered themselves over to moral flashiness for the high-handed business of all uncleanness. But you, my friends, did not learn Christ like
20. that—if He did "register" in you and the teaching that you actually embraced in Him comes up to the truth as it is shown in Jesus. It provides that you should lay aside the old man who is true to your former kind of life and is being ruined as he steps along with deceitful desires; let the spirit of your mind be constantly toned up; fling on the robe, I mean the man who is ever new who was created at the divine level in righteousness and the holiness of the truth.
25. Hence you should get rid of the false and each of you speak truth with his neighbour, because we are members of one another. Keep up the anger, but not the sin; don't let the sun find you still angry when it sets; don't give any scope to the devil—squeeze him out. Let the man whose fingers are in other men's pockets take them out; let him rather toil, producing with his own hands what is good, so that he may be able to give a series of shares to the man who feels the drag of need. The stream of rotten speech which passes your lips must dry up; let pass only what is good for the solid building up of the requirement, so as to give grace to the
30. listeners. Do not pain the Holy Spirit of God any more, by Whose seal you were marked for the day of redemption. Let all bitterness and anger—gust of passion and settled resentment alike—and clamouring and abuse be shifted from you, together with all spite: make a clean sweep of it. In your dealings with one another show yourselves easy to get on with, with flexibility fitting in with others, not forcing them into your own strait-jacket; let men find that you are large-hearted, pardoning one another, just as God also in Christ gave you His pardon.

A good deal of this needs to be justified or at any rate explained. "You'll see the point of that" was inserted because of the particle (*ge*) following "if". It is a highly subtle little word, with no one English word corresponding to it, and we have to be sensitive to its spirit. It here emphasises the "if", and the inserted clause shows us the reason for the emphasis. "Heard tell of" (v. 2) attempts to bring out the pinpoint. "Management" seems to be the best of a poor selection. "Dispensation" suggests too much the giving of a "dispensation" by the pope, or "dispensational truth"; "steward-ship" is rather out of date in spite of its current use; "administration" is better, though perhaps a little political. Everyone knows what a "manager" does in a large factory: giving orders, arranging policy, and making payments. He is in a position of responsibility though not the owner. To transliterate and say "economy" savours too much of parsimony or of the science of economics. "Grace" is repeated so as to show quite clearly that here it was the grace that was given to the apostle, not the management.

"Pressed into my hands" is a pinpoint, and with the preposition (*eis*), suggesting ultimate destination, it calls to mind a report of one of the great Foundations, one of the biggest public trust funds in the world, with resources of about two hundred and thirty million dollars. They are to be devoted primarily to activities that promise significant contributions to world peace and the establishment of a world order of law and justice. Any of the trustees might say, as he addressed the peoples whose lands have been devastated by war and who have been denied the stability which law and justice bring, "These vast resources were pressed into our hands—for you". Such is the spirit of the apostle's language.

"On the top deck" (v. 3) is a particular case of the preposition "according to", "on the level of" (*kata*), with its picture of the horizontal line. It is higher than the level of speculation (see pages 79*f*). On that high promenade a man has the sky above him, and the light is all around him not merely coming in at the sides, so to speak, as it would be if he were on a lower deck; still less coming in through a porthole. "Pierced" is a pinpoint, and "reached" is added in anticipation of verse 5. "Reference to which enables you" (v. 4) is a neater inversion of "by reference to which you are able" and is justified by *pros*. Notice the contrasted tenses; "to realise" (aorist, pinpoint) and "as you read" (present). "Realise" is the sort of thing which happens when a man is reading and suddenly shouts "Got it!" "Ability to put two and two together" is an English phrase which almost reproduces the Greek. "*Sunesis*," often translated by "intelligence", strictly means "putting things together", and there is fortunately available the very phrase we have used.

"Did not reach" (v. 5) picks up the allusion to light and to the deck of the ship in verse 3, and "minds" was added to show that knowledge was involved. "Burst into the open" is a pinpoint. "The secret means this" (v. 6) is a legitimate way of introducing the accusative and infinitive construction which follows (indirect discourse), and it enables us to break up the long sentence. "Along with the rest", used three times, gives a weighty emphasis to the preposition *sun-*, used three times in the three adjectives.

Verse 7 is tricky, at any rate from the point of view of our present method, as it contains two pinpoints ("Stepped into position" and "given") and two uses of the preposition *kata*, and it is difficult, if not impossible, to give four suitable renderings without mixing metaphors too much. But it does illustrate the fact that every translation loses something. For instance, we can hardly say "grace which fell into my hands", as a fall suggests something vertical, and we have twice to think of the horizontal line. "Along the line of" and "in continuation of" are both horizontal, and as visualised when first written here were pictures from the railroad. In some places on the coast the trains can go directly on to the ship: where the track ends on land, it begins on the ship, and the train can continue without being derailed. For this purpose the ship must be very still, and its side must be *in line with* the quay. It is true that *kata* is often rendered "in virtue of", almost "because of", but even so it is in virtue of the railroad lines being in the right position that the train can proceed.

We might have used something like "grace fell into my hands" in verse 8. Observe then the vivid contrast: grace, mighty, massive, like a bolt from the blue, descends to him who is "leaster" than all the saints—note that the apostle takes the superlative, "least", and then "compares" it. "To sound the note" is a pinpoint: the one note of the horn. "Unexplored" stands for an adjective containing the word "track", "footprint". Wealth is not only money; it may be territory, and the wealth of Christ is virgin soil waiting to be occupied, without the footprint of any earlier explorer. The old words might be said to the preacher with new force; "Go west, young man". There is land in abundance in Christ that human feet have never yet trod.

"Throw a spotlight" (v. 9) is a pinpoint. So, too, is "touched off the creation", which is a metaphor from explosives. There is a school of opinion which speaks of "creation with a bang" and our pinpoint makes an allusion to it. "Catch the eye" is a pinpoint, a variation of "be made known" (v. 10). "To square with" is the horizontal *kata*. "Brought to a head" (v. 11) is a pinpoint standing for the rather colourless verb "to do" or "to make". "Free speech" or "saying everything" (v. 12) is a type of all boldness. The naval metaphor after this has been stated explicitly. "I ask you to give me" (v. 13) emphasises the middle voice and is neater than "I ask for myself that you do not go on losing heart. . . ." "On those occasions" is an interpretation of an abstract noun in the plural, just as in Latin *irae* means not "angers" but "outbursts of anger". But instead of saying "occasions of persecution" we find it more vivid though still true to speak of life being squeezed out: the corresponding verb means "to make narrow by pressure".

"For this cause" (v. 14) harks back to 3: 1; hence our resumptive parenthesis. "I am kneeling" stands for a present tense. A spark of imagination will see the apostle break off his writing or his dictation for the purpose of prayer . . . "In prayer that" (v. 16) resumes the thought of kneeling and introduces the content of the prayer. "Put into your hand" is a pinpoint, as when a merchant hands to another man a diamond or other precious jewel. "On the scale of" is, of course, *kata*. "By means of His Spirit", speaking of the agency, is made into a subject, and the pinpoint is suggested by the electrical completion of the circuit: once that is done, the electricity does not "come": it is there! "Settle" (v. 17) is an ingressive aorist (pinpoint). "With roots spreading and foundations deep" (see page 115) brings the perfect tense up to the present moment. "You have been rooted" means that "you (being alive, not mere bricks and mortar) are spreading your roots". "May get the strength" and "to grasp" (v. 18) are two pinpoints. "Come to know" (v. 19) is an ingressive aorist (pinpoint), and means "find out", "discover", though we have to retain some form of the verb "know" in order to chime in with "knowledge" a little later (see page 113).

"Produce" is purposely a little vague. It stands for a pinpoint. A conjuror or "magician" will "produce" with startling suddenness a card from under your hat or a coin out of your sleeve. That kind of "produce" is a pinpoint. But it also suggests today the massive plant of a factory, industrial "production" and so on. Paradoxically, God's production is a "massive pinpoint". The horizontal *kata* almost compels us to add "on the production line."

"Am beseeching" (4: 1) is a continuous present: compare 3: 14. Two pinpoints are preserved by "make your step" and the monosyllable "Come!" The abstract nouns in verse 2 have been re-written as imperatives, not unfairly as verses 1–3 breathe the atmosphere of command, or at least exhortation, which is persuasion with authority. Notice how the two ideas "lowliness" and "mind" have been retained. Gentleness is not weakness or flabbiness. We do not speak of a gentle sponge, a gentle custard, a gentle newborn puppy; but we do speak of a gentle police dog, if that is its temperament, or even of a gentle lion or elephant, if they are tamed and exhibited in a circus. Gentleness is strength held back and not used. Hence "restrain your strength". In "long-suffering" the emphasis is on the "long", not on the amount of pain endured, and it implies the postponement of a violent reaction. Hence "go on and on without an explosion" (of wrath). "Keep your hands off" (see page 63).

"Ever show swift zeal" (v. 3) reflects the continuous present tense ("ever") and combines the two ideas of speed physically ("swift") and mentally ("zeal") inherent in the verb. "To keep uncut" is due to the present tense, and the clause which follows elaborates the genitive of material—"the bond which consists of peace". If the oneness is "in" the bond, then the bond must tie the parts together. "Come!" (v. 4) represents the pinpoint, as before.

In verse 6 the prepositions suggested the verbs: "through" brings to our minds the idea of "penetrate", and "in" that of "dwells" (For "over" cf. Acts 8: 27). Notice how three great ideas of the Christian faith are simply expressed. God is "on" (*epi*) everything. He is therefore outside everything: He is God transcendent. But He is not shut out, as He is "through" everything: He is God immanent. But He is not shut in, either, as "through" implies emergence as well as entrance. With this firmly settled the apostle goes on to speak of religious experience: the transcendent and immanent God is not so transcendent that He is remote, not so immanent that He is overlooked, but is "in" us all: He is God intimate. God: transcendent, immanent, intimate: the universe does not exhaust Him (the answer to pantheism); it does not escape Him (the answer to deism); and we do not perish in a cold intellectualism, in a bare philosophy (the answer to the needs of the human heart). All from three prepositions!

"That reached . . ." (v. 7): *kata* once more. Think of the lock of a canal. A ship enters it, and the lock fills, bringing the ship up to the higher level, at which it can sail on into the heart of the country. The grace that we were given in Christ raises us to the level of His abundant free gift, a veritable continent. As an alternative *kata* might be rendered "commensurate with".

The parenthesis was inserted in verse 9 for the sake of clarity.

E

A man can only go *up* if he is first of all *down*: if you are already at the top of the skyscraper you cannot go up. You must first be down, to some extent at any rate, if the elevator is to take you up. Hence the apostle's argument in verses 9 and 10. If we do not bring this out, some people will be puzzled by the apparent statement that going up means going down.

Notice the words "He did give" in verse 11. It is a pinpoint, but we have to retain the actual word "give" to show that it is a quotation from verse 8. The "as" is important. The meaning is not "He gave the apostles to some groups and prophets to other groups . . ." He gave to the whole church. That is why it is wrong for some ill-disposed persons to assert that the clergy are in receipt of charity. They are not: they are a gift by Christ to His church, and it is the church that is in receipt of charity. He gave to the whole church the ministry: in this, some are apostles, some are prophets, and so on.

"Fitting" (v. 12) is related to a verb used for mending fishing nets (Mark 1: 19) and elsewhere for repairing and equipping ships. We read sometimes that units of the navy or merchant fleet have returned to the home port for a "re-fit" and this accounts for the choice of "fitting", as it combines the repair of damage and taking aboard new stores. "To go on" facilitates the introduction of "until". The verb which follows immediately (v. 13) is an aoristic pinpoint, used of arriving at a destination. An air-minded age will understand the pinpoint of "touch-down", though "put in" or "tie up" would preserve the naval metaphor.

"Triple destination" enables us to break up the sentence a little. We have heard of twin cities, such as Nishni-Novgorod, situated at the junction of the Oka and the Volga rivers, or Minneapolis and St. Paul, Minnesota. Why not a triple city? "The purpose is" (v. 14) again helps us to manage the long sentence. The present participle, suggesting the series of dots, justifies "successive waves", though there is no need to repeat "successive" with "gust" because of the word "every". "In the sea of" continues the metaphor: immature minds are tossed because they have no ballast, swung round because they have no engine or rudder, in this fearful sea.

We have written "who stop at nothing" instead of "in craftiness" because the Greek word (*panourgia*), from *pan*, "all" (compare "*Pan*-American Airways") and *ergon*, "a deed", gets its meaning of "craftiness" or "villainy" from the spirit that is willing to "do anything and everything". In addition, the preposition *pros*, with its idea of "direction towards", almost of motion, accords well with the "movement" of men who "stop at nothing".

"Maintaining the truth" (v. 15) is sufficiently vague to cover both speech and life. The parenthesis in verse 16 gets rid of the awkward relative pronoun, though still preserves the sense. "Assembled" is reminiscent of the "assembling" of the parts of an automobile. We are "building the body"—a mixed metaphor. The continuous present justifies "goes on growing". "Tends" brings out the direction in the preposition *eis*.

"I am telling . . ." (v. 17): compare 4: 1 and 3: 14. The perfect tenses in verse 18 have been brought up to the present, on lines already familiar. "Persistent" was put in to be true to the present participle of the verb "to be". "Hardening" reminds us of the hardening of the arteries. (Aristotle uses *pōros* for "stalactite".) "True to type" (v. 19) is a locution for the generic relative pronoun ("who are the sort of people to . . ."). "Past feeling" brings the perfect up to date. The adjective "high-handed" represents the phrase containing the noun *pleonexia*, which means having, or getting, *more* than is one's due. A high-handed person takes *too much* upon himself, and disregards the right of others.

"My friends", (v. 20) has been inserted in order to emphasise the "you". The italic of "if" stands for the untranslatable particle *ge* (v. 21). When we say that anything "registers" we think of the "click" which takes place in a man's mind when he suddenly says "Now I see your point". "Embraced", like "register", is a pinpoint. "Comes up to", as in an elevator "coming up" to a certain floor, represents the *kata* in *kathōs*. The verb "to be" is more here than a mere copula: hence "shown" in Jesus. "It provides" (v. 22) is a legitimate introduction to the accusative and infinitive of the dependent command (indirect speech). "Lay aside" is a pinpoint. "True to" stands for the frequent *kata*. Think of bricklayers making a wall with its top perfectly level with the horizontal. "As he steps along with": *kata* again: like one man keeping on the horizontal sidewalk with another, and not stepping down alone into the road. Notice the present, continuous tense in "is being ruined."

"Toned up" (v. 23), instead of "be renewed", suggests a pinpoint, but the tense is present. Actually a series is called for, and so we have added "constantly". Think of a lady who pays a regular visit to the beauty parlour: the renewal does tone her up every time she goes. "Fling on the robe" (v. 24) makes the metaphor in "put on the new man" quite explicit; it is a pinpoint, and conveys the sort of meaning which a mother has when she hastily urges her son to "tumble into" his clothes. A man can "fling on" a university gown in a pinpoint. "Ever new" is perhaps better than the mere "new", because the word *kainos* means "new" in quality rather than in time, "fresh" rather than "stale". (The opposite of "new" is "old".) "At the divine level": *kata* once more. There is sometimes talk of a meeting between heads of state: in current language, this would be discussion "at the highest level", not a meeting of Foreign Secretaries or Under-Secretaries or Ambassadors.

"Get rid of" (v. 25) is an alternative pinpoint for "lay aside" in verse 22. In verse 26 the two imperatives have purposely been retained, though the former, "keep on being angry" is probably conditional in meaning, though not in form. "Find you" is in place of "come down *upon* you". "Do not go on giving" (v. 27) means "stop giving". This, together with the fact that the word translated "scope" also means "room", justifies the added "squeeze him out".

The constant demands for money by officials, charitable organisations, missionary societies and churches have led some people to say that their hands are always in their pockets. They mean that they are constantly giving. The present tense in verse 28 ("The man who steals") suggests a like continuity and repetition, and we therefore have translated by "the man whose fingers are in other men's pockets". "Take them out" continues the figure and stands for "let him no longer go on stealing", that is, let him stop, a normal way of dealing with a negative and the present imperative. "Give a series of shares" recalls the series of points which illustrates the present tense. "Feels the drag" is an attempt to give force to the continuity. For instance, if an automobile has been involved in a smash and has to be towed home, the "pull" is continuous—otherwise it is a jerk.

"Rotten" (v. 29) is used purposely, one might almost say literally. "Let it not continue to go out" means "let it stop", hence "dry up". Noticed the contrasted "building", the contrast made clear by the addition of "solid"—as opposed to "rotten". In ancient churches in England it is sometimes found that great beams have been attacked by the death-watch beetle. The beams are rotten, and cannot be kept in the structure as they fall to powder. Speech can be like that. There is a pinpoint in "by Whose seal you were marked" (v. 30). The stamping with a seal is a momentary act.

"Shifted" (v. 31) is really a pinpoint, though so far this is not very clear. Influenced by this fact, and the word "all", we have made sure of the pinpoint by adding "make a clean sweep of it".

The beginning of verse 32 has been greatly expanded. *Eis*, expressing direction towards, justifies "in your dealings with", and

dealings may be intermittent and regular. Hence the present imperative may be represented by the series of points—"*show yourselves*".
(For this rendering of the verb, cf. Luke 10: 36.) The rest, "easy to
get on with, with flexibility fitting in with others, not forcing them
into your own strait-jacket" was suggested by the use of the adjective
in Matthew 11: 30, "my yoke is easy". The yoke of Christ is com-
fortable, does not fit too hard, does not chafe, is supple. Such is
something of the meaning of the Greek word which we have tried
to bring out in what is admittedly a long paraphrase. "Gave you
His pardon" is a pinpoint.

Chapter 8

NEAR NEIGHBOURS

THE preacher will find in the New Testament certain passages or phrases where the most unlikely words are brought together. It is said that adversity makes strange bed-fellows, but it is not always adversity which brings words together. It is rather the richness of the content of the Christian faith, and a (perhaps unconscious) skill in expression. The juxtaposition imparts a certain piquancy, which is found in our own language and indeed even in some situations. Some years ago I was struck by a newspaper headline, "Rain Stops Rain-Making Experiment." And once, one of my children as a very small child woke up in the middle of the night sobbing his heart out. "What's the matter?" we asked. "I'm tired!" he wailed. When it was suggested that he might find it helpful to go to sleep he sank back on to his pillow, quite satisfied. The arresting contrast between words and situation, or words and words, especially when the words are side by side, invites comment.

Think, for example, of the phrase in Hebrews 4: 16, "the throne of grace". The throne suggests authority, the right to rule, the support of force if need be, and all the majesty of royal power. In utter contrast grace, the unmerited love of the lovely for the unlovely, dwells less on the idea of authority and seeks to win men, not force them; to bless them, not to make them obey; to inspire them to follow, not to conscript them.

The association of these two ideas yields two thoughts for the preacher. First, grace is enthroned; the love of God is armed. His is not the unhappy love which sees its children tortured and can do nothing about it, as with King Zedekiah (2 Kings 25: 7) and a host of parents in the Europe of the twentieth century. It can intervene when it wills: it can right wrongs. It has agents and servants everywhere. "Thousands speed to do His bidding." It can listen to the suppliant and grant his request. It can relieve the distressed, encourage the faint-hearted and defend the innocent.

Second, authority has a heart. It is not bare naked will; it is far from vulgar tyranny. It not only can but will listen to the suppliant. It is power and might, directed by love, and will descend from its throne. Thus we have the two complementary thoughts; love has power and the right to use it; authority is ever guided by love. We tend to think of the throne of power and of the tenderness of grace, but Christianity unites them in the throne of grace.

There is an analogous paradox in the words "the wrath of the Lamb". This is indeed a triple juxtaposition. We are to come to the throne of grace "with boldness" (see p. 128)."Boldness to the throne" suggests a third point to the preacher. Faith has encouragement (Rev. 6: 16). The title "Lamb" suggests the submissive Christ, the willing sacrifice for sin, the innocent sufferer Who bears the sin of the world (John 1: 29). (The Greek words differ: in John it is *amnos*; in Revelation it is *arnion*. But see also Rev. 5: 6, "the Lamb as it had been slain" and Acts 8: 32—*amnos*—both of which texts seem to refer to Isaiah 53: 7.) Which is the more impressive? the wrath of the bully, the uncontrolled mouthings of a Hitler, the anger of the utterly base and selfish; or the wrath of love which is angry not because its pet schemes have gone awry or because it has been thwarted, but because those whom it loves have turned away from the best?

The One Who emptied Himself for us, died for us, is not the One Who is ruffled or filled with chagrin. His wrath is love blazing at white heat; it is moral goodness roused by the very evil and ugliness of sin. Take the righteous wrath of an Abraham Lincoln, take the words "If ever I have power to strike this thing, I'll strike it hard", purify it of all dross and unworthiness and raise it to its highest power, and you then have some faint resemblance to "the wrath of the Lamb". You can see it in action in John 2: 15, "He made a lash out of cords."

Such wrath is not ill temper, not uncontrolled passion or malice, not a mere gust of fury. It is the moral reaction of infinite goodness and love when goodness has been trampled on and love mocked and rejected with scorn; it is like the blaze of the father who finds grown men, grown in body but mites in moral stature, torturing his six-year-old son with knives or a red-hot poker. The wrath of the Lamb is the wrath of One Who studies our interests; Who bore the doom of our sin that we might escape it; Who would lead us to all that is good and noble and save us from our folly, our vulgarity, our ugliness and our evil; Who would bring us into fellowship with Himself.

An interesting juxtaposition occurs in James 1: 25, "the law of liberty". Now law is binding, and must be obeyed. However inconvenient it may be to us, however it may conflict with our plans, we have to do what it says. It seems thus to limit our personal freedom: we want to do this or that, and we are not free to so do. The law forbids it. On the other hand, freedom suggests that we are free from our shackles. Do we want to say this or do that? Is it our purpose to go here or go there? If we are free we may. Law and freedom: though they are near neighbours in James's text they seem to be like neighbours who are ever quarrelling. They are very like opposites.

But deeper reflection will reveal a truth not lying on the surface. It is law which makes freedom possible. It is law which gives us freedom to use the highway. If everyone were free to drive precisely where he liked there would be no "rule of the road"; traffic would not proceed in line but would be all over the road at the whim of the various drivers and there would be accidents galore. No one would give way—why should he? He is free—and the result would be chaos. The speed with which automobiles travel in the Holland and Lincoln tunnels in New York—as I remember—depends on an absolute obedience to the highway code. One slight deviation at speed and there is a smash. Law takes away a proportion of our freedom in order to give us more. Our Lord takes away our freedom to do anything and everything we like, in order to build up an ordered life of true freedom. Psychologically, we are free to sin; morally we are not free. And when we truly obey Him we find that "His service is perfect freedom". We are not indeed "under law" (Rom. 6: 15) but we are involved in Christ's law (1 Cor. 9: 21).

The paradox is illustrated in a virtual juxtaposition in Galatians 5: 13. We were called for freedom, but freedom itself is restricted. It must not be used as a beach-head, bridgehead or foothold for the invading flesh. "Through love be slaves to one another." Cf. Eph. 6: 7, "with goodwill—be slaves. . . ." Revelation 7: 14 speaks of those who washed their robes and "whitened them in the blood of the Lamb". They made them white—with blood. This is as expressive as Milton's violent phrase, "blind mouths", and as startling. The puzzle may be resolved, of course. Milton is thinking of men without discernment or insight; they are thus "blind". But they take it upon themselves to speak in public, and are thus "mouths". "Blind mouths" speaks of a noise which is no message, a leading which is but a direction from the ignorant.

Now when men whiten their robes by washing them they remove what might be termed the routine dirt, the grubbiness which has soiled the garment through ordinary wear and tear. They also take away the stains, or the marks that are concentrated in one or another place—if, for example, they have upset the inkpot. The robes of the people of God have been washed white: clean, glistening, snowy white. They are "presentable" in the sight of God—in Christ; and through His grace their very characters will eventually be so, to match His righteousness with which they have been clothed. Notice the cost of all this. The blood of the Lamb has to be shed to be available. Through the death of our Lord His people "are clean every whit". If we may speak, in terrible words, of "routine sins", they are washed away; and outstanding sins also, which mark the wrecked life, are blotted out by the same means. By His death we live, and may become partakers of the divine nature (2 Peter 1: 4); with His stripes we are healed (Is. 53: 5); by His blood our robes are made white.

A similar paradox occurs a little later (Rev. 7: 17), where the seer speaks of the Lamb Who will shepherd them. The Lamb as the Shepherd! Is not this a new way of speaking of the doctrine of the Incarnation? The Lord became Man and lived our life, knows it from the inside, and is therefore not a High-priest Who cannot feel the touch of our infirmities. He Who shepherds His people leads them in the light of His own experience as the Lamb.

We have already translated Hebrews 11: 27, "he held out, as seeing the Unseen One" (see p.25). Notice the use of the same root, "seeing" and "Unseen", and notice, too, the fact that it is "as seeing", not "as if seeing". The Greek word (hōs) here rendered "as" is often subjective: it reflects what is going on in the mind of the subject. We might therefore translate "held out, *in the conviction that* he was seeing the Unseen One." The contrast, even the contradiction, reminds us of the apostle's prayer that the Ephesians may come to know the love of Christ which goes beyond knowledge (Eph. 3: 19).

All such passages are a help and an inspiration to men faced with the contradictions of life. There are always impossibilities; but they can be done. If you are with men they are impossible, but if you are with God everything can be done (Mark 10: 27). Nobody has ever yet seen God (John 1: 18); but the eye of faith has seen Him. The dead are very dead, incapable of anything; but with Christ standing by even the dead are only asleep. How dramatic is Luke's verse (8: 53), "They laughed Him to scorn, *knowing* that she was dead." And she stood up! The dead are very deaf, but the Lord said to the dead son of the Widow of Nain during the actual funeral, "*To you* I am speaking; arise!" (Luke 7: 14). And he sat up and began to talk. The dead are very still, but our Lord said "Lazarus, come out!" (John 11: 43). And he who knew the experience of death (mark the graphic perfect tense) came out.

In Hebrews 11: 9 there is the verb *katoikeō*, which suggests a permanent residence (see Gen. 37: 1 LXX). It is paradoxically associated with tents, of all dwellings surely the most impermanent. We have rendered the clause (see p. 24) in a way which draws attention to the contrast: "he took up permanent residence in impermanent tents." It is a text which helps us to realise the "permanent impermanence" of our life here below. As we grow older the truth sinks in more deeply that the possessions of earth are not lasting: they wear out or we lose them, increased activity of the state may diminish them or even confiscate them, a revolution may turn everything upside down; and apart from all this, we cannot take them with us. A tent is a fitting symbol of our life. In all our thinking we should not fall into the secularism of concentrating on this world to the exclusion of the next. Cf. Luke 16: 9 with its striking expression, "eternal tents".

There is a striking juxtaposition in Romans 16: 20. "The God of peace . . ." We expect some soothing, comforting word, and perhaps it is comforting: but it is hardly what we might have imagined. "The God of peace will shatter, smash, Satan under your feet quickly." (The verb is *suntribō*.) He is indeed the God of peace, but not the God of peace-at-any-price. And here He works through human agency. Have you ever seen how different men will kill an insect? Some just tread on it: others tread on it and then swing themselves round as if on a pivot, squashing, shivering, smashing, grinding it to pieces. Such could be the scale of the victory of the church over evil, if she had the faith and the devotion.

We have already referred to the word *perissos* and its compounds (see page 99). It is finely used by St. Paul in 2 Corinthians 8: 1–2 in vivid contrast with the context. "I am making you to know, brothers, the grace of God which has been given among the churches of Macedonia: when they were sorely tested by the grip of affliction, the *overflow* ('surplus' is the idea; but 'overflow' prepares us for the same word in the verb) of their joy and their down to depth *poverty* together ('together' shows that the subject is 'overflow' and 'poverty') *overflowed* in the wealth of their liberality." ("Liberality" in the Greek is literally "simplicity" or "one-foldness". When a man has but *one* idea, that of giving, he is not two-fold, three-fold, or mani-fold, but one-fold, which is what "simple" means. Hence "simplicity" comes to mean "liberality".)

Note, then, the picture which is suggested. There is a river of joy, overflowing its banks. It meets another river, poverty, which is down to the very bed: resources are but a trickle of a stream. The two rivers converge and the one resulting river is the wealth of liberality which overflows its banks. It may be that St. Paul is thinking of a liberality which is to be measured by the spirit behind it, by the proportion of their money which was given. The poor widow (Luke 21: 3–4) gave two mites and it was all she had. She gave more than all the wealthy, who were giving out of their *overflowing* (same word) wealth. If this is the right interpretation, the overflowing joy transformed the little stream of cash into a torrent of liberality which refreshed a very desert.

On the other hand the apostle may mean that the overflowing joy was so real a treasure that little else mattered, so that the Christians in Macedonia gladly gave out of their poverty, and the many little gifts became one large gift. To keep to the figure of the river, the many little tributaries contributed to the one overflowing Mississippi. Whatever his ultimate meaning, St. Paul has brought together vividly for our instruction and inspiration the two ideas of "surplus" and "poverty".

1 Peter 4: 8 has an interesting juxtaposition: "before everything having your love to one another fervent, because love covers a multitude of sins." The literal rendering shows that the love is regarded as already present, but Peter wants it to be "fervent". Now this last word is the adjective *ektenēs*, which really means "stretched out". (Look up the verb *ekteino*.) When people pray "fervently" they are stretching their whole personality so to speak. As the present day colloquialism has it, they are going "all out". A football team after a strenuous match is said to have gone "all out". Some sporting journalists used to say that they were "fully extended". Similarly a fast driver sometimes goes "all out".

Love, then, when it is stretched out, covers a multitude of sins. Presumably if it is not so stretched the sins may be so many that the love will not cover them. We need the elasticity of love, or at any rate a love which is not folded up but spread out. The reader will see that I am feeling my way towards an illustration which will combine the ideas of stretching and covering. During World War II the blast of a bomb would sometimes ruffle the tiles of the roof, and sometimes blow half of them off, leaving a gaping hole. It was the aim of "first aid repairs" to put a roof on so as to keep out the rain until proper repairs could be done. In many cases canvas was used, a tarpaulin, something in the nature of the hard cloth of a sail. If it were kept folded up it might cover a square yard or so; if it were unfolded it would cover a wider area; if it were stretched and made taut it could be roped down and cover the whole roof.

So love, if it does not remain folded up, huddled up in itself, can cover many sins. It keeps them out of sight: the silence of love can "hush up" a scandal and save distress to a repentant sinner and prevent cynicism on the part of outsiders. In the fellowship of the church it can hide the misdeeds of the unseemly by treating him as if he had not sinned; it can avoid a clash and thus bring him back into the inner circle of them that love God. Our love will not "cover" sins in the sense of making atonement for them, but God's love has already done that. Stretch then your love, and spread it over the sins of others, for that is precisely what God has done. It needed a good deal of love to cover the sins of all mankind, but "God so loved the world . . ." (John 3: 16). The obvious application is to gossip. We could preach on "Stretched Tongue or Stretched Love?"

There is a play on words in 2 Thessalonians 3: 13, *mē enkakēsēte kalopoiountes*, with—*kak*—meaning "bad" and—*kal*—meaning "good". It is frequently rendered "be not weary in well-doing", though the same verb is often translated in 2 Corinthians 4: 1 "we faint not". It refers not to involuntary fainting but to the coward's "easing up" or slackening his energy. The immediate task is to bring out the contrast between the *kak* and the *kal*, the "bad" and the "good". Now if a runner in a long race becomes short of breath and on the verge of collapse as he struggles along, we say to ourselves "He's in a *bad* way." So the apostle tells the Thessalonians "don't get into a *bad* way when doing *good*." A pretty little pun! Cf. Galatians 6: 9.

In 1 Thessalonians 1: 3 the apostle speaks of "the work of faith". Each word has been a battle-cry. They are mutual enemies when either of them trespasses on the other's ground. If "works" invade the domain of faith we may anticipate a Galatian blast. If "faith" regards itself as a work and lolls in spiritual laziness it will be attacked for giving aid and comfort to antinomianism. Works do not bring us to God; they do not justify. But faith must still work; faith, in the language of industry, must "produce", and a living faith does. Works may be regarded as the evidence of faith; faith is the inspiration of works.

If a non-Christian says, "What must I do to be saved?" we must not answer in terms of "works". If a Christian asks what he must

do to be sanctified, then we must refer to works, adding that as he
out-works his salvation God is at work within (see Phil. 2: 12–13).
In the language of academic examinations, works do not count for
a pass but they do for honours.

A not dissimilar juxtaposition occurs in 2 Thessalonians 1: 8,
where Paul speaks of people who do not "obey the gospel." The
word here gives us a start of surprise. The law is to be obeyed. The
gospel is good news. But it is not merely God's good advice; it
is not merely His offer which we are at liberty to accept or reject.
The gospel is a command of grace as well as an offer of grace. This
has an obvious connection with "the throne of grace" in Hebrews
4: 16. Cf. Romans 10: 16; 1 Peter 4: 17.

After Peter had "escaped" from prison Herod sought him in
vain. He examined his guards and commanded them "to be led
away" (Acts 12: 19). This is a clear euphemism for it means "to
execution". So "they led Him away" in Luke 23: 26. (We have
an analogous use in English. We say that "he was put away".
Where? A favourite animal is "put down".) Now in Mark 14: 53
"they led Jesus away to the high priest". This may be a legal
technical term for bringing a person before a court. But it is
ominous and in the light of the Passion story the association is startling. What have high priests to do with executions? "They led Jesus
away . . ." What thoughts do these words engender? ". . . to the
high priest"!

The high priests figure in another juxtaposition in Mark 15: 11.
"The high priests . . ." Took counsel in a solemn and prayerful
meeting? Took thought for the welfare of their people? Called the
people to repentance? Far from it: "The high priests stirred up the
crowd . . ." If we wish to receive the full impact of this, we must
imagine in the present day the archbishops shouting as agitators in a
demonstration in front of some foreign embassy—which is un-
thinkable. The picture of high priests giving encouragement to mob
rule is not a pleasant one but, as with other features of the Passion
story, it gives great scope to the imagination.

The English versions in 2 Timothy 3: 13 speak of men who will
"wax worse and worse." The Greek is much more lively. They will
"advance—to the worse." We hear much about progress and it
seems to be often assumed that progress in itself is automatically
good. But it is possible to progress, to advance, even to pioneer, on
the wrong road. Sometimes the only valuable advance is to go back.
Ask any motorist who has taken the wrong turning into a cul de
sac!

St. Paul tells the Romans to present their bodies (i.e. their persons) as a "living sacrifice". We are reminded of the hymn,

> Not all the blood of beasts
> On Jewish altars *slain*.

The sacrifice of our Lord means the death of Christ and as a result of this His one act Christian men are under obligation, not to repeat His work (which is impossible) but to follow His example: to give themselves. There is both loss and gain in the translation "a living dead thing", but it brings out the startling juxtaposition. We read at times of men who after some dangerous expedition return "more dead than alive". Christians are "both dead and alive". Cf. Galatians 2: 19–20; Romans 6: 13. ". . . you died, and your life . . . Put to death . . ." (Col. 3: 3–5). Perhaps the clue to the paradox lies in the death of self and the life of service. As an illustration we have Acts 5: 41. ". . . rejoicing . . . Considered worthy . . . to be dishonoured."

A humorous example of juxtaposition occurs in 1 Peter 2: 15. It is the will of God that by doing what is right we should "gag the ignorance of foolish men". The ignorant will talk! If the ignorance in question has special reference to the lack of spiritual experience (cf. 1 Cor. 15: 34) we might recall with interest Matthew 22: 34. The Pharisees heard (no doubt with relish) that the Lord "had gagged the Sadducees", though it was with words rather than deeds.

In Acts 15: 14 opposite words are placed side by side with remarkable effect. God took action to get "from the gentiles a people" (*ex ethnōn laon*). The preacher will find his imagination working at full pitch here. He can begin historically with Gentiles and Jews. He can then "amplify" and "expand". God recruits His people from the unpromising, the unprivileged, the inferior. ("For after all these things do the Gentiles seek," Matt. 6: 32.) When they are His through their faith in His Son they inherit the promises, enjoy the privileges and occupy the "superior" position of knowing where they are, where they are going and in Whose hands they are.

Changes can be rung on this theme; the same tune may be rendered with variations. Obvious examples are: "from outsider to insider" and "from no start to having a start." Perhaps it is unwise to suggest "from self-reliance to (the spiritual) welfare state" though with care it has possibilities. Cf. Romans 15: 10.

In the story of the Transfiguration we learn that "a *bright* cloud over*shadowed* them" (Matt. 17: 5). We might expect a dark cloud to cast its shadow: its brightness is towards the sun rather than to the earth. On the road to Damascus Saul of Tarsus was blinded by the light. Does this point to the richness of God's revelation and to our own incapacity? The same kind of "contradiction" is present in 1 Corinthians 15: 44, "spiritual body".

Examples are piled up in 2 Corinthians 4: 17. "The momentary lightness of affliction . . . produces for us an eternal weight of glory." We should note the contrasts between "momentary" and "eternal," "lightness" and "weight" and "affliction" and "glory". There is a further hidden juxtaposition in "weight of glory." The Hebrew word for "glory" is from a root which means "heavy". Glory is not as evanescent as a sunset; its "heavy solidity" cannot be removed.

Three final instances make use of the verb *blepō*. I know that in some contexts it means "take heed", "look carefully at", and even "beware of". But the Greek reader still has before him the one verb and we translate literally to show the effect. "See what you hear" (Mark 4: 24); "seeing the wind" (Matt. 14: 30); "to see the voice" (Rev. 1: 12): all these arresting expressions suggest an "imaginative consideration." It may be wrong, as when Peter "saw the wind". Its tempestuous effects turned his thought to danger and death. Instead of keeping his eyes and his thoughts on Jesus he attended to the "circumstances."

On the other hand "imaginative consideration" may be right. What we hear is not to be mentally tape-recorded, as it were, uncritically. We should reflect and imagine: what does it mean and how will it work out? Can we visualise the possible consequences? "Always take a look at what you hear."

Or such a reaction may be demanded and be all but inevitable. The Christ Who spoke to John was the transcendent Christ and His voice came to him with compelling power. We should notice that in verse 10 the loud voice was "as of a trumpet speaking." It is odd to say that it was the trumpet which was regarded as speaking, not the voice; but such is meant by the grammar. It suggests the loud blare which falls upon our ears and which we cannot help hearing; and the revelation which is thus heralded. We *must* "see the pictures" which are suggested by the voice. An appropriate comment would be Ephesians 1: 18, "the eyes of your heart being illumined."

Let us turn to Ephesians 5 and try to make our own translation.

V.1.   Therefore: let every event make you imitators of God, mindful that you are beloved children; keep moving, on

love's highway, parallel with the love which Christ also gave you and the life which He delivered up for you as an offering and a sacrifice to God redolent of fragrance. Fornication, all kinds of impurity or "going too far", should cease being even mentioned in your circle, as befits holy members; so with baseness and foolish talking or ribaldry, which are
5. infra dig.; rather let thanksgiving be on your lips. For let this knowledge sink in: no "loose" or impure person or one who "goes too far", i.e. idolater, has an inheritance in the kingdom of Christ and of God. Nobody must go on deceiving you with talk which has nothing in it: for this is the reason why the wrath of God is coming upon the family of the Disobedient. Therefore: do not turn out to be partners with them; for you were at one time darkness, but now in the Lord you are light; show by your walk your kinship with light—for light begets all manner of goodness and right-
10. eousness and truth—as you elicit by scrutiny what is well-pleasing to the Lord. Break away from the unproductive deeds of darkness: do not go on with the fellowship, but take rather the line of unmasking them, for even to talk of their secret goings-on has an ugly sound. All things when unmasked by the light are brought within our vision; in fact everything so brought is (in turn) illumination. Hence the hymn says:

> Awake O thou sleeper,
> Arise from the dead,
> And the glory of Jesus
> Shall shine on thy head.

15.   Therefore: let there be no blur in your moral vision: take heed how you go on your way, not as unwise, but as wise, cornering the market in opportunity because the times are bad. Because of this, show yourselves not at folly's windows, but in the full light of understanding what the will of the Lord is. No bouts of wine, in which is squandering, but keep up to the top the level of the inner spirit, talking to yourselves in psalms and hymns and spiritual songs, singing and psalming with your heart to the Lord, giving
20. thanks to God and the Father on every occasion for everything in the Name of our Lord Jesus Christ, taking your places in subordination to one another, in awe of Christ.

Wives, go on being subordinate to your own husbands as
to the Lord, because a husband is head of his wife as also
Christ is head of the church, Himself the saviour of the Body.
But you wives should continue in subordination to your
husbands in everything as the church does to Christ. You
25. husbands, go on loving your wives, rising to the way in
which Christ also gave His love to the church and delivered
Himself for her, in order that He might plunge her into the
laving waters in the context of the Word, holy to emerge,
that He might present the church to Himself in her glory,
free from blemish or wrinkle or any of such marks of faded
loveliness, but that she might be holy and above criticism.
Husbands also are under obligation to go on loving their
own wives as their own persons. The man who loves his
own wife loves himself; for no-one at any time vented hatred
on his own flesh, but a man tends its growth with the warmth
of a father's love just as Christ also tends the church, because
30. we are the limbs of His body. In view of this a man will
abandon his father and mother and will be joined to his
wife and the two will be one flesh. This mystery is a great
one, but my point is that I am speaking in regard to Christ
and the church. But let each individual also among you go
on loving his wife as he loves himself. I bid the wife to go
VI.1. on standing in loving awe of her husband. Children, answer
the calls of your parents with obedience—in the Lord; for
this is right. Let your attitude be one of honour to your
father and mother—this is the first commandment which is
embedded in a promise—in order that it may turn out well
for you and you may be long-lived on the earth. And you
fathers, do not give your children a succession of irritants,
but bring them up in the culture of the Lord: put something
5. into their minds. You slaves, obey the commands of your
human masters with fear and trembling; let your heart be
fully in the job, remembering that you are giving your obedience to Christ. Rise above the level of a service to please
men only when their eyes are on you, but, mindful that you
are Christ's slaves, do the will of God spontaneously, not
mechanically. Do the work of a slave with goodwill—"for
the Lord and not men" is your motto. You know that each
man, if he does some good turn, will get it back from the
Lord, whether he be slave or free. And you masters, pursue
the same policy towards them: relax your threatening; for

you know that their Lord as well as yours is in heaven, and
He pays no regard to face values.

10.   In future, take in new power in the Lord and in the might
of His strength. Fling on the martial dress of God, so that
you may be able to make a stand against the cunning tactics
of the devil; because we are locked in a hand-to-hand struggle
not with flesh and blood but with the rules, with the authorities, with the cosmic lords that control this darkness, against
the spiritual forces of evil in the heavenly realm. Because of
this, pick up the set of soldier's gear which God provides,
in order that you may get the means to show fight in the
evil day, and when you have done everything still to make
a stand. Make a stand, therefore: but first hitch up your robes
in the belt of truth, and clamp on the breast-plate of right-
15. eousness. Don't be barefoot—and slow: slip into the readiness of the gospel of peace; at every alarm pick up the shield
of faith: under its cover you will be able to put out all the
incendiaries of the evil archer. Close with the offer of salvation's helmet, and the sword of the Spirit, which is the word
of God. Do this, leaving out no prayer or petition, but offering prayers in the Spirit at every opportunity. Keep your
eyes open for Him, with vigilance unrelaxed, and with a
prayer for all the holy members, and for me, that speech,
through God's gift, may burst forth when I open my mouth,
so as without reserve to make men realise the open secret
20. of the gospel, for which gospel's sake I carry on my mission,
an ambassador bound in a chain. Pray that in the gospel I
may let loose the whole flood of good tidings, as they ought
to gush forth from me.

You also, should know my situation and how I am getting
on. For this purpose Tychicus my beloved brother and faithful servant in the Lord will tell you all the news. I am sending
him to you so that you may find out all about us and that he
may give your hearts a dose of encouragement.

Peace to the brothers, and love with faith from God the
Father and the Lord Jesus Christ. Grace be with all those
whose love for our Lord Jesus Christ grows and does not
decay.

Many of the renderings in the above translation or expository
paraphrase have been suggested by the very grammar, and the reader
will probably have been prepared for them. Even so, a comment or

explanation may not be out of place. In 5: 1 and elsewhere, the "therefore" has been put first to make sure of it, and so to leave us free to look for a phrase which will not be unduly cumbered. "Become imitators . . ." is a present tense, and may be represented by a series of dots. What do the dots stand for? "Every event" leaps naturally to the mind. I wrote first "let every event *find* you imitators of God", but this would imply that their imitation continues in an unbroken line. This might be the meaning; but it seems better to think of a succession of challenges to faith. Hence "let every event *make* you. . ." "Mindful that" is used to give force to the subjective *hōs*, to express what is in the mind of the (Greek) subject.

"Keep moving" (v. 2) is true to the present tense. "On love's highway" continues the metaphor and is not untrue to the preposition *en*. The gospel not infrequently used the phrase "*in* the way" when the meaning is "on the road". "Parallel with" is an attempt to do justice to the *kata* in *kathōs*, and introduces the punctiliar "the love which Christ *gave* you". Think of the swift movement of a gift from hand to hand, and you have the pinpoint implied in "loved". The aorist, a past tense here, sums up the love concentrated in the Cross. The construction is continued and the pinpoint repeated in "the life which He delivered up". "Life" balances "love" and is a fair variant for "Himself". A negative with a present imperative means "do not continue to do . . ." and this justifies "cease" (v. 3). "In your circle" stands for "in you" (*en*), "among you".

"Infra dig." (v. 4) is a colloquial expression suggested by the Greek *anēken*: the verb "are not convenient" (KJV, AV) or "are not befitting" (RV) means "do not come up" to something. Either they are "infra dig." i.e. "below (the) dig(nity)" of Christians, or, still colloquially, they "do not come *up* to scratch". "Be on your lips" continues in thought the present imperative. If it had been an aorist we should have needed to say "let it fall from your lips", to preserve the pinpoint. "Sink in" (v. 5) is for the two verbs for knowing, "be aware of this by continually taking in knowledge".

"Nobody must go on . . ." (v. 6) is a stylistic variant for "let nobody . . ." Notice the continuity of the present tense. "Empty words" is more vigorously expressed by "talk which has nothing in it". "The sons of . . ." is a Hebraistic expression: it suggests that the persons in question, the "sons", are such striking examples of the quality of which they are "sons", e.g. "sons of disobedience", that they bear a family likeness to it. Hence we have boldly rendered "the family of the Disobedient".

"Turn out to be" or "prove to be," instead of the bare "become", is reminiscent of a similar use of the same verb in the parable of the Good Samaritan: "which of these three, do you think, has turned out to be a neighbour to him who fell among thieves?" (Luke 10: 36). If we emphasise the present tense we must add "do not prove to be partners every time they are exposed", "every time" being suggested by the series of dots. "Kinship with the light" (v. 8) may be explained on the same lines as "family of the Disobedient" (v. 6). "Show" is a sign of the subjective *hōs*, as in verse 1. It means "walk, knowing that you are children of light"; hence, "show by your walk . . ."

As we may have the "fruit" of trees, or of a man's loins (Acts 2: 30), so we may have a fruit of righteousness (Phil. 1: 11; Heb. 12: 11; James 3: 18). The idea is that there is a "parent" which produces the fruit; and so we have translated "the light begets . . .", which is an alternative for "the fruit of the light consists in . . ." Scrutiny reveals from time to time what will please God, and this will determine the manner of one's "walk". In particular (leaving behind the parenthesis in v. 9), scrutiny or testing will afford guidance as to direction of travel, speed, times of halting, whether travelling alone or in company, and so on. When our Lord said "Follow Me" He implied that He is the moving Christ, and the apostle is concerned that the disciples who move behind Him should do it in the right way.

"Break away from" (v. 11) is another way of saying "do not continue to . . ." which the present tense suggests. In a boxing match the referee sometimes commands the boxers to come out of a clinch, to "break". But this rendering has only partly translated the rich content of the verb, and we have therefore added in explanation, "Do not go on with the fellowship". "Take the line of unmasking them" draws attention to a custom or habit, advocated by the present tense. Similarly, "goings-on" reproduces the continuity of the present, and has an added air of vagueness not inappropriate to the verb (*ginomena*). Verse 14 seems to be a quotation from an early Christian hymn, and in order to reduce it to a stanza I have taken a few liberties. "Glory" is almost implied by the verb "shine", "Jesus" suits the rhythm better than "Christ", and "on thy head" is poetic licence for "on thee".

"Blur" (v. 15) requires a little explanation. The adverb *akribōs* has been used in older Greek with the meaning "with clearness of outline". If we see in this way there is an absence of blur, and our vision, here clearly moral, is not distorted. "Go on your way" reflects the present tense. "Cornering the market" (v. 16) : see page 63. "Days" is the original meaning, of course, at the end of the verse; but Paul is not insisting on periods of twenty-four hours, and "the times are bad" is a common expression. In these difficult days let the church gather in all the opportunities: there are plenty of others who will do so if we do not.

The rendering of verse 17 is a useful example of how a rendering came to me. For a whole day I pondered it, when lying in bed with influenza. The verb is in the present tense, and I could see a series of big dots. But what did the dots mean? First came the idea, "avoid these bursts of folly"; then a peremptory command, "no chain of follies!" But they failed to satisfy, and I lay like a log, with head and eyes aching furiously, sometimes awake, sometimes asleep, sometimes dreaming, but always confronted by a series of dots.

In the evening I picked up Canon Roger Lloyd's *Church of England in the Twentieth Century*, and began to read. He describes the intervention of Bishop Westcott in the coal dispute in Durham in 1892.[1] The Bishop invited owners and miners to his home, and after a meal sent both parties away into separate rooms, and went to and fro himself between them as an intermediary. A large crowd waited for five hours outside, trying to follow the course of the negotiations by *observing the movement of the heads in the windows*. As I read of this the series of dots which had been worrying me all day suddenly were transformed into a row of windows, and the translation suggested itself.

The miner's dispute was completely forgotten: all I could see was windows. Hence the rendering, "show yourselves not at folly's windows, but in the full light of understanding what the will of the Lord is." Some people think that they can "see life" from the poor entertainments of the world and from the habitations of sin. They look out from the separate windows and see but little. But let them come into the open country, as it were, and the handiwork of God is all around them. Which is a parable for those who can understand.

The rule, then, is clear: whenever we have a present or an imperfect tense, let us ask ourselves if it may be represented by a continuous line or by a series of dots. Then let us ask what the line or dots represent or can represent. So in verse 18 we have said

[1]Roger Lloyd: *Church of England in the Twentieth Century*: Vol. II, pages 86–87.

"no bouts of wine", which reproduces both the negative and the
dots. There is another present in "keep on being filled with the
spirit". When we tell the man at the filling-station to fill up our
tank with petrol we do not necessarily mean that it is empty: it may
be half full. To keep on filling therefore means "keep the level up
to the top". What follows is illuminating.

The thought of drunkenness and its opposite, being filled with
the Spirit, has suggested to the apostle a very bold line of thought,
and he states the Christian equivalent of four stages of drunkenness.
Drunken men first begin to talk to themselves: let Christians employ
psalms and hymns and spiritual songs for this purpose. Then they
get rowdy and start to sing, generally out of tune: Christians should
avoid the rowdiness by singing to the Lord, with their heart, that
is, either silently or sincerely meaning the words. At the third stage
drunken men are "touchy", take offence, complain, grumble loudly:
the Christians, in contrast, are ever to give thanks, for everything.
Finally they are spoiling for a fight, "chucking their weight about"
and ordering people about, confident in themselves and in their own
high position and their right to lord it over others. Christians are
to be subject to one another. It is a very daring illustration for an
apostle to use.

Notice the fine delicacy with which he passes from the rough
picture to the continuous presents: go on being subject, go on
loving. In verse 25 we have tried to combine the *kata* with *hōs*
(indicating manner), in *kathōs*, by rendering "rising (as in the illustration of the elevator, p. 79*f*) to the way in which". For the rest of the
verse, compare 5: 2 (pages 144, 147). "Plunge" and "emerge"
(v. 26) are both pinpoints. The metaphor in verse 27 is that of the
youth and loveliness of the church, as opposed to the wrinkles of
age. Hence the valid interpretation, "marks of faded loveliness."
"Any of such things": the literal rendering would be pedestrian
and dull. "In her glory" is a fair rendering of the predicative
adjective. "Above criticism" follows the same metaphor. Women
can be very "catty" in describing the faces of other women.

"Are under obligation" and "go on loving" (v. 28) are both
expressive of present continuity. By contrast, "vented hatred"
(29) is a pinpoint. Two metaphors follow, perhaps sunken ones, but
still metaphors, though perhaps a little mixed. The first is concerned
with bringing up children and the second means to warm or to
heat. We have tried to bring in all the ideas by saying "tends its
growth (this is part of the one metaphor) with the warmth (this is
the second metaphor) of a father's love (this completes the first

metaphor: without it somebody could easily imagine, say, the care of a farmer)". The present tenses in verse 33 will explain "go on loving" and "go on standing in loving awe of". The latter is preferable, in a Christian home, to a bare "fear".

In 6: 1–2 there seem to be two uses of the present tense, one represented by a series of dots and the other by a continuous line. This has been shown by translating "answer the calls with obedience"; each separate act of obedience being represented by one dot; and by saying "let your attitude be one of honour to": an attitude is continuous, aptly figured by a continuous unbroken line. "Turn out well" in verse 3 is punctiliar; if it had been ingressive it would have been a temptation to render the pinpoint by the American expression "get a break".

"A succession of irritants" (v. 4), and the "commands of" (v. 5) are suggested by the present tense. "Heart fully in the job" is derived from "singleness" or "onefoldness". "Rise above the level of" (v. 6) results from a combination of *kata* and the negative. "Remembering that" (v. 5), the purposive "to please men" (v. 6), "mindful that" and "is your motto" (v. 7) are all suggested by the subjective *hōs*. "Goodwill" (v. 7) seems to be the best word here: note its juxtaposition to the horrid word "being a slave to".

Sir Ronald Storrs thinks that there is no word in ancient Greek which will exactly express the word "loyal" to describe the attitude of a servant of the state.[1] He thinks that the nearest is *eunous*, which is the adjective cognate with the noun which we have rendered "goodwill". If he is right, and we are thinking of an under-officer, a subordinate civil servant, or some such person, who disagrees with a policy and yet carries it out, we might learn from him and say "carry out your slave-duties with loyalty". "Good turn" (v. 8)— as done by a Boy Scout—is punctiliar. "Pursue the same policy" (v. 9) expresses the continuous line of the present tense. "Relax your threatening" might have been written "not being strict when you threaten" if only we could be sure that English readers would know that "strict" (from Latin "stringo") means "to draw tight".

"Fling on" and "make a stand" are pinpoints (v. 11). *Palē* (v. 12) means a wrestling bout, which does not quite accord with the metaphor of "the whole armour" of God. Wrestlers are stripped, not armed. We have tried to overcome this difficulty by toning down the metaphor and yet keeping it in language common to our day: "we are locked in a hand-to-hand struggle". We still speak like this—or the newspapers do—even with regard to modern

[1] Ronald Storrs: *Orientations*, p. 471.

armies. "Pick up" (v. 13), "get the means", "show fight", and "make a stand" are all pinpoints. So, too, at the beginning of verse 14.

"Make a stand" has reminded me of a story of World War II. It concerns a chaplain who was returning to the line from his base, with orders to report at what we will call "Hill 50". He made his way forward, and met some men running towards him. They proved to belong to his own unit, and in surprise they asked him where he was going—"the enemy is on the other side of the hill". "My orders are to report at Hill 50". Soon he met yet more, running towards him and away from the hill, and these, too, tried to persuade him to accompany them further back. And so it went on: more and more of his own men appeared, all in flight, and all trying to get him to join them. To every man he gave the same reply: "My orders are to report to Hill 50, and I am going to." In time panic was arrested, the noble example of an unarmed chaplain fired the imagination of the retreating soldiers, and they turned round, *made a stand*, and fought their way to Hill 50. So the apostle wants his readers when they "have done everything, still to make a stand."

Note the succession of pinpoints in verses 14–17: "make a stand", "hitch up", "clamp on", "slip into", "pick up", "put out" and "close with the offer". By contrast, "offering prayers" (v. 18) represents a series of dots. "Keep your eyes open" is a variant for the continuous "keep awake"; may we add "for Him", taking the neuter *auto* as referring to the neuter *pneumati*? If so, we have a picture which reminds us of detectives set to watch, say, the entrance to a great building, to await the arrival or departure of "Mr. X." "Keep your eyes open!" The Holy Spirit may come in an unlikely moment or unlikely event. "With vigilance unrelaxed" was suggested by *proskarterēsis*, the corresponding verb of which occurs in Acts 8: 13, where Simon Magus would not let Philip out of his sight; and in Acts 10: 7 of the household slaves and soldiers of a retinue, who again would presumably not let their master Cornelius out of their sight for fear they did not receive his orders.

"Burst forth" (v. 19) is a pinpoint: the meaning of the verb has been retained in the phrase "through God's gift". "Make men realise" is also a pinpoint. "I carry on my mission" (v. 20) emphasises continuity. At the beginning of World War II the British Ambassador in Berlin, Sir Nevile Henderson, came home and wrote a book, *Failure of a Mission*. We have shown the kind of mission by inserting the corresponding noun, "*an ambassador* bound in a chain." "Let loose" and "gush forth" are both pinpoints.

"I am sending" (v. 22) is an epistolary aorist. In such matters we take today the point of view of the time of writing; in Greek they thought of the time of the reading of the letter by its recipients, who would think "the apostle wrote it." So Paul uses the aorist. "Give a dose", another pinpoint. "Grows" (v. 24) represents the continuity of the present tense.

Chapter 9

NO!

WE have already noticed in our translations the way in which Greek expresses a prohibition, and the time has now come for us to study it more closely. Greek uses two methods for the purpose of dissuasion, the negative *mē* with either the present imperative or the aorist subjunctive. We shall first examine instances of the present imperative.

To state the rule very simply, the negative with the present imperative forbids the continuation of a state or action. In many cases the action of the verb has already begun and the command is that it should stop. "Do not continue to . . ." clearly implies "Stop doing . . ." This fact leads us to some interesting renderings.

Romans 11: 20, for example, may be translated literally "Do not go on thinking lofty thoughts." (AV, KJV, and RV give "Be not highminded.") As a first step from this we may say "Stop having superior ideas", perhaps even, in this psychological age, "Get rid of your superiority complex." But there is another way, not without its attractions. Why should we not say "Come down from your high horse"? There is something arresting about this, which is always of service to a preacher, and it is not really straying from the Greek. "Stop doing . . ." is reproduced by "Come down from . . ."; "high" is a literal rendering of the Greek adjective; and "horse", *in this context*, implies the possession of superior *ideas* which is true to the Greek verb. The individual preacher may or may not feel able to use this text for a sermon; but it is a useful study in method.

The command to "fear not" seems to have been often on our Lord's lips. In Matthew 10: 31 the present tense means "Do not continue to fear", that is "Cease your fear". Now fear may at times be completely irrational. It is one thing to tell a man not "to get into a panic" when he is in a rational frame of mind. But it is another to deal with him when he is already distracted, even incapable of rational argument. What manner of Man is this, that not only the winds and the sea obey Him, but the stormy and illogical fears are stilled by Him? (Matt. 14: 27; 8: 27) He is no isolationist in the storms of the human heart. Indeed, He breaks into the thoughts of men, and into their actions as well. "Permit the children to come to Me; stop preventing them" (Mark 10: 14).

It is not only fear that makes men irrational: there is such a thing as blind prejudice and hatred. Pilate had written a superscription for the cross on which our Lord suffered, and it was read by many of the Jews. The high priests therefore said to Pilate, "Stop writing 'The King of the Jews', but (put) 'He said, I am the King of the Jews'". For them the question was still open, as open as if the Roman Governor were still engaged in writing. For him the matter was closed: "What I have written, I have written". (John 19: 21–22) Evil, thank God, is sometimes too late. When Hitler attacked Russia, General Smuts is reported to have said "It is the function of evil to make mistakes". The present imperative, uttered by the malignant high priests, illustrates this.

We hear sometimes of crumbling thrones and tottering monarchies, of tyrants slain and kings relieved of their royal responsibilities; of punctured potentates whose swelling pride has been their doom. There is an example of this line of thought in Romans 6: 12, "Let not sin go on reigning in your mortal body . . ." It is not a question of refusing admittance to a pretender, but of kicking out the unworthy occupant of what can be a noble throne. From the opposite point of view we have a picture of a local leader possibly being brow-beaten by older men. Young Timothy is a sort of Apostolic-Deputy, and he is urged (1 Tim. 5: 19) to "cease entertaining a charge against a presbyter", except on the evidence of two or three witnesses. Again, Paul pokes a finger into the tangled matrimonial affairs at Corinth. "Have you been bound to a woman? (As the perfect tense may be re-interpreted as a present, we may paraphrase, 'do a woman's apron-strings fetter you?') Stop hankering after freedom. Are you free from a woman's snares? (Again bringing the perfect tense into a present.) Stop hankering after a wife" (1 Cor. 7: 27).

A lofty moral standard is required in Luke 6: 30, where the present tenses are striking. "Make it your practice to give to everyone who keeps coming to you with requests." ("Match a chain of requests with a chain of gifts." "Pair off every request with a gift.") "And put an end to your custom of asking for your property back from the man who takes it." The continuity is most marked: the moral imperative is ever with us.

There is a courageous word in Luke 14: 12. Our Lord was "dining out" and He said to His host, after a miracle of healing and some wise words of counsel to the other guests, "Whenever you are arranging a breakfast or a dinner, refrain from inviting (as you do now) your friends or your brothers or your relations or wealthy neighbours, lest they on their part invite you back some time and you get a return for your hospitality". This is a startling challenge to a modern host, but it contains the possibility of great reward. "Let love of the brotherhood go on. No more forgetfulness of hospitality! By means of it some people entertained angels without realising it" (Heb. 13: 1–2).

There is a moving example of the construction under discussion associated with the Agony of our Lord. The hallowed words, "Not My will, but Thine, be done" (Luke 22: 42) may be more deeply analysed. With the phrase "Not My will" we must understand the Greek present imperative (*ginesthō*) which appears at the end, after the phrase "but Thine". See how it works out: "Let not My will go on being done, but let Thine go on being done." "Will" (*thelēma*) strictly means "that which I will", so that we may make a paraphrase, to avoid the awkwardness of beginning with "let not". "What I want: let it cease to happen; what Thou dost want: let it go on happening."

This is a mystery into which mortals can barely enter. It seems to imply that hitherto our Lord has seen His desires brought about— He has always delighted to do the will of His Father, and so far the wills have been one. Now the temptation assails Him, to desire that the bitter cup may pass from Him. In so far as it has any pull on Him, temptation as it is, it is "His will". Hence the prayer from the battleground of His soul: our two wills have been one and have come to pass: but let them now diverge. Let My will (the passing of the cup from Me), cease to have effect; let Thine (My drinking of this cup) go on having effect. The psychology is rudimentary; where can there ever be a final psychology of Christ? But our brief study has shown that our Lord's original Temptation, a battle re-fought time and time again (Luke 22: 28) throughout His ministry, came to a climax in that fierce engagement in Gethsemane. It has unveiled to us something of that faithfulness with which He was "obedient as far as death, even death of a cross" (Phil. 2: 8), for us.

One more instance must be considered before we pass on to the other Greek construction. It suggests a character study of a man who was wiser than His Lord, and concerns the story of Simon Peter on the roof at Joppa (Acts 10: 13–15. cp. 11: 8–9). A voice said to him "Rise, Peter, slay and eat", and he answered "Not so, Lord . . ." It is important to notice that this is not a refusal but a protest. A point-blank refusal would have been *oudamōs*, whereas the Greek is the corresponding form, *mēdamōs*, which is the appropriate, negative for a prohibition. We have to understand a verb with it something like *lege*; "do not by any means go on speaking (like that)". "Cease making such a request."

The voice comes back to him, "do not go on regarding as unclean what God purified." "Stop defiling what God pronounced clean." Peter, in fact, is continuing in impetuous, bungling fashion what he has already done before, and it is all the more striking, and indeed tragic, because he has risen to such heights. After Caesarea Philippi, when Peter had declared his Master to be the Christ, the Son of the Living God, our Lord spoke of His impending death and its necessity. He protested vehemently (Matt. 16: 22) "Be it far from Thee, Lord". (The Greek suggests a deprecatory provincialism, "Mercy on us!" or "Lord 'a' mercy!") It was sufficiently bold—and foolish— to call forth our Lord's sharp rebuke, "Get behind Me, Satan". So he who had climbed so high fell to the depths.

We find the reverse in John 13: 8–9. Peter has said "Thou shalt never wash my feet." When he learnt that without it he had no part with Christ, he soared: "Lord, not only my feet but also my hands and my head." It was Peter who had been so sure that he would in no circumstances deny the Lord (Mark 14: 27–31). And when he had denied Him (Luke 22: 34, 60–62), and the Lord had turned and taken a look at him (note the aorist), he went out and burst into bitter tears outside. Even in this humiliation there is a redeeming greatness: the bitter sorrow of an honest but mistaken man. There is a lesson here in this complex character both for the preacher and for his congregation. Be slow to contradict or protest to God: He may have a wider revelation for you of His love. Be slow to show confidence in yourself: it is misplaced. Be slow to refuse the ministries of grace: refusal of them may separate a man from Christ.

The other method in Greek of expressing a prohibition is to use *mē* and the aorist subjunctive. In contrast to the former "do not continue to . . ." this construction, perhaps a little peremptorily, says "don't . . .", i.e. "don't start to . . ." Sometimes in the home I used to say to my young sons, who were both learning Latin and Greek, "don't talk". When they indignantly replied "I wasn't!" the playful rejoinder was made: "*Mē* with the aorist subjunctive, my son. I didn't say 'don't go on talking,' but 'don't start to talk.' "

This has great possibilities for the preacher. When the first Christian martyr, Stephen, was being stoned (Acts 7: 60) he knelt down and cried with a loud voice "Lord, don't start to put this sin down to them." The implication is that the Lord is longsuffering, and delays taking final note of men's sins and wickedness, in spite of their unbelief and cruelty. The Recording Angel, so to speak, had been ordered to "hold his pen," and at the moment of Stephen's prayer he has not yet started to make his record. "Delaying Grace" is an idea which many a preacher might put into the minds of those who think that God is ever looking at men with a watchful, critical eye, ready to "jump on" them at once for their misdeeds.

And what light it throws on to the character of Stephen! For all this has opened a door into his mind. It was he who implied that the Recording Angel's work was not yet begun, and it is a sign of that charitableness and dignity with which a wronged man can regard his persecutors. It is by no misadventure that we speak of Saint Stephen: even his inmost thoughts have been redeemed.

We have already seen the text "Cease your fear" (Matt. 10: 31). In Matthew 10: 26 our Lord uses the aorist subjunctive, "don't be alarmed by them." He Who can still the storms of fear that rage can also prevent their rising. There is a vigour in the speech of Christ which should be preserved, particularly when He had in mind an act which has not yet begun. "Don't get the idea that I came to cast peace upon the earth . . ." (Matt. 10: 34). "Don't get into a flutter (of anxiety), saying 'what food are we to push in?' or 'what drink are we to toss down?' or 'what dress are we to fling on?' " (note the punctiliar aorists.) Matthew 6: 31. "Don't succumb to surprise that I said to you, 'You people must be brought to birth again' " (John 3: 7). "Don't *you* take the name 'Rabbi' " (Matt. 23: 8).

The commandments quoted in Mark (10: 19) and Luke (18: 20) differ from their strongly legal form in Matthew (19: 18) and in the Septuagint (Exodus 20: 13–16), and using *me* and the aorist subjunctive, suggest that actions not yet begun should be prohibited. "Do not take away a man's life. (Not, "Stop killing him".) Do not break up a marriage by adultery. (Not, "return to your wife—or husband".) Do not transfer other people's money to your own pocket. (Not "take your hands off".) Do not give a word of evidence which you cannot substantiate." (Not "put a stopper on your lying tongue".)

John the Baptist is equally vigorous at times. To the Pharisees and Sadducees (Matt. 3: 7–9) he said "Who gave you the tip (aorist) to get out (aorist—compare the American expression on the movies 'Let's get out of here') from the coming wrath? Produce therefore

fruit worthy of repentance; and do not take a fancy (*mē* plus
aorist subjunctive) to dwell on (to go on saying within yourselves—
present) the privilege, 'We have Abraham as a father' ". It is perhaps
worth observing that apart from this text and 1: 20 all the 39 instances of *mē* and the aorist subjunctive in Matthew are in sayings of
Jesus (J H M: I, 124).

When Tabitha died in Joppa the disciples sent two men to Peter
in Lydda (Acts 9: 38) with the urgent—and polite—message "Do
not hesitate to come right through to us". The suitable reply is
not "I will stop hesitating" but "I will avoid hesitating". There
is a courtesy in the very use of the verb "hesitate" which we may
paraphrase by the stock expression "I beg you". Their meaning is
thus "We beg you not to adopt a policy of delay". They do not lose
their heads in the emergency, any more than Paul did at Philippi.
His words to the Philippian gaoler show a keen foresight: "don't
do yourself an injury" (Acts 16: 28). The gaoler had thought that
the prisoners had escaped, for which he would pay the penalty with
his life. He had drawn his sword and was about to kill himself. The
apostle's words imply therefore "don't fall on your sword" or "don't
run yourself through". Seeing that it was dark and that the gaoler
was outside (v. 29) it speaks much for the coolness of Paul. May we
not infer that a sound Christian discipleship helps to preserve both
politeness and foresight in a sudden emergency. Neither are to be
despised. Note the two uses of the word *kurios* (verses 30–31).

The gaoler says "Sirs (*kurioi*), what must I do to be saved?" They
answer "Believe on the Lord (*Kurion*) . . ." Bengel's comment is
apt: *non agnoscunt se dominos*: "they do not recognise themselves as
lords."

One last example combines the two constructions under review.
In Acts 18: 9 the Lord said to Paul "Do not go on fearing, but keep
on speaking and do not begin to be silent." This is very literal:
the meaning may be put "Fade out your fear; (this is a radio allusion:
most of us know what is meant when a programme is 'faded out').
Keep the wheels of speech turning; don't shut your mouth". Good
counsel for a preacher of Christ!

There is a choice passage in Philippians of which we shall now
attempt to give an expository translation (Phil. 4).

> And so, my brothers, loved and longed for, my joy and
> crown, keep your foothold in the Lord in this way, beloved
> brothers. I urge Euodia and I urge Syntyche to maintain a
> common mind in the Lord. Yes, and I ask you also, true

comrade in my team, to prolong your help to them, since in
the gospel struggle they linked their effort with mine, with
Clement as well and the rest of my colleagues, whose names
are in the book of life. On with the joy in the Lord—always!
I will say it again: on with the joy! Let your sweet reason-
5. ableness strike home to the minds of all men. The Lord is
near. Tone down all anxiety; in everything combine thanksgiving with your requests and then let prayer and petition
wing their flights to God. And the peace of God which over-
tops all reason will garrison your hearts and your reasonings in
Christ Jesus. Finally, brothers, whatever is true, whatever
makes you want to worship, whatever is just, whatever
is pure, whatever attracts your love, whatever is high in
men's regard, wherever you find excellence and wherever
you find approbation, keep all these in your calculations.
Go on reproducing the plan of life: the lesson that got home
to you, the truth you embraced, the message that sank into
your ears, the life you glimpsed in me; and the God of peace
will be with you.

"Keep your foothold" (v. 1) draws attention unobtrusively to the
continuity of the present imperative. So with "maintain a common
mind" in verse 2, though the present in this instance is an infinitive.
"To have a common mind" is "to think the same thing", and it
avoids the use of the colourless "thing". "Prolong your help"
(v. 3) once more is true to the present tense. "Linked their effort"
is a pinpoint and represents the *sun-* and the aorist tense of the verb.
But this leaves out the idea of competition inherent in the Greek
verb. We have therefore combined it with the adverbial phrase,
"in the gospel struggle."

"On with the joy" (v. 4) has a small personal history behind it.
I was ransacking my mind for a phrase to serve better than the
pedestrian "Continue the joy", "Resume the joy", when there came
hammering into my mind the phrase "On with the dance." Over
forty years ago at school we learnt by heart some lines, snatches of
which came back to me:

> There was a sound of revelry by night,
>   And Belgium's capital had gather'd then
> Her beauty and her chivalry . . .
>   . . . And all went merry as a marriage bell;
> But hush! hark! a deep sound strikes
>   like a rising knell!

The revellers pause, wondering. (It is the eve of the Battle of Water-loo.) Then:

> On with the dance! let joy be unconfined;
>   No sleep till morn, when Youth and Pleasure meet
> To chase the glowing hours with flying feet.

A little search traced all this to Lord Byron's *Childe Harold*, but my point is that a few lines had been dormant in my mind for years; then, when I was "feeling" for a phrase to bring out the force of the present imperative, "resume your joy", "continue your joy", Byron's words forced their way to my attention. Each preacher has stories, poems, experiences, locked in his unconscious mind. Brooding on a Greek text will at times release them, to give freshness of understanding and treatment. This is here but a passing incident, but it is included as a small illustration of method.

"Strike home" (v. 8) is a pinpoint; but as this does not adequately translate the verb "know" it has been necessary to add "to the minds of", which is sufficient compensation. "Tone down" (v. 6) as a rendering of the negative and the present imperative, may be compared with "fade out your fear" (p. 159). The structure of this verse has been altered so as to avoid the accumulation of phrases. "With" justifies the innocuous verb "combine" and once we have said "combine thanksgiving with your requests" we are free to devote our attention to the present imperative. It suggests repeated action, but the third person "let your requests repeatedly be made known" is much too cumbersome. The datives ("by prayer" and "by petition") seem to be instrumental. Why not turn them into subjects? If we think of them as the two wings of a bird we can say "let prayer and petition wing them (i.e. thanksgiving and requests) to God." But the idea of repeated action has not yet been brought in. Then we should add "let them wing *their flights*". Note the plural, "flights". There is a repeated action in the flights of trans-Atlantic aircraft, so many times a month. As prayer and petition imply thought and language, we need not press the idea of "making known" to God as we did with "strike home" in verse 5.

"Keep all these in your calculation" (v. 8): continuous present imperative. "Go on reproducing" (v. 9) also stands for a present imperative. An object was needed for this, so as to avoid a long relative clause and give us freedom to express the pinpoints of the four aorist verbs. It had to be a somewhat vague, general term to include the specific ideas of learning, receiving, hearing and seeing. "Plan of life" seems to be as good as any, and after the brief pause

F

indicated by the colon we have four pinpoints. "Got home" and "embraced" are momentary actions. "Sank" is not the settling down of a great ship before she slowly sinks to the depths, but the swift descent of a stone. "Glimpsed" is also a pinpoint. Notice that "lesson", "truth", "message" and "life" are suggested by their respective verbs, "learn", "receive", "hear" and "see".

Chapter 10

YES OR NO?

THERE are three ways of asking questions in Greek: you may merely ask for information; you may ask in such a way that you imply that you expect the answer "yes"; and you may ask in a manner which expects the answer "no". With the first method we shall not be greatly concerned here, as it is the last two which are more suggestive for the preacher. In Greek *ara ou*, or simply *ou*, expects the answer "yes". This corresponds to such an English expression as "Are you not a member of the Church?" or "You are a member of the Church, are you not?" (Answer expected: "Yes, I am".) By contrast, *ara mē*, or simply *mē*, expects "no". As an example of this we may take the sentence "You are not the President, are you?" (Answer expected: "No.") If we examine some of the New Testament instances we shall find that the text frequently takes on a new vigour and sometimes is the source of fresh insight into spiritual truth. We shall begin with those which expect an affirmative reply.

In Matthew 7: 22 we have the deluded question "in that day": "Lord, Lord, did we not prophesy in Thy Name, and in Thy Name cast out devils, and in Thy Name do many mighty works?" (Yes, we did.) They are sure of themselves, convinced that they have been right, certain that they have a claim on the Lord. "We prophesied, didn't we, in Thy Name? We are sure we did." Blind leaders of the blind! "Will not both parties fall into a pit?" (Luke 6: 39.) They will. There is a peril about certainty in religion, no less than a blessedness. It must be based in Christ, not in ourselves; and it must show itself in deeds as well as words; and they must be deeds of obedience, not merely deeds, or they may be deeds of lawlessness (Matt. 7: 23).

Matthew 13: 55f shows us a genuine certainty and a false conclusion. "This is the carpenter's son, isn't it? (Yes, it is.) Isn't his mother called Mary and his brothers James and Joseph and Simon and Jude? (Yes.) And his sisters are all with us, ar'n't they? (Yes, they are.) Whence, *therefore*, does he get all this?" The speakers were right in their view of our Lord's relationships: these people were indeed His kith and kin. But their assumptions were sheer folly. There is an argument tucked away in that word "therefore", and when it is stated explicitly it reveals the prejudice of men:

1. All sons of carpenters are devoid of wisdom and mighty works.
2. This is the son of a carpenter.

Therefore

3. This man is devoid of wisdom and mighty works. (I.e he is a fraud; we may well stumble at him.)

Proposition 2. is perfectly true. 1. is a wild assumption. 3. is a conclusion logically drawn but wrong in fact because one of the premisses is untrue. If this conclusion is wrong, their last one is ridiculous, as their implied argument will show.

1. All men with sisters like this are devoid of wisdom.
2. This man is a man with sisters like this. (They are all here, ar'n't they? Look at them!)

Therefore 3. This man is devoid of wisdom . . . As if sisters had anything to do with it! Think of the folly of saying "a man can't be anything or know anything or do anything if he has sisters like that." It is good to have a certainty; but beware of linking it to a false assumption and drawing a conclusion, and then calling yourself a thinker or a rationalist.

Matthew 13: 27 may be regarded as a study in Christian conviction. "Lord, you sowed good seed in your field, didn't you?" God's people are convinced that God is the Author of good; they are not blind to facts before them, and are not afraid to exercise their reason; (notice their use of "therefore"—always a sign of thought) and they address their questions to God. It is significant that in spite of the evidence before them they retain their basic conviction. The "tares" cannot be spirited away, and they are growing bigger. Even so the Lord's servants turn to Him with faith unshaken: You sowed good seed, didn't You? We know you did. There is plenty of evidence today of the activity of another; ample opportunity for the use of reason. But above all men need this foundation truth: God is good and His works are good.

There is a vigour in the language of St. Paul, a robust confidence, which must have carried along with it many a hesitant Christian. He is dealing with the vexed question of "speaking with tongues" (1 Cor. 14: 23) and he puts the hypothetical question: "if the whole church meets at the rallying-point and all are talking with tongues, and unskilled folk or unbelievers walk in (note the return to the aorist—like people who suddenly 'put their nose round the door'), won't they say that you're crazy?" (Yes, they will.)

There is a great place in the Christian faith for sheer common-sense; there ought always to be a "sanity of saintliness". It has been said that a former British Prime Minister, Ramsay Macdonald, went to the King in great despondency: his followers would not follow, and he himself was a failure. Instead of accepting his resignation the King told him that he was overwrought and must go home to bed. From that injunction was born the National Government. Archbishop Lang's comment was "That 'Go to bed' saved the country". Similarly, Miss Evelyn Underhill, the authority on mysticism, sometimes advised people who came to her for spiritual direction to go to bed early with some hot milk. To embrace the Christian faith does not mean saying goodbye to common-sense, and some people and indeed some congregations, need to be reminded of this.

The apostle's energetic question also touches on the place of prestige in religion. We must not limit the Holy Spirit of God, but even so in a rational universe there are considerations which must be kept in mind. St. Paul can ask "how are they to hear apart from a preacher?" (Rom. 10: 14) and we do not accuse him of limiting God. Similarly his sharp question, "Won't they say you're crazy?" (Yes, they will!) may be interpreted thus: "if you make religion look ridiculous won't you keep sensible people away from the Christian faith?" Missionary strategists have long seen the necessity of beginning in the great centres rather than in outlying villages. (See Acts 16: 6–7; 19: 10; 1 Pet. 1: 1.) Converts in the cities will themselves take the gospel to the scattered population.

In like manner there is something to be said for winning to the faith the people of influence. This is not meant to be snobbery, for the humble and simple have souls to be saved as well as their greater brethren. But who can tell what might be done for evangelism if leaders of thought are converted? The Roman Catholic Church is well aware of this. It applies particularly in a hierarchical society. From the point of view of prestige, then, avoid the ridiculous. But we must add one caution: we must not "tone down" the faith in the interests of a social or intellectual class.

This apostolic vigour, this depth of conviction, this confidence which seeks to carry others along with it, is seen also in 1 Corinthians 9: 1. "Am I not free? (Yes) Am I not an apostle? (Yes) I have seen Jesus our Lord, haven't I? (Yes: note the perfect tense: 'the vision of the risen Lord is still before my eyes, isn't it?') You are the

product of my work in the Lord, ar'n't you?" (Yes) If this is conviction, elsewhere we see grim determination. When Saul of Tarsus,
the persecutor, was converted to the Christian faith, his strength of
mind was not blotted out but turned into fresh channels. Guided by
the Holy Ghost he gave the Church a forceful leadership. Faced with
opposition, affliction, danger, persecution, he could still press on,
stout-hearted, bowing to no blows.

It has been said of Martin Luther that the man who denied that
the human will had any power at all was himself the strongest will
in Europe. This is partly the paradox of St. Paul (Rom. 7: 18b).
Listen to him as he deals with Elymas the sorcerer (Acts 13: 10):
"O full of all trickery and of all unscrupulousness, thou son of the
devil, thou enemy of all righteousness, you will stop making crooked
the straight roads of the Lord, will you not?" (You will stop, my
friend!) The apostle is dominating the wretched man by his own
spiritual power. It is not mere invective, though it is that—magni-
ficent invective; but it is more. Paul, redeemed and sanctified, is
imposing his will on one who would oppose, not a personal rival,
but the gospel itself. It is through the mercy of God that the early
Christian community had so strong a personality, so forceful a
character, when the battle of evangelism was being fought. Like
Elijah (2 Kings 2: 12) and Elisha (13: 14) before him, Paul was the
chariot of the new Israel and the horsemen thereof. His spiritual
authority was mightier than the sword: "you will stop, will you
not?" (You will!)

In contrast to the above questions we have now to consider
ara mē or simply *mē*, which introduce questions which expect the
answer in the negative. We continue to notice the vigour of the
apostle Paul. In distinguishing the different kinds of ministry in the
church (1 Cor. 12: 28–31) he asks "They are not all apostles, are they?
(No!) They are not all prophets are they? (No!) Are they all teachers?
(Take a look at them at their lessons!) Have they all got powers?
(Look at the weaklings!) They don't all have gifts of healing, do
they? (Count the invalids!) Surely they don't all speak with tongues?
(Listen to the silent churchmen!) They do not all interpret, do they?
(Try to explain something to them!)"

All these questions "expect" the answer "no", and we have tried
to suggest in parenthesis the manner in which the preacher might
convey the decisive negative. The various commands are all ways
of asserting "No" in accordance with the way in which the question
has been framed. Equally impressive is Paul's question in 1 Corinthians 1: 13: "Paul was not crucified for you, was he?" (No.) The

apostle was a true John the Baptist: "He must increase; I must decrease." For all his brilliant gifts, organising genius, theological insight, powerful preaching and missionary statesmanship, he was at heart a humble disciple of our Lord.

Rather different in atmosphere is the question asked by the portress in John 18: 17 (cp. v. 25). It has sometimes been wondered how a slip of a girl could have led to the undoing of a man. It is to be noticed how she put the answer to her question into Peter's mind. "You too are not one of the disciples of this man, are you?" She expects the answer "no" and she gets it. We should mark here the subtlety of temptation. At times it may come to us with all the glittering splendour of the world: it may lure us with the gleam of gold. But on other occasions it seeks not to stupefy us with massive pictures or grandiose schemes, but to catch us unawares, to trick us so that we agree almost before we know what we are doing. "You're one of us, ar'n't you? You're not one of this man's men, are you? Of course not!" And the word leaps out of our mouth in answer: we have been briefed in a moment, primed to say what may bring on our very ruin.

If only she had said "You are a disciple, ar'n't you?" Peter might not have fallen into a trap; if he had taken his cue from her he still would have given the right answer. Later on (v. 26) one of the highpriest's servants, a relation of the man whose ear Peter had cut off (18: 10), gave Peter his chance: "Didn't I spot you in the garden with Him?" He expects to be told "yes", but it is too late. Perhaps Peter was overawed by his danger, if he knew of the relationship between this man and Malchus, both of them in the service of the highpriest. But in any case he had already committed himself, a fact which shows that temptation may be not only subtle but progressive. Some temptations grow out of earlier ones, and at the later stage they can dispense with subtlety and even give the tempted man a chance. "You were there, weren't you?" But this is the freedom which the cat gives to the mouse which has once been caught. No wonder that our Lord told His disciples to "Watch and pray" (Mark 14: 38), to "keep on the *qui vive* and to keep on praying, that you may not cross the line into temptation."

Observe the uses of the word "therefore". The first question of the maidservant in John 18: 17 follows hard on the entry of Peter. The "other disciple" (v. 15) entered in with Jesus, leaving Peter outside; he then returned, "had a word with" (note the aorist) the girl who kept the door, and brought in Peter. She *therefore* said to Peter, "You are not . . . are you?" There are some situations which discipleship or Christian fellowship involves, which bring peril to us. Be on your guard! But later (v. 25) "Simon Peter was standing and warming himself. They *therefore* said to him 'You are not . . . are you?'" Some situations may not be due to Christian fellowship or discipleship: we may be mingling with the crowd, warming ourselves. Flee!

There are several examples of this mode of interrogation in the Fourth Gospel; indeed, it is almost a feature of the author's style. The man born blind, when questioned a second time (John 9: 24-), said, "One thing I know, that 'blind man' though I am, I now am seeing . . . You too don't wish to become disciples of His, do you?" (In verse 25, "being blind I now see" might be rendered "though I was blind . . .", as the present participle *ōn* can do duty for the non-existent imperfect participle. Such a use is by no means unknown in Greek. But it is more attractive to say "Being a 'blind man' I am now seeing." Note that 'blind man' must then be in inverted commas.) Blind though he had been, he was not blind to human prejudice. Such an experience of healing was hardly likely to inspire him with any sympathy with objections based on sabbatarianism (v. 16). Some of the Pharisees said to our Lord afterwards (v. 40) "We also are not blind, are we?" But He refused to be drawn into argument.

The familiar words should also be noticed, "Will ye also go away" (AV, KJV) or "Would ye also go away?" (RV, John 6: 67). As they stand they suggest a pathetic last appeal of a man who sees his following breaking up and fears that he may be left desolate. In point of fact our Lord is really paying His disciples a compliment. The fickle crowd is melting away, but the men nearest to Him will remain loyal. "You too do not wish to go away, do you?" The preacher has here something of the force of suggestion as opposed to direct commandment; of believing the best about people rather than the worst; of putting one's trust in minorities rather than in the big battalions. There is rich comfort here for the preacher in the modern world. Our Lord suggests, does not bully; when we are sore beset He looks to the love deep down in our hearts, not to our possible desertion; He trusts His cause to us, and does not criticise us for not holding the masses at our side.

Some vivid touches are given to the Fourth Gospel if we translate in harmony with the Greek. "The rulers never really recognised that this is the Christ, did they?" (John 7: 26) "When the Christ comes, he will not do more signs than this Man did, will he?" (7: 31) "Many of them were saying 'He has a demon and is mad. Why do you go on listening to Him?' Others were saying, 'These words are not those of a man in the power of a demon; a demon cannot open the eyes of the blind, can he?' " (10: 20–21)

But we are not limited to the Fourth Gospel. In Mark 2: 19 our Lord says "The wedding guests cannot keep up a fast while the bridegroom is with them, can they?" In Luke 22: 35 He asks "When I sent you without purse and travelling-bag and shoes, no supply was turned off, was it?" (This gets round the ingressive aorist, "did you become short of anything?") James, protesting against faith without works, asks indignantly "Faith cannot pluck him into safety, can it?" (Jas. 2: 14—note the aorist infinitive of the verb "save".)

Sometimes we have *mē ou* apparently as a single expression. In such cases the *mē* introduces a question expecting the answer "no", as before, and the *ou* goes closely with the verb. Thus in Romans 10: 18 we must say "They did not fail-to-hear, did they?" "Israel did not fail-to-know, did he?" (v. 19). Three verses later Paul uses the simple *mē*: "God did not give His people a push away from Himself, did He?" (11 :1) Further examples of *mē ou* are found in 1 Corinthians 9: 4–5: "We are not without authority to take a meal or a drink, are we? We are not without authority to take on circuit with us a sister as a wife, are we?" And in 11: 22 "You are not without houses for eating and drinking in, are you?"

There is an extension of *mē* in the word *mēti*, which is the same negative with the addition of the neuter singular of the indefinite pronoun—probably the adverbial accusative. It imparts a measure of hesitancy and uncertainty. Thus in John 4: 29 the simple *mē* would involve a translation something like this: "Come, have a look (aorist) at a man who told me all I did; this is not the Christ, is it? (No)". But *mēti* is not so dogmatic as this; it has not already judged the question. It asks somewhat vaguely "It is not somehow the Christ, is it?" i.e. "I suppose this isn't the Christ?" The woman is planting a seed thought into the minds of her fellow-citizens, and leaving them to think it out. In fact we have run up against suggestion once more in a slightly different form (p. 168).

Compare the hesitancy of a beggar's question, "I suppose you haven't a coin to spare, have you?" and that of the crowd in Matthew 12: 23, "I suppose this isn't the Son of David?" There is a pathetic uncertainty and doubt in the minds of the disciples in Matthew 26: 22. At the Last Supper the Lord had told His men that one of them would deliver Him up. Instead of an angry protest, as we might have expected (see v. 35), they were filled with grief, and each one began to say (Mark 14: 19 says "one by one") "*mēti egō eimi*": "I suppose I'm not the man?" The awful doubt seems to suggest that each man had recognised the traitor—not the actual historic traitor Judas, but the potential traitor—in his own heart. Each man knew that he could be the one to betray his Lord. Judas, who had already begun the fell work of betrayal (Matt. 26: 14-16; 24 "is being delivered up"; 25 "Judas, who was in course of delivering Him up"), followed suit and asked the same question, "I suppose I'm not the man?" But what were his secret thoughts?

To revert to the Woman of Samaria—John 4: 29. My mother once told me a story of a woman who in England long years ago died an atheist. While alive she said that if there were a God a fig-tree would grow out of her grave. When she was buried there was erected over her a massive stone super-structure, to prevent the growth of anything which might conceivably spring up from beneath. But there seems to have been something in the grave, perhaps even the seed of a fig-tree. At all events, something grew up, split the stone of the tomb, and grew into a fig-tree. In like manner the idea which the hesitant, undogmatic woman left in the minds of the Samaritans—"I suppose this isn't the Christ?"—may have split the entombing prejudice of the Samaritan mind. The seed was later watered by Philip (Acts 8: 5) and the city received the Word of God (v. 14). Even our tentative suggestions can be blessed by the Holy Ghost.

Let us now try to translate John 7: 37-52, a passage which contains a number of questions.

In the last and great day of the feast Jesus was standing and He uttered a shout, saying "If any man has a thirst raging, let him come on to Me and drink deep. He who keeps the steady beam of faith towards me, just as the text of scripture said, rivers of living water will flow out of him." He said this about the tide of the Spirit which they were going to receive who had trained their faith on to Him; for not yet was there Spirit,
40. because the light of glory had not as yet fallen on Jesus. A hum of talk arose from a section of the crowd when these words fell on their ears: "This is truly the Prophet"; others were saying "This is the Christ". But an opposition was countering: "No; for the Christ does not come out of Galilee does He? Didn't the scripture say 'of the seed of David', and 'from Bethlehem', the village where David was, 'comes' the Christ?" Division therefore split the crowd because of

Him; and some of them were desirous of putting Him under arrest, but nobody laid hands on Him.

45. The underlings, then, came to the highpriests and Pharisees, and the former barked at them "Why did you fail to produce Him here?" The underlings flashed in answer "Never did a man strike a note in his speech as this Man is doing." The Pharisees therefore retorted "You also are not on the wrong track, are you? No-one of the rulers or of the Pharisees swung round his faith in His direction, did he? But this mob that does not know the law are accursed every

50. one." Nicodemus, who had come to Him on a former occasion, said to them (because he was one of their number) "Our law does not judge the man without first hearing a word from him and getting some light on what he is doing. It doesn't, does it?" They made rejoinder to him "You too are not out of Galilee, are you? Make a search and take a look to see that a prophet does not arise out of Galilee".

A few comments will explain some of the expository phrases which have been adopted. "Uttered a shout" is the nearest to a pinpoint that seems desirable. "Has a thirst *raging*", by contrast, expresses the continuity of the present tense. So, too, with "drink deep". A pinpoint would have required something like "have a drink" (rather undignified here) or "toss down a drink" (which is similarly lacking in dignity). "Keeps the steady beam of faith towards Me" (v. 38): the beam is not intermittent but, like a search-light or spotlight, "shines steadily". It is thus a mode of drawing attention to the continuity of the present tense.

"Receive" in verse 39 was rather a problem. It is present in tense, but "keep on receiving" or "receive one after another" and similar attempts seemed pedestrian and dull. In the end it seemed wiser to transfer the idea of continuity to the "Spirit". An estuary "receives" the incoming tide, and if the tide takes about six hours to come in it is continuous. If we want repetition, tides are repeated. "Trained their faith on to Him" stands for an aorist, a pinpoint. It does not mean "those who had believed and had got it over and done with", as when we speak of "those who had eaten their breakfast". It is an ingressive aorist, marking the entrance into the state of faith. "Trained" might suggest a gun, pointed at a target, but I had in mind rather a telescope. Those concerned "swung round the telescope on its swivel so that it pointed to the moon," and so we may understand the initial act of faith. "The light of glory . . ."

is yet another pinpoint: when an electric switch is pressed, light falls on to the face.

"Fell on their ears" (v. 40) is a similar pinpoint. "A hum of talk" brings out the continuity of "they were saying". "A section of the crowd" represents the partitive use of *ek* and the genitive. There is no need to repeat "hum", so that "were saying" is enough in verse 41. Note that there were really only two parties: those saying that He was the Prophet, and others, still favourably disposed, that He was the Christ: and in contrast, secondly, the sceptics. The contrast (*de*) and the continuity (imperfect) are brought out by "an opposition was countering". "No;" is implied by the *gar* (for) early in their question, which gives the reason for their negation. They expect agreement with their negative attitude as they allude to scripture.

Observe that the unscrupulous, the prejudiced, the blind, can use scripture to prove anything that suits them: "Judas went out and hanged himself; go thou and do likewise." Everything turns on the meaning of "come". Did not the scriptures say. . . .? Yes, it did. (v. 42) The minutiae of prophecy are not so significant as its general tenor, interpreted in the light of the historic Christ. "Division . . . split" (v. 43): "split" is a pinpoint. Compare Matthew 27: 51, and think of the sudden sharp tear (pronounced "tare") as a woman in one brief movement rends a piece of cloth in two. "Were desirous" (v. 44): continuity; "put under arrest": pinpoint. ("Putting" ends in "-ing" because the English idiom demands it: "desirous *of* putting" But this may be disregarded, as the general idea of "put under arrest is a pinpoint.)

"Barked" (v. 45) is a pinpoint: not the long howling of a dog but the staccato of a single bark. "Produce" is also a pinpoint for the aorist "bring". If it had not been too much out of harmony with the dignity of the desired Prisoner, and unnecessarily long, we could have had recourse to the temporal pinpoint (see page 16) and said "bring in one jerk". The pinpoint is indeed there, but this is going too far. Other pinpoints are "flashed in answer" (v. 46), "strike a note", "retorted" (v. 47). "Are on the wrong track" is a perfect tense, re-interpreted as a present. "Swung round" (v. 48) is a pinpoint: the figures of the telescope once more. Note that "no" is expected as the answer to both questions. *You* deceived by talk? Men sent to make an arrest are not usually talked round ("I didn't do it, officer"). Ask any policeman how many men he has failed to arrest when under orders to arrest them, just because of the prisoner's talk! The very words of our Lord are deeds. The second question reveals the impregnable fortress of prejudice. "Are accursed every one" (v. 49) draws attention to the plural verb and complement, though the subject is the singular "mob".

"Hearing a word", "getting some light" (v. 51) are pinpoints. "It doesn't, does it?" sums up the whole question, which expects the answer "no". The opponents of Nicodemus have already made up their minds. Justice has little chance against hatred, organised fanaticism and the status quo, when men whose bodies are "on the bench" have minds that dwell in a rut. They cannot conceive that our Lord is capable of winning one of their own number. "You don't come from Galilee, do you?" (52) Perhaps; but Nicodemus assisted at the burial of Jesus (John 19: 39). The Lord has His surprise for those who will not believe in Him: some of their close associates are on His side. "Make a search" and "take a look" are pinpoints.

Chapter 11

POSTSCRIPT

WE have now completed our survey of the possibilities of the Greek Testament for the preacher. It may be that there are some Aramaic originals; it may be that some of the Greek is Semitic. It is far from my purpose to run counter to the devoted toil of Semitic scholars, and we must not ignore their findings. But a man must give his own testimony, and this is mine. When I read the Greek Testament, pictures move before my eyes, stories incidents and sayings read elsewhere speed into my mind in illustration, and the written words flash with light and life. In the preceding pages an attempt has been made to show how the Greek language itself suggests such picture and movement, and the translations have been made to show to a preacher something of what the text has meant to me. This is perhaps what might have been expected, if "each word is the centre of a whole cluster of meanings and *associations*."[1] But there is a deeper reason.

In an impressive and indeed a moving book[2] Lord Eccles has reminded us again that the gospels are great works of art. Place them in the company of the great masterpieces of literature and they are at home. They are not poor relations. This is virtually the view of Dr. E. V. Rieu[3]. The canonicity of the gospels enshrines the excellent literary judgement of the Church. In other connections I should want to go on to speak of their spiritual value but that is not the point at the moment. If any person does not take kindly to the idea of scripture as a work of art he should reflect on the fact that there is (or was) a right way and a wrong way of writing a gospel. (The "wrong" ones did not attain to the canon of scripture.) This is what is ultimately meant when we refer to a work of "art" or skill (*technē*).

Now it is a characteristic of a work of art that it elicits a response. Dr. Rieu speaks of an "over-all effect". The gospels evoke feelings. In striking language Lord Eccles tells us that in common with all

[1]NEB Introduction ix. The italic is mine.
[2]*Half-way to Faith* by Lord Eccles (1966 Geoffrey Bles).
[3]*The Four Gospels* by E. V. Rieu (1952 Penguin Books). Introduction ix.

great works of art the gospels "will not keep quiet". They "hold fresh conversations" with readers old and new, and reveal their own deeper meaning. They thus say more even than their original authors intended. (This is not unrelated to a doctrine of inspiration.) And, again in common with works of art, they are catholic. That is to say, in principle the door is open to all. There is no price of admission. The expert is not the only possible interpreter. Obviously certain qualifications are necessary: the reader must at least be able to read. But the principle holds. God has yet more light and truth to break forth from His word.

We have been speaking in particular of the gospels but all that has been said applies to the New Testament as a whole and indeed to the whole Bible. It is true that there is such a thing as "correct exegesis" but it may be doubted if in the final analysis it is static and fixed. Knowledge grows indeed and academic fashion changes. But the fact remains: the "effect "of reading the scriptures varies and grows. Hence in this book I have tried to set out something of what the Greek Testament has meant to me. Certain principles should be kept in mind in estimating the worth of any of the English versions here offered.

To begin with, a knowledge of theology and of ethics has been assumed. It is open to question what benefit a "preacher" would derive from a minute study of a text in Greek, if he knew nothing of theological or ethical doctrine. The preacher who has no theology is a menace, and the more influential he is the greater the menace. That is not to say that he is to give his people great slabs of meat, great chunks of the writings of, say, Barth and Brunner. He has to make the nourishment of the Christian soul appetising. The mind that is stored with theological truth will find that the Greek suggests a hundred ways of presenting it.

Secondly, it should not be assumed that anything written so far is to be applied mechanically. This book has tried to show certain methods of interpretation and it is hoped that the preacher will use them. But he still needs the guidance of the Holy Ghost, Who will take these dead bones of grammar and syntax and make them live.

Thirdly, the translations given are not necessarily literary or ecclesiastical. A literary rendering may give aesthetic pleasure but it may miss the point of the original. An ecclesiastical rendering may be suitable for public worship in the church, like the noble words of an ancient prayer which has been consecrated by centuries of piety; but it may yet omit what is vital in the text. In short, our renderings have not aimed so much at dignity as at truth and vividness; hence they are not seldom colloquial and vigorous. They are not meant for *littérateurs*, still less for use in the reading of Holy Scripture in church. They are translations made by one preacher to show other preachers something of what the text has meant to him; to bring out a thought, to draw an outline, to paint a picture, to represent a little of what he sees with his mind's eye as he reads the Greek. The skilled teacher of souls will not therefore bluntly say "the Greek means so-and-so", but will take the thought or the picture suggested and weave it into his own thought and illustration.

Fourthly, a Greek word has not necessarily been always translated by the same English word. Here we rest on the great authority of Sir Arthur Quiller-Couch, whose lectures *On the Art of Writing* (Cambridge, 1916) are still a joy to read. A decision "to use one and the same English word, as representing one and the same Greek word . . . is the most gratuitously unwise" decision a translator can take, "for in any two languages few words are precisely equivalent" (p. 131). I have tried to be faithful to the spirit of the original *in its context*.

Fifthly, at different times a different translation may be given of the same text, to suit one's mood, to convey the picture and movement suggested at one time rather than another. There is an illustration of this on page 21. Many renderings of a text may be wrong, but it is doubtful if there is one correct translation, and one only.

Sixthly, sometimes it will be thought that we have over-emphasised and exaggerated one aspect of a meaning. This charge may be brought particularly with regard to our rendering of aorists. But it is a charge which can be answered. Exaggeration is sometimes necessary for the purpose of bringing out what otherwise would be lost. Much translation loses something. For example, "the King of kings" in 1 Timothy 6: 15 loses by comparison with "the King of those who are actually exercising royal power." It is not literary grace that is lost, but *meaning*. Why should we lose more than is necessary? A Greek sees or hears an aorist, and the punctiliar aspect is but one element in a number, such as basic meaning, person, number, voice and mood. An ordinary English translation does justice to all these with the exception of the punctiliar. *It can sometimes only be shown by what is an exaggeration in comparison with the other aspects of meaning.* Then show it. Quite apart from the fact that the only way to make some people understand a truth is to exaggerate it, in the work of translation sometimes the only way to pay a few pennies is to hand over a large silver coin—and expect no change.

Such, in outline, are the principles embodied in the work of translation here submitted. It is a difficult task to reduce pictures to words, especially when the pictures are moving, instinct with life. It is too much to expect that every scholar will agree with every rendering given, but in the general method of approach I cannot but believe that God is speaking; cannot be disobedient to what is the heavenly vision (Acts 26: 19). To say otherwise would not only deny belief in the prophetic ministry; it would mean going back on forty years of Christian service. And I covet for all preachers and ministers of the Word the joy in the ministry of the pulpit which I have found, and those seals of ministry which come to a preacher from time to time from appreciative listeners who have found the minister to be a "helper of their joy."

We plead guilty then to exaggeration. Sometimes this is apparent in the mere process of "making heavy weather" of the punctiliar aspect; and sometimes by bringing in a totally new figure of speech which is not present in the original. There is precedent for it.

What we have called "exaggeration" is to be seen in some renderings of the New English Bible. In Acts 14: 5 the Greek preposition *sun* is represented by "with the connivance of." The conative present receives full treatment: "this is not another attempt to recommend ourselves to you" (2 Cor. 5: 12); ". . . we try to recommend ourselves" (2 Cor. 6: 4). The force of the present tense is brought out in "the gospel which I am accustomed to preach" (Gal. 2: 2); and in "Let us then keep to this way of thinking" (Phil. 3: 15). The conative imperfect is seen in "tried to destroy it" (the church. Gal. 1: 13; cf. v. 23) and the inceptive imperfect in "began to hold aloof" (Gal. 2: 12). The repeated action which is characteristic of the imperfect is explicitly stated in the story of the importunate widow, who "constantly came before" the judge with her plea for justice (Luke 18: 3).

Punctiliar aorists are rendered with clarity and vigour. ". . . their misguided minds are plunged in darkness" (Rom. 1: 21). ". . . in order that . . . we might set our feet upon the new path of life" (Rom. 6: 4). ". . . when first we believed" (Rom. 13: 11). "You have come into your fortune already. You have come into your kingdom . . . ." (1 Cor. 4: 8).

We have seen that the perfect tense expresses the abiding result of a past act and can therefore be interpreted as a present. This is done in the N.E.B. in 1 Corinthians 7: 18, "Was a man called with the marks of circumcision on him?" Cf. 2 Corinthians 5: 11, "To God our lives lie open, as I hope they also lie open to you in your heart of hearts."

I have no criticism to make of all this. Some will not even regard these renderings as exaggeration at all. My point is that where I have exaggerated I have continued a process already apparent in the N.E.B.

In bringing in a new figure of speech I have once more maintained a tradition—or at least have done what is done in the N.E.B. (The qualification is important because most of this book was written before the N.E.B. was published.) Perhaps the most famous example is James Moffatt's "maintain the spiritual glow" in Romans 12: 11. "Glow" suggests a dry heat, without flame, like that of a red-hot poker. The Greek implies a wet heat, boiling. The change of metaphor is quite justified: the impact is the same and the law of equivalent effect[1] is observed.

The N.E.B. does the same. Thus we read in Acts 8: 9, 11 that Simon Magus "had swept the Samaritans off their feet" and that "they had . . . been carried away." In Acts 8: 31 the Ethiopian eunuch asked his famous question, "How can I understand unless someone will give me the clue?" Now there is nothing about brooms, carriages or detective stories in the Greek, but the impact on the reader is vivid and vital: the effect is "equivalent."

Other examples are: " . . . they are stifling the truth" (Rom. 1: 18), though there is nothing in the Greek about suffocation; "Love keeps no score of wrongs" (1 Cor. 13: 5): it does not record every "run" hit by a wicked man nor does it treasure a musical score to be played over and over again in resentful mood. But is the game or the music in the Greek? The "old human nature . . . is sinking towards death" (Eph. 4: 22) brings out the force of the present tense but "sinking" is an imported metaphor.

The punctiliar aorist is admirably expressed in ". . . his heart sank" (Luke 18: 23), though the Greek has nothing in it of heart or of sinking; and in "they got wind of it" (Acts 14: 6), though the Greek is visual (*sunidontes*), not olfactory. Is it the picture of a deer which suddenly scents its stalker?

Now I am far from criticising these and similar renderings. My point is that some new metaphor has been introduced to facilitate the rendering. I may have been guilty of greater exaggeration or of using figures which do not appeal to all. But in principle I should like to think that in some places I have been in line with the work of those translators who have spurned the word for word method and have aimed at translating according to the meaning.

In a work such as this, designed as it is to help preachers, there

[1]See F. F. Bruce: *The English Bible: a History of Translations* (Lutterworth) p. xii.

are four canons of interpretation. There should be a *fidelity* to the Greek text. Literality is not always the best method of retaining the meaning. Secondly come questions of *taste*. This has not been my prime concern, though a translation should not fall below a certain level. Of chief importance are *vividness* and *vigour*. I hope that something of the picture and movement suggested by the Greek has been conveyed to the preacher and that all of us can not only "listen like a disciple" but also "see like a disciple".[1]

[1]Cf. p. 122.

SELECT BIBLIOGRAPHY

Liddell and Scott: *Greek-English Lexicon,* new edition revised by Jones and McKenzie, Volumes I and II. Oxford: Clarendon Press.

W. F. Arndt and F. W. Gingrich: *A Greek-English Lexicon of the New Testament.* Cambridge University Press and University of Chicago Press, 1957.

W. W. Goodwin: *A Greek Grammar.* London: Macmillan 1924. *Syntax of the Moods and Tenses of the Greek Verb.* London: Macmillan, 1889.

Moulton-Howard-Turner: *A Grammar of New Testament Greek.* Edinburgh: T. & T. Clark. Vol. I, 1919. Vol. II, 1960. Vol. III, 1963.

Blass-Debrunner-Funk: *A Greek Grammar of the New Testament.* University of Chicago Press, 1961.

C. F. D. Moule: *An Idiom Book of New Testament Greek,* second edition. Cambridge University Press, 1959.

A. T. Robertson: *A Grammar of the Greek New Testament in the Light of Historical Research,* fourth edition. New York: Hodder & Stoughton and George H. Doran Company, 1923.

H. P. V. Nunn: *A Short Syntax of New Testament Greek,* fourth edition. Cambridge University Press, 1924.

N. Turner: *Grammatical Insights into the New Testament.* Edinburgh: T. & T. Clark, 1965.

Moulton and Geden: *A Concordance to the Greek Testament.* Edinburgh: T. & T. Clark, 1897.

Hatch and Redpath: *A Concordance to the Septuagint.* Graz, Austria: Akademische Druck-u. Verlagsanstalt, 1954. Two volumes.

INDEX OF SCRIPTURE REFERENCES

INDEX OF SCRIPTURE REFERENCES